WATER DRAWN BEFORE SUNRISE

FORTHCOMING

Luminous Heart of the Earth, Opening to the Luminous Awareness in Your Heart through Direct Experience in the Natural World, by Robert and Rachel Olds

Path of Joy, Images of Inner Radiance, by Robert and Rachel Olds

WATER

DRAWN

BEFORE

SUNRISE

A Journey of Return

Spiritual Memoirs

Robert *&* Rachel Olds

Heart Seed Press

Published by

Heart Seed Press

www.acircleisdrawn.org

robert.rachel@acircleisdrawn.org

Printed in the United States of America

ISBN 978-0-615-37628-8

Cover photo: high desert prairie sunrise in Stanley, New Mexico, Robert and Rachel Olds

Cover and book design: Robert and Rachel Olds

Homage
to luminous inner radiance,
primordial awakened heart,
seed of your very being,
essence beyond concepts,
all encompassing, beyond all that is,
all embracing, beyond going beyond,
nothing not nothing, spontaneously arising.

Water drawn from a well or stream before sunrise is considered numinous and endowed with special powers of regeneration and transformation in European folk wisdom. This catalyst and expression of the journey of return to origin is invoked at times of collapse and decay, when the world order as perceived by a culture or an individual has broken down and renewal through genuine reconnection with the *essentia*, the primordial source, is called for.

CONTENTS

PREFACE

This is an account of a spiritual journey, a portrait of two lives with the same purpose that came together, a picture composed of moments along our way, moments of inner radiance bursting forth, and moments in between, pushing, pulling, and prodding us to remember a recognition vast and fluid. Our search led us to spend nine years in retreat together at a Tibetan Buddhist lay monastery in the mountains of northern California. For five and a half of those years we lived in a simple pit dwelling which we built in the forest above the monastery, and even after moving to a one-room cabin close by, the rhythms of hauling water and hiking steep forest trails continued to shape our daily lives. Our practice in retreat was the union of luminous awareness and Tögal, the ancient visionary Path of Joy. The blessings of the practice and our backgrounds as artists color our account of our journey in the same way the mountain, the forest, and the creek helped shape our days in retreat.

We began writing at the request of our lama. As we approached the completion of the path of Tögal, he urged us to consider writing about our experience and advice for future practitioners in the West. Within the oneness that comes from the resolution of the path, we saw the depth of the seamless quality of all experience. We looked back at the situations, choices, and recognitions that arose throughout our lives and helped us along the path. We wrote these memoirs to express the importance of recognizing the natural wholeness of spiritual life and Earth, and to honor the myriad teachers and teachings that our lives offer us at every moment.

This is not a guidance manual, and yet it is an expression of the same observations and advice, clothed in events of our lives. The memories that presented themselves and the ones we choose to write about are strongly influenced by the culmination of the path towards which they were leading. There is now no other way to see them but in the light of their release. Without writing about techniques and details of the practice, we want to evoke the texture of our experience of Tögal and of retreat and the life preliminaries that brought us there. We want to share some of the joy of these far countries of the heart to encourage all those who may feel compelled as we did to embrace a spiritual path, and especially now, in these times of great change, to remind that there is a potential for opening and renewal that naturally arises within decline and decay.

We gratefully acknowledge all the many teachers we have had in this life, everyone and everything, the vast display of this great vision. Friends, plants, animals, relatives, the Earth, fire, air, water, and space all carry precious teachings ready to be revealed if you are open and allowing. This life is already sacred and holy beyond all knowing. Awakened heart, the heart of this vast display, is here now, yet the whole wonder hinges on recognition and how we attend to our lives, freeing ourselves of all the wants and desires into an open, fluid, and aware state, so that the true gift of recognizing, this luminous wonder, arises within us.

WATER DRAWN BEFORE SUNRISE

TWO SOLITUDES

Everything is offered to each of us at any moment, for everything is the essence and the call to return. Our forms, this Earth, the progression of light and darkness, the tidal forces of our world, moving, mixing, and changing us, are all here as essential agents of this call. This world's experience, the whole of it, the good and the bad, all speaks to us through the voice of this call.

What are the memories of a yogi? The charnel grounds, a visceral experience of life and death, Earth, rock, fire, and water, mountains and open sky, a freedom outside of boundaries and a knowing grace, the inner radiance that arose for us like a clear mountain lake touching that which is beyond time or space, beyond the ordinary structures of a personal history. Yet this entire visionary dream we call life unfolds in a seemingly linear fashion. We arise, grow, and progress towards a goal, and so growing up in the fifties and sixties in America, we followed as best we could what resonated with our hearts, two solitudes, apart and waiting.

WIND RIPPLING IN THE GRASS

Rachel

The narrow coast highway turned inland again. Tall trees lined the road on either side. We were approaching the quaint bed and breakfast place in Big Sur, our destination on a three-day college weekend organized by a proctor in our dorm. Orange and red nasturtiums and geraniums were blooming in a patch of sunlight out front, as we arrived at a collection of rustic cabins at a forested bend in the road. We got our rooms and then I walked alone down the highway to where the land suddenly opened out into a plunging view of Earth and sky and sea.

I climbed a few feet down from the roadway and sat nestled in the narrow space between an aging barbed wire fence and the raised roadbed, surrounded by lupine bushes in full bloom and fragrant wild sage. I was wearing a bright yellow blouse, but as I settled in, I was utterly convinced that I was invisible. I had become a bush rooted in this Earth, one with this place in an inexplicable way. I had never been here before, but I had always been here. Steep pasturelands fell away below me to the edge of cliffs closer to the sea. Light shimmered across the surface of an ocean inseparable from the sky. Wind rippling through the grasses carried a pungent tidal scent upward in the warm spring air.

As I sat, my mind merged with the whole of this living vastness. I was the fullness of this union of land and sea and sky enveloped in the sweet breath of sage and the fertile ocean air. I was the grasses, the lupine flowers and the sage, the plunging Earth and soaring sky, the endless level sea. I was their unity and I wanted to stay here for all time, never apart from the gleaming oneness of this place and the oneness of my heart that opened here as naturally and as easily as the lupine and the sage growing at my side.

Two years later, my mother came to visit me at school and we took a trip to Big Sur. She wanted to stay at the same inn of cabins by the road; this was where I was conceived. She had never told me this before.

We arrived late in the afternoon. The light was falling fast under the redwood trees. We got a room and started to unpack, then sat on the beds talking for a while in the deepening twilight, trying to bridge the uneasy distance that always seemed to be between us.

The room was growing cold. As I got up to go to the office to ask for extra blankets for the night, my mother looked up at me and with fearful eyes and a small voice she said, "You won't leave me alone here will you?", a question startling in the soft darkness of this temporary room. Was she asking me, her daughter, growing up, growing away from her, asking me not to leave? We had pulled apart from each other so many years ago.

Don't leave me alone. She looked very scared. In her eyes, she was not just asking me, she was asking others, others who were no longer here, her mother or her father perhaps. An aunt told me that when my mother was an infant her parents had moved to a new house and believing it was the best way to get the baby accept the new place, had let her cry alone in an unfamiliar room at night. Don't leave me alone.

She was also afraid of something else. Here in this place, if not this room, was a window into a part of her she never talks about. This was where I was conceived, and she was caught, pressed by her memories and her fear. My father was back from the war then, and they were both caught in different ways, never moving beyond certain moments in their hearts. My mother was trapped there now

6

in this room, with a shadow welling up in her eyes from the depths of the troubled love she and my father still had for each other. The shadow about which she never wanted to speak, this shadow was present then, at the time I was conceived. So was the brightness of their love, so was the molten union of the Earth and sky and sea, so was the timeless purity of the holy ones, the primordial mother and father consorts in union that engender worlds, so was everything, present at every moment, even in my parents' pain, all there encoded in my heart, to heal and to be healed, layers of union, wounded and divine, inseparable.

I could feel my head above me, big and heavy and round. My perception was centered wholly and tangibly in my heart, as a brightness there, floating very softly not in liquid or in air, just floating being one with something all-encompassing and kind that held me on all sides so that I could not fall, I could only be there. I was in a pink wrinkled valley with steep rounded sides that came together above the roundness of the big head. I could see pink boulders and folds in the sides of the valley; they were clearly illuminated by the soft light of my heart, but the head seemed shadowy, remote, not yet a part of this world.

Remembering is a fluid motion, ever changing and alive, circling between the dream-like points we call then and now. Within the living energies that form the patterns of this or any life, who are we now, no one and everything, sunlight shimmering on a sea, wind rippling in the grass. Remembering is woven through with strands of so many others' lives, where does anyone begin. Perhaps in summer in Big Sur, or later, in the spring of the following year, in Palo Alto, California, in 1947, yet each time we appear we are also a timelessness expressed inside of time. We are a reflection of a radiance that embodies itself through us effortlessly. We offer memories like shining beads or small stones passed from hand to hand, as reminders of the flowing brilliance of which, in which, we all abide.

Beyond the low stone wall, a clear sky opened out above the trees and houses on the slope below. My mother helped me climb the last few steps to the empty courtyard in front of the tall ornate important-looking building. When we reached the top, I was suddenly fascinated by the head of a grey stone lion in a small alcove to one side of the courtyard. The grey unseeing eyes and the broad curves of the mane were all the same color and texture. The lion had no body, just a head emerging from a flat grey wall at the back of the alcove above a shallow pool.

When I asked my mother about it later in my life, she said the lion was a fountain at the Pacific School of Religion where we would walk when I was small, but I do not remember any water pouring out of the lion's mouth that day. The mouth was hollow and empty, even more startling than the eyes, a shadowy compelling space, a mysterious hollowness hidden inside the heaviness of the carved shapes.

We lived just north of the U. C. Berkeley campus then. We could see the big clock face on the Campanile straight out one of the kitchen windows. The neighborhood was on a steep hill and our street ran straight up and down the slope. The flat terraces for houses on either side were contained by high retaining walls overhung with ivy. It was a world of compartments, of small worlds opening unexpectedly into other worlds. The window of my bedroom on the second floor looked right into the next-door neighbors' dining room on the uphill side. I could see people moving in the darkness behind the glass like fish at the aquarium. I thought England was over there. At the park there was a dark echoing tunnel to walk through that opened into a sunlit amphitheater of rose bushes. At the very back of our backyard under a grove of tall thin trees, the ground ended abruptly at two straight edges that met at a square corner, the top of a retaining wall with a drop of twenty feet to the street below.

The house in Berkeley was a duplex and the owners lived in the other half. They were an older couple, world travelers, with a large collection of beautiful Oriental rugs. In their front room, carpets covered every wall as well as the floor, and when we visited with them I do not know which interested me more, the colors and the patterns of the rugs, or their walls that looked like floors.

The landlady's father was an elderly Swiss gentleman I called Grandpa Bachi. He was my best friend. He would take me for walks up and down the steep street and let me help him in the garden. He had been a builder of large telescopes for observatories in Europe, but he had developed palsy in his old age. His hands shook so badly he could not drink tea from a cup; he used a glass straw instead, which shook in his hands and made a rhythmic clinking sound in his cup as he drank. His room was filled with big overstuffed leather upholstered chairs, and floor to ceiling shelves filled with books. He gave me a sky chart, a map of the night sky printed on a wheel that you turned around to see the stars for different seasons. He was kind and patient. He was the one who would walk with me to the very back of the yard and hold my hand while I looked over the geometric edge of the Earth there, and one day we walked all the way around the block, so he could show me what the edge looked like from the street below.

He gave me a wonderful book, *Let's Go Outdoors*, with close up photographs of small creatures in the garden: sow bugs, snails, and toads, spiders, dragonflies, and ants. They were all printed in the velvety sepia tones of rotogravure that heightened the strange beauty of the details: the huge, round, disc-shaped eyes and spiraling tongue of a butterfly, the shiny, slick trail from the single foot of a snail across the craggy surface of a brick. On the back pages of the book, written in my mother's hand, were the complete dictionary definitions of "plant" and "animal", apparently I would ask. Grandpa Bachi taught me to be curious and to explore. He was encouraging and reliable, with a wholesome rootedness like a plant or a tree. I loved him. He gave me, just by being who he was with his centered openness, a sense of a great basic goodness inherent in all life.

The wide meadow in the forest sloped upward to the crown of the hill ringed on three sides by tall trees. It was a special place, set apart. I walked with my parents toward the big round structure with a pointed roof like a tent that was perched by itself at the top of the meadow. We could hear the music as we got closer, and I ran ahead toward the whirling colors and the joyful churning sounds. The big merry-go-round was still in motion. I could see the horses gliding up and down as they went by inside a blur of shiny poles and dazzling colors, rhythms of light and sound, and then the whole display slowly began to wind down.

I had a passion for merry-go-rounds. I waited until forever for it to stop, and then I climbed up on the springy suspended platform as the riders dismounted. I was looking for a special horse, a different one each time. I passed by the splendid orange and black striped tigers and the graceful swan boat longingly, but they did not go up and down, they were stationary. I was looking for horses, horses that moved: a blue one with golden spots, or a white one with pink and green bridle and braided yellow hair, or a black one with fierce red and blue green eyes, horses with legs outstretched, horses with legs folded in a leap. This huge grand vintage merry-go-round in Tilden Park was filled with elaborate beautiful horses, four or five abreast.

I moved quickly up and down the aisles of horses. Other kids were looking too. Suddenly you knew, you picked the horse in front of you, stepped up on the stirrup, threw your leg over its back, grabbed onto the shining golden pole and held your little ticket out in one hand for the ticket-taker man, the only person who was allowed to walk on the quivering floor after the ride began.

Then the music started up again. The ponderous floor began to creak and move; the pipes overhead that carried the horses up and down began to turn. Your horse soared upward, not too far, and gently brought you down again, you stood up in the stirrups, you sat in the saddle, you were riding, a glorious exuberant ride of spinning painted colors and revolving mirrors and other horses moving up and down all around you. You saw your parents up ahead outside, watching for you to go by, sometimes you wave, mostly you ride. This was earnest sacred joy; you rode with all your heart, lifting impossibly, descending gently, over and over, turning on an endless wheel revolving around the mysterious, mirrored, golden and multicolored center you could not see inside.

Then the turning would begin to slow, the horses taking longer to rise each time, longer to fall, still falling to rise and lift once more, slower and slower each time, not yet coming to a stop. The undulating movements would be in slow motion now, time was slowing down, and you melted into the easing rise and fall, stretching out the end. Then the music stopped and the horses and the spinning floor would come to rest.

Each night when I was four or five, as I began to fall asleep, the walls of my room would expand and contract as if the room and the grainy twilight air were breathing together, a living form of space. I would watch the walls moving for a while, and as I came nearer to sleep, my body would begin to shrink. I would feel my arms and legs growing smaller and smaller from inside. I would be slowly sinking too, until I was no longer in my head. Then I would be in the pink valley again, looking out from the small light at my heart with my head looming large above me. There would be an exquisite counterpoint between the weightless tenderness of the soft light at my heart and the apparent weight of the big round head, and a wondering how my tiny shoulders could be strong enough to support the heaviness of the head. I would ride the floating and the weight, the solidity and the light, deeper into sleep.

SINGING BLUE

We were living in Walnut Creek, California by then, in one of the first subdivisions in the hills overlooking the valley. All the newly built modest ranch style homes were awash in a sea of adobe mud that first winter when it rained. Gradually my parents and the other new home owners tamed the land, planting lawns, trees, and gardens, building patios and barbecues, and putting up swing sets for the kids, but I loved the undeveloped wild land, the open rolling hills that started right on the other side of the back fence.

Our small neighborhood was surrounded by grasslands on all sides, endless untamed hills, oceans of long grass rippling in the wind. The hills were blond with summer heat, green with winter rain, and in the spring, wild sweet peas with colors like the dawn bloomed all along the banks where the roads cut through. I loved the hills, and I loved the sky that was so much a part of the hills, the blue, blue singing sky, blue beyond all time, a soaring vibrant blue, bell-like clear and vast.

I had no brothers or sisters. I moved within the hidden currents flowing between two complex adults. My parents seldom talked about their lives and I heard few stories about their childhood memories. Years later, a favorite aunt told me a little about their early life together. My parents met in college. They were very much in love and were always holding hands when they were first married. My mother was unprepared when her tall handsome philosophy major turned Marine lieutenant came back from Guadalcanal sickened by what he had experienced there. She wanted a large family but she had a miscarriage of an almost full term child before I was born and a hysterectomy for uterine fibroid tumors, the pink boulders of my memory, when I was two or three. I did not know these stories about my parents when I was young. I felt their sadness and their struggles in my dreams instead, and inside their words and gestures so often intended to mean something other than how they felt.

I looked for nurturing outside, in Grandpa Bachi and in the land. In the California hills and especially the sky, I found what many people look for in family, a sense of belonging. I found something else as well that transcended family, a spacious brightness that opened in the company of the hills and sky, independently of my age, my life, my time.

I liked to get up very early before my parents were awake, and go outside and sit quietly before the sun came up over Mt. Diablo to the east. I loved the dawn. Our backyard had an unobstructed view of the rolling hills sloping down to the valley below, a valley that almost disappeared at dawn, becoming hidden in the mountain rising up beyond. The whole Earth was in the mountain then, in the dark blue color of the massive shape, and in the bright flickering edge that met the pale no color sky slowly giving way to pink before the blue of the day began. The air was soft and new. The distant rumble of heavy trucks on the highway in the valley below sounded like invisible machinery in the sky that opened the day. There was a specialness before the sun would rise, of waiting for something and not waiting for anything at all, both at the same time, a freshness and a stillness at the beginning of the day, as if everything was recreated anew, waiting to reappear along with the sun.

There was also a mysterious power in the colors of the dawn, a generative power that had something to do with the reappearance of the daytime world. One day I put all my pink, blue, purple, and turquoise crayons in a small cough drop box and carried them around with me. For several months I drew every picture in these potent colors of the dawn, no matter what the subjects were. Then one day I started using all the other colors again.

I loved to draw. When I was not outside, I would be drawing. I was given a large set of colored pencils, although I did not like to draw with pencils then. The points were too hard and fine to put a lot of color thickly on a page, but I loved the individual colors painted on the outside of each pencil. I would spill the pencils on the floor and reassemble them again in perfect rainbow order in their box, again and again. The progression from the reds, through the yellows, the greens, and the blues fascinated me, a natural ordering that seemed to come from the colors themselves.

Early childhood can be a time of great openness and subtlety of perception, unencumbered by the learned responses of the society you find yourself within. Many people have profound spiritual experience then. Some are met with incomprehension or disapproval from the adults around them intent on shaping their world. For others, the ties of past lives and the progress of the present life can dull or cover the openness from the inside, and the experience can be explained away as not being real. These imprints of the divine, however they come to you, can also form a simple secret trust instead that lasts throughout your life.

We went to church on Sundays and my parents would buy me a big round puffy glazed doughnut on the way home each week. The doughnuts were sweet and greasy, golden brown, with a lighter color around the rim where the dough was pressed when the shape was cut out, and they had a tantalizing hollowness built into their form. I would put my finger through the empty place and eat the rim all the way around, saving the hole for last.

From what I had heard at Sunday school and from my parents, God was an old man with a white beard who was everywhere and saw everything, and I became very interested in just how he could do this. I had already realized that my parents were Santa Claus. I had not told them. I was not sure if they wanted to be found out, and I did not want to hurt their feelings. I was certain that God was also not an old man with a white beard, but he was not my parents either, and as for his being everywhere and seeing everything, I considered these carefully.

I decided that God was like the sky overhead, larger than anything, and he was like the air, because he was inside rooms too. He was an invisible space around everything, with holes in him for

14

all the objects, for people, mountains, tables and chairs. God was also aware; he knew what you were doing and what you were going to do, so the miracle of God was that when you were going to move a chair, God moved the chair-shaped hole over too, so you had a place to put it.

This God with hollows in him big enough for mountains, intricate and small enough for an insect or a plant, was an interesting idea to me, but it came from adjusting a definition given to me by adults. Both the definition and the adjusting seemed limited and limiting compared to the feeling of the heart light at the edge of sleep or the mysterious power of colors.

That year the small Christmas tree in our kindergarten classroom was set up on one of the tables so that you had to look up to see it. The tall windows in the gabled wall behind the tree opened into a soaring blue sky, and the little tree seemed inseparable with the vastness outside.

We had made chains of colored construction paper to decorate the tree and a paper angel with silver glitter for the top, and as I stood looking up at the tree, the colored hoops linked together in the paper chains were suddenly inexpressibly holy, filled with an overwhelming tenderness and a power like the dawn. I was enveloped from within by an endless silken radiance, my heart opening into a memory intangible outside of time, everything else fading away, only this wordless certainty, absolute blessing, luminosity. Enfolded in the brightness, I knew what holiness meant, from inside. Beyond any ideas of God or spirituality, I knew that this living brilliance was what blessing is, and I remembered that my heart knew that it was always there, even when unseen, an ephemeral embrace.

These moments of spacious radiance, so certain and complete, feel as if they will never end. I did not know how the brightness opened, nor how to ask for its return, but it left a trace as indelible as memory and timeless in its own way, a secret in my heart. I knew instinctively to never mention these experiences, or even to dwell on them with my mind. They were the province of my heart, outside of words.

STAYING GRACE

Rob

The brilliance of father and mother consorts in union glowing in inner radiance makes up all phenomena of the vision we call this life and abides in the hearts of all beings waiting to be recognized and kindle an open heart. Are we aware, are we really looking? If the eyes of your heart are open, you are surrounded by inner radiance. This recognition can arise suddenly, especially in childhood, but not always in gentle ways or circumstances. It can reveal itself in the midst of truly wrenching experience.

The beginning can be said to be in 1955 in a hospital in Los Angeles, California, but even an insect's life is vast in the scope of endless lives. Undefined space outside the concepts of beginnings or endings is filled with beings in constant flux, coming into and being torn from life in endless unremitting rushing cycles. Where did it all begin, or is it all present, and the vastness beyond anything comprehensible plays itself out in a cycle understandable as a life? And so I was taken home along with my twin brother John to grow up, comfortably enough, in Encino, California.

One of my earliest memories was of crawling down a narrow rug along a passageway separated from the living room by a tall balustrade. I was crawling toward Elena, who was standing beside a clothes hamper in the hallway near the room I shared with my brother John. Her dark brown face was round and soft. She was a heavy-set woman, part African-American and part Cherokee. I loved her deeply; she was real, a genuine good heart. Elena came three times a week to clean and do the laundry, and so my memories of her are while she worked around the house. I remember her openness, her deep joyful laugh and her profound sense of patience and forgiveness. She had a strong enduring quality like the Earth. She calmly kept going even during difficult times.

As I crawled toward Elena I heard my mother's outburst of anger coming from my room, then she rushed past Elena and quickly disappeared down another hallway. My mother had white hair even when she was young, and a fair complexion. She was slender, always elegantly dressed with nylons and high heels. She was very quick with her mind and her body; she had a hot temper. I always wondered at my mother's formal wedding photograph, her white hair setting off her sharp featured profile, stern and cold. She had a collection of very fine porcelain figurines. I felt my mother was like these fragile representations of people, refined, elegant, and frozen within a costume from another time. She was proud, noble, and sad. I loved her in a different way.

I was still very young, clinging to my mother's skirt in a sea of legs and skirts going and coming. We must have been at the market. At one point, I noticed a different set of legs, the nylons were sagging and loose, the legs were swollen and heavy, with visible sores. I felt a strange pain all over my body. The sensation of pain subsided and from that time onward whenever I saw someone with visible wounds or sore angry skin I would have the same sensation.

Around the age of three, I had a medical procedure performed on me, an experience that was a major jolt, a dream-like mix of nightmare and epiphany. I was in a darkened office with my mother. I was too young to grasp what she and the doctor were talking about. Then we went to the Children's Hospital. In a large room, we were ushered into a curtained stall where my mother filled out forms and I was to get undressed and into a little outfit with teddy bears on it. I was very unhappy and I let my mother know. I was placed in a wheelchair, and my mother and I were taken to a room with a large glass window facing the hallway, with a crib inside which was for me. This also did not make things better.

I guess I got a bed, for I soon found myself waking up in one, but something was very wrong. I had a tube exiting my penis going to the foot of the bed, connected to a bag hanging off the railing. My mother was sitting in a chair at the end of the bed. She talked to me as I came out of the anesthesia but soon got up and left. I was very uncomfortable, nervous, and afraid. A nurse arrived in a big hurry; she was upset and told me to get out of bed. I was naked and hesitated. She would have none of that, whipping the cover off me and demanding that I get out of bed and into the wheel chair. The chair was cold and clammy as she plopped the bag of warm dark red fluid from the end of the bed into my arms. She dropped the cover on my lap and away we went, down corridors, elevators and more cold empty concrete hallways. The nurse parked me in the hallway, alone. I was numb, just looking at the polished floor shining in the dim light. I did not know what was going on; I felt I had done something wrong.

I sat for what seemed an eternity with my bag of blood on my lap. In front of me were two very large steel doors with no windows. All of a sudden, they opened wide to reveal a little boy younger than I was, screaming uncontrollably, naked on top of a steel table with a large lamp over him. There was a plastic bag over a bloody mass where his penis should be. A man beside the table was yelling at the boy who was convulsing in fear. Suddenly my heart literally cracked open, and as if hands emerged from my heart, I embraced the boy. It was as if the air of my lungs and the beat of my heart were offered to him. The doors closed as suddenly as they had opened. I was left shaking, concerned not only for myself but also for someone who was even more shaken and afraid than I was. There was a certainty I never forgot from this brief experience: that you need not do something physically to touch another. There was a power within my heart that could actually comfort others.

Despite the intense circumstances, the procedure was resolved to the satisfaction of the adults, but I was no longer focused on it. The ephemeral power of my heart became a staying grace throughout my life. I knew I had touched the boy.

The following Sunday I went to church for the first time I can remember. The stages of entering this space were tantalizing, as I dipped my hands in the holy water and was told to make the sign of the cross. My mother and father guided us to a pew. I must have seen Jesus on the cross, although all I recall was the quiet. Everyone whispered. It was all very important, special, almost scary. My parents were most serious. I must have been told this was God's house.

In our pew, we all knelt to pray before the Mass began. For me there was only this precious moment, refreshed by the blessing that quieted these unruly people. Kneeling, alone within one's closed eyes, below the level of the pew, I entered a radiance like a spark becoming a flame, becoming the sun. I was embraced, held for an eternity, on the warm sand of an endless beach, and yet adrift in a calm vast sea which knew no shore, no boundary. Brilliant, engulfing, I dove into it not wanting to come back. Abruptly I was jerked out into an inferno of reproach I could not understand. My neck hurt from being pulled to my seat, and told in sharp whispers to stop playing around! I had no idea what I could have done wrong.

I loved to wake early before dawn. It was exciting, a joyful time in the cool, early morning dark, the thrill of things becoming apparent again. The birds knew it; they all sang praises and blessings when first light brought out the shapes of everything, which had vanished into the night like ships sinking at sea. This day was even more special. My mother woke my brother John and me in the night, long before we usually got up. We had to get an early start;

this was the day the family was to drive to the mountains. It was still dark as we pulled out of the driveway. The atmosphere was moist, cold, and exciting. The roads were empty, the houses and buildings closed. Everything was calm and quiet; we were free to leave the usual chaotic smoggy order.

The buildings dropped away as the sun rose. The road narrowed and we entered a world of trees, rocks, and mountains. Then we had to wait in a line of cars, requiring patience. Finally, we arrived, free to move and be greeted by elemental fresh air smelling of pine. And there was a cabin made of trees, just as much a wonder as the forest.

Shattering this delight my mother exploded in fury, screaming and yelling in a cataclysmic rage. I did not know why she was screaming. I found a log to sit on not far from the cabin. I sat within the shelter of the forest allowing the tempest to pass. The forest air was alive with a simple kindness, and so I sat, open, enfolded by this essence for quite a while, until my mother, who had calmed down by then, came over to take my picture. The photo shows me looking at her. I was neither happy nor sad. I was just sitting there.

Years later, my father told me why my mother had exploded into a rage that day, saying it was the most shocking, horrible experience of his life. My father loved the wilderness, and he tried very hard to find comfortable elegant ways to share this love with her. He said he had rented a very nice cabin near Yosemite with a large deck overlooking a rushing river below. When my brother and I ran to the railing, my mother thought we would fall to our death and still crushed by the loss of her second child who had died of an internal congenital defect a few years before, she had been terrified she would lose us too.

As I sat in the forest that day, open and aware of the beautiful energy of life around me and embracing me, I looked at my mother taking the picture, knowing that like my experience in the hospital or the church, I was seeing something that she did not see. The

21

caption in my mother's perfect handwriting beneath the photo in the family album reads "Solitude".

It was early morning, damp from a light rain, as we drove up a wooded country road. A buck with a large set of antlers bounded across the road just ahead of our car. We were on our way to visit my mother's sister, Sister Miriam of Jesus o.c.d. who had founded a Carmelite convent near Eugene, Oregon. I remember the sound of the gravel of the driveway as we parked, and at the garden gates, my mother speaking on an intercom; you could not just walk in. Then we were walking on a garden path. We found a green tree frog; my sister touched it and it stuck to her finger; she screamed trying to shake it off. After her scream, I could feel a quiet that was not just there because there was no scream. It was a presence like in church, and then from behind a fence came Aunt Mary's hearty laugh.

We came into a plain room and sat on chairs looking at an iron grill that separated the room into two halves. Soon Aunt Mary walked in and greeted us warmly through this partition. I was truly surprised and fascinated by this separation. As I understood things then, Aunt Mary was the church, she lived in it, and when you do that, you never touch or live with ordinary people. Everything spoke of this sacred order and special existence, calm, quiet, peaceful, orderly. She and later, all the nuns, exhibited the same behavior; they laughed warmly, but they were restrained.

We stayed the night in their guest room and went to Mass the next morning. We sat in their chapel with them, but the nuns remained inside a glass partition. I never stopped wondering about this separation; I wondered why we all could not live like this. A peaceful existence in God's house seemed a good idea compared to the hurried smog-choked intensity going on back home, but the life within the cloister, though praised and supported, was said not to be for everyone, only those chosen by God.

RAMPARTS

On weekends when my parents slept in, I would get up very early before sunrise. I did not usually do this during the week for my father and mother would get up early then; it was their time and I would be greeted by cold anger. My whole family would be asleep. I was fascinated and a bit shocked. Why sleep when such a glorious dawn is occurring? I was careful so I would not wake them. I would wander around the house and finally into the family room, which my parents called the keeping room, a colonial phrase for a common room, where we had a large TV built into the cabinetry with controls over by the couch. I would turn on the TV making sure the volume was very low. Television broadcasts did not run twenty-four hours a day then, so I was greeted by the static fuzzy cloud, sort of a dry rushing fog, specks of black and white that were moving yet nothing could be seen, just this violent rush of light broken into a dust cloud with a whooshing static sound. I sat on the floor and watched this cloud for a long time. Then columns of grey tones or a circle with radiating lines of grey tones or a profile of a Native American with a feathered headdress would spontaneously appear. All of them had a similar strange high-pitched sound. I would sit and watch these pictures for another long time. Then, inevitably, a rerun would start, *Buck Rogers* or *Gene Autry*. The cartoons would come another hour later when my parents woke up.

My poor parents, they truly wanted a well-behaved little boy with no problems, good-natured, and excellent manners. My brother, sisters, and I were never allowed to feed ourselves until we could hold a knife or fork properly. I can remember my mother coaching my brother and me on the proper way to use a soup spoon, an advanced practice, which I never fully mastered.

I had my share of physical problems some of which I have carried through my life, childhood asthma, illnesses of all kinds, broken leg, various operations. I seemed to be at the doctor's every week. My mother could not deal with my problems. She would sometimes scream at me in utter rage, "What's wrong with you!" Those early experiences of the little boy and my epiphany in church were like a stone rampart that could not be breached. I may have been falling inward but my eyes were open.

From very early on in my life I had a strong inner sense of who I was, what I wanted, and how I saw the world. My parents saw the world in a very different way, and after a while, I learned which parts of their world were not to be transgressed. The highest most important aspect of my parents' world was Society. My grandmother belonged to the L.A. Country Club and my mother was involved with her sorority and high-class charity. Elegant parties were an absolute necessity for my parents.

Education on the other hand was of a lower category. My parents did not take a daily interest in our schoolwork, rarely helping with our homework, although they later got us tutors and took us to summer school. My parents really were happy and content if we were not running around or asking questions. My mother's temper was a strong impetus to stay in the family room where television and sugar treats were a daily routine. We were out of the way.

Since parties were almost a weekly event in our lives my brother and I began to help cleaning and organizing the house and garden to prepare for them even when we were little kids. My parents were very quick to praise this behavior.

Around our fifth year, my brother and I were enrolled at the local Catholic grade school. My sisters were taken out of a private school that they passionately loved and were also enrolled. My father had recently started his own glass contracting business along with a partner. Even though my mother received some money from a family business in the Midwest, it was not quite enough. The elegant parties continued but my mother would now sew her own ball gowns.

I did not like the parochial school, which relied on corporal punishment to discipline the students. There were over fifty students per class so strict order was always enforced. Inquiry was discouraged. If you got anything wrong, you were hit with a ruler or a rosary. I always got good marks for conduct but my low grades reflected my true feelings about the school. The teachers were always considering whether to hold me back but my mother would not allow this. I was just passed along year after year. The rigidity of the school and the church were the same to me. It was all so solid and fixed. Everything you learned was so absolute and inflexible, the verb goes here, the numeral there, and the belief is this. There was no room, no movement and no heart.

I did not like school but I did have a great private interest in space travel, the space race, and science fiction. I collected every newspaper and magazine with pictures of planets, stars, and spaceships. All of it fascinated me, but my true sense of cosmology came out of the Sci Fi movies like *Forbidden Planet*, *Them*, and *The Body Snatchers* and numerous movies about encountering new and bizarre worlds. My mind was consumed by the notion of traveling through space, going to other worlds, not stuck in this ordinary world's perceptions. I watched cartoons of all kinds. They were so molten and unfixed. I fell away into myself and drew a world and experience from these fluid images of strength moving beyond the ordinary. Television programs added to my library of space adventure. I never felt this life to be a solid reality. My experience was a mix in the mind of a daydreamer who also felt and saw spirits and light.

Then there were the movies of war, battles, hills, last stands, the last torpedo, the last bullet. There was Spencer Tracey playing an old mountaineer saving a "Hindu lady" after a plane crash in the Alps, or he was an old priest comforting a dying convict who had saved the orphans from being trapped on a volcanic island about to explode. His words were soft yet laced with a knowing that this was his last moment on Earth, his last act. So many movies and actors battling for freedom, marching up the last hill, and as the smoke clears they march off victorious though beaten and bloody to the next battle, the horizon, the sunset. I was always affected and moved to dream again another molten dream with honor, belief, and faith, as a new dream begins and ends within this fluid world.

Smoke hung low over the battlefield close to a large dam and reservoir system for a whole nation. Troops were massing with a sense of urgency on both sides, a sense of vital decisions being made far off and waiting through a dense atmosphere of fear. A flash of light streaks across the sky, blinding the troops. Flames shear through the land and the men as the dam bursts, engulfing the lives of all in its path. Long flaring flames streak through the sky as silence descends on the survivors.

It took a long time to shovel the sandy soil from the road out front of our house. Our extensive dam across the drainage channel had backed up water past my grandmother's house, and my father had taken a dim view of our sense of apocalypse. The rose garden did survive the war at the end of time. We picked up our remaining soldiers, raked the reservoir system back around the rose bushes, and threw away the empty cans of my mother's hair spray and the spent matches, while the air raid sirens blared their warnings in the summer of 1962.

My mother and father loved each other very much. My father became Catholic in order to marry my mother, and children came as a matter of course. My father would say many times to us, "We love you kids, you better know that." They were frustrated by the demands of a family and their love of elegant social gatherings and so they tried very hard to bring the children into the matrix of their social lives.

My parents along with my grandmother had built a large ranch style house in the foothills of Encino. My grandmother lived in her own section of the house in the back. All around the property were old orange orchards. The scent, liquid and edible, would pervade the air in spring. The house had no views to speak of; the emphasis was on entertaining. The formal living room and dining room, even the family room, were decorated in antiques, comfortable but refined. Don't spill anything!

The focal point for my parents' lives were their elegant parties which really were beyond their livelihood but something they had to have and could not live without. The preparation for these events would begin weeks in advance with my mother sending out personal invitations in her calligraphic handwriting. My father would be engrossed in preparing the menu; his hobby was being a gourmet cook. As time came closer to the day of the event, my dad would buy boxes of liquor and adornments and set up the bars inside and out on the patio. He would also buy and plant all new bedding plants for all the borders of the gardens, which was a great deal of work. My mother would have Elena polish all the silver as she prepared the centerpiece in the dining room. The specific type of china and crystal would be chosen and arranged for use during the party.

My mother would be finishing the details of her gown or cocktail dress, and making sure that all the children had the proper clothes to wear, everything cleaned, pressed, and polished. My brother and I would have our hair cut, which was always a struggle for me; I just could not stand it.

As the day arrived, my brother and I would clean the front yard, hose down the driveway, and rake up any fallen leaves or debris of any kind. The backyard was manicured by the gardeners days before but John and I washed the patios down and cleaned all the elegant wrought iron furniture. The whole facade was in place and gleaming with a strong smell of window cleaner, furniture polish, and insect fogger, to be topped off by room freshener.

By the time the guests began arriving the whole family was scrubbed and in suits and party dresses. When my brother and I were very young, we were trained to greet the guests with formal bows from the waist. After all the greetings, the guests would settle into the living room and the kids would help serve the cocktails and hors d'oeuvres. If it were a large party, more than thirty people, it would be catered, but many times just Elena was asked to come and help keep the kitchen clean and organized. My brother, sisters, and I found refuge in the kitchen then, talking and laughing with Elena; she was the evening's bright star for us. After the dinner was served and lauded by the guests, they retired to the living room for after dinner drinks. When we were very young, my mother would be coaxed to sing opera with my uncle Alden playing our Steinway piano. Not all the parties were so formal but even our birthday parties were an excuse for an elegant get together, for the adults.

SIGNS

Driving along Route 66 in the summer of '65, the two-lane highway was laid down upon the ground following the ridges as if riding along the back of an immense dinosaur. My mother, sisters, brother, and I were on vacation, going across the country in the family station wagon. We would spend most of the day on the road, and then find a motel for the night, where the stillness of the desert was cut only by an occasional rushing sound of a car going by on the highway and the rattling hum of the air conditioner.

I loved the drive along these long open spaces, the changing light of the day playing upon the rolling land and the billboards. The desert seemed filled with signs of all kinds, telling of the two-headed snake only 5 mi. ahead, with snow cones, cafés and gas stations 45 mi. ahead. Every mile after that was a countdown to this incredible place where enormous arrows, taller than the billboards, were stuck in the ground as if shot from a giant bow, huge concrete teepees, arrowheads, panning for gold, petting zoo, gift shops with ice cold soda pop. As you drove away these amazing places would be swallowed up by the vast desert, becoming only dots upon a map.

During that stretch of America, I remember picking up the book my sister Mary was reading for her religious studies class, *The Autobiography of a Yogi,* by Yogananda. The black and white photographs were amazing and compelling like a dream that would not surface. They had a strangely mysterious quality, the yogis seemingly appearing on their own accord rather than being captured on film by a camera. One photo of an old yogi with a long white beard gave me a chill. I had once seen myself in a mirror at our house as an old man with a long white beard rather than my own reflection as a child. The picture of Babaji was mesmerizing, as was the one of a white yogi with a cobra on his head sitting in front of the tallest mountains in the world, and yogis in strange postures, eyes half shut, and long hair. I would pick up the book, leafing through this album of forgotten ancestors as we drove up and down the thin ribbon of asphalt. When my sister left home, I kept this copy of the book.

DISTANCE

Rachel

My maternal grandmother's front porch in Wabash, Indiana, was deep and wide, with big hydrangea bushes like a battlement in front protecting the house from the quiet street. The humid air of the hot Midwestern summer night had cooled down suddenly with the approach of my first thunderstorm. My father and I sat together on the porch swing as lightning flared in the dark sky and thunder rolled and crashed all around us. He was sitting with me not to reassure, but to introduce me to a stupendous wonder, a great wild joy.

I loved my father very much. He was a troubled man in some ways, consistent with his times, a sensitive thoughtful spirit injured by a world war, and injured again by his successful corporate climb, but sitting on the porch swing, suspended inside the gleaming darkness of the thunder and the rain, he gave me a precious gift, the courage to be unafraid, not because the world was safe and good, but because it was unpredictable, dangerous, and challenging. He gave me the willingness to fall in love, to stay open even to the fierceness of a storm.

My mother's gifts to me were subtler and harder to unveil, tangled up in the unspoken things she kept concealed in her heart, but I remember a day in grade school, coming home for lunch, just the two of us together, the soft light of early autumn seeping through the closed slats of the venetian blind at the window by the table as we ate, and the clear pure shape of a fresh pear cut in half. I had heard at school that if you taste one thing while smelling another, you will taste the one you smell, so we cut an apple in half too, and took turns mingling the apple and the pear, laughing, an unusual moment of playfulness between us, but that was not the heart of her gift. It was the soft light, and the clear shape of the pear, and a moment when our minds met in gentle silence, just simply being there.

My parents had sold the house surrounded by grasslands in Walnut Creek. We stayed in Wabash with my grandmother until my parents found a new place to live, and then we moved to an older suburb on the west side of Cleveland in the fall. I was in exile. I knew that then. I belonged in California; I was supposed to be there. I missed the open hills, the long grass rippling in the wind, the sunrise over the mountain, the great soaring singing sky. I missed California and all that it meant to me, an openness and a freedom simply called "The West".

In the California of my memories, the sky was always a brilliant turquoise blue, like the flat oval stone set in a silver sunburst on a bracelet that my mother had. The bracelet and the stone were from the West too, a West as ancient and far away as the blue sky.

The sky in Cleveland was capable of many amazing things, thunderstorms, and the eerie yellow and greenish purple light before the big tornado that uprooted huge oak trees up and down the street. An oak fell right next to our house parallel to the wall and from my bedroom window that night I saw a long jagged flash of lightning run straight down the middle of the street a few feet above the pavement, just before my mother came to get me and take me downstairs when the power went out. These were dramatic and exciting, but they quickly passed. The basic sky, the one you relied upon, was rarely blue; it was most often grey and heavy with low clouds.

31

I was willing to connect with a different kind of land and sky, but there was no distance in the part of Cleveland where we lived. The land was flat; there were no mountain peaks to testify to far away, and the houses and trees all crowded up close to your eyes. I was eight when we moved to Cleveland, but I was already sensitive to visual space. An uncle who had been an artist when he was a young man had taught me about perspective when I was five or six, when he visited us in California and saw how much I loved to draw. Like most children, I would draw objects, horses, people, and trees directly on the horizon line, which in one sense is the way things are. My uncle told me to look with my eyes, to see what my eyes see. The horizon line was actually at a distance; most objects closer in were below the line. I went outside and looked at the mountain, the valley below, and the trees in our yard, and he was right. I started drawing his way. Other kids at school would criticize, asking why I was putting the sheep inside the ground. I tried to explain what my uncle had said, but they were usually unconvinced.

Years later when I was invited to give a slide lecture about my paintings of dreams for an audience of art therapists, the therapists were confounded too. One woman came up to me afterward and said, "What are you anyway?" She explained that they understood artistic expression as having two modes: people who were more expressive, drawing how they feel the world to be; and people who were more visual, interested in exactly how and what they see. My paintings were such an equal mix of these two forms of expression that the therapists were both enthusiastic and surprised. The seamless integration was from my sense of childhood exile mingled with my uncle's gift, from a simple longing to reconcile how you feel with where you are.

Cleveland was disappointing not only in terms of visual space. I knew that outer distance was also a connection to the inner brightness at my heart, and in that way especially, I felt an oppressive heaviness here. An excess of gravity or some other force seemed to pull down on everything. It held the sky down, kept it low and close to the Earth. It concentrated the toxins from the sewage and industrial waste in the rivers and the lake. It pulled down on the people too. When we rode public transportation, the buses and commuter trains to go downtown, the faces all around looked so joyless and sour. They looked to my eyes then as unripe fruit picked to soon to rot, just drying out from inside. Perhaps moving from one part of the country to another, not belonging to either world had created a gap, and I was seeing the traces of others' hopes and fears more clearly. The weight of sadness and unlived lives seemed to be everywhere. Cleveland in the fifties was showing me the spaciousness I so longed for turned inside out, revealing the anguished hollow space that arises when hearts pull away from each other and from the inner brightness, and take their separation to be real.

My parents tried. We walked around our neighborhood in the fall, picking up bright colored autumn leaves from red maples and yellow oaks. We pressed them between the pages of the heavy books, the big dictionary and the gold embossed volumes of the encyclopedia that had belonged to my paternal grandfather. For years every time you looked up anything in one of those books, broken bits of brittle leaves would fall out on the floor. But my parents were disappearing, turning farther away from each other and away from themselves. My father was molding himself into a perfect corporate lawyer; he wanted to succeed. My mother was treading water as a proper housewife; she wanted to survive. I was somewhere in between.

We were living in a duplex again. The tall oak trees in our yard had left years of small pointy acorns embedded in the lawn like sharp tacks; you could not practice cartwheels or sit easily on the grass. The owner would not let us have a dog. I began to spend more time inside, inside my room, inside my mind, drawing and reading, looking there for a landscape for my heart, for the expansive vivid quality I had found in the California hills and sky. I would finish a picture or put down a book after reading for a while, and be surprised to be in my body and my room again. At times when I walked on our street, I would look down and be startled; my arms and legs would seem so strange to me, like waking momentarily from a dream, oh, that's what I am this time.

My parents joined a country club, and they bought a new car, a two-tone Imperial with a lot of chrome, power windows, and white sidewall tires. When they washed this gleaming ornate vision of a car, my dad would park it next to the curb on the side street by our part of the yard so the hose would reach. We would polish the blue and white enameled and chromed curves and scrub the white circles of the tires until they glowed. One day I was standing in the yard alone, facing the empty place where the Imperial would be washed and all that it signified to me. As if a veil pulled apart, a deep assurance arose from within that I came into this life to do something specific, something familiar I had done before, something very different from going to grade school in Cleveland, Ohio, and I felt it was both inconvenient and tedious to have to learn a whole new culture and a complex language like English before I could do it.

WISH BOATS

We had only a few days left of our two weeks at Girl Scout summer camp. I joined the other girls, and as we started down the trail to the lake, we began to sing. This had been my first time away from my parents and their world, my first time living in the woods, and I loved the camp. I loved being with the other girls. I loved the musty army tents, the trees, the smoky campfires, and scrubbing the blackened pots. Most of all I loved the songs, with the high clear voices of girls singing in harmonies and rounds.

There was the round of overlapping names of French cathedrals that made the sound of tolling bells, and another, a few simple Latin words set to a simple tune, like clear stones immersed in light. Even in translation, it was the most unadorned of prayers: I am poor, I have nothing; I will give my heart.

Then there were the songs; there was "Peace I Ask of Thee O River", stately, gentle, wide, with deep slow harmonies on the low notes, and bright rippling unison on the high. Words alone on paper are not enough to convey how much this song meant to me. The singing gave the simple poetry a majesty and grace, but there was also a wisdom behind the words, from an unknown voice who knew as I did, that land, a river, or a hill, could be your parent, teacher, friend. My longing for California came from that same place, an openness inside the singing of the song.

On the last day of camp, we held a wish boat ceremony. Each unit of girls received a wish boat, a short flat wooden plank with angled cuts on one end like the prow of a boat and a candle mounted in the middle. We decorated our boat with wildflowers and forest leaves and wrote a group wish for peace and happiness in our families and the world. Each group of girls elected a girl to launch their boat, someone to represent their experience of the camp and the intention of their wish. I was elected to launch our boat. I was completely surprised and touched, so accustomed to spending time by myself, disappearing into schoolwork, drawings, projects, and books. Here, in my great enthusiasm for the camp, I had found another place for my heart.

The evening of the ceremony, the whole camp gathered on the shore of the lake. Some of the counselors spoke until it was dark. Then one by one, we launched the boats as the wishes were read. When it was our turn, I lit the candle and waded out into the shimmering darkness of the lake, moving slowly so the flame would not blow out. I set the little boat gently on the water and let it float out of my hands. The surface of the lake was very still, but the current from the small creek that fed the lake carried the boat farther from the shore. I watched the little light of our boat join the other little lights of prayers drifting quietly into the night.

When all the boats were launched, we stood together in the dark, and sang the kindly hopeful harmonies of the river song; our hearts were floating there, in the shining darkness with the little lights and in the clear tones of our voices carried on the song.

For a year, our Girl Scout troop had planned a trip to the White Mountains of New Hampshire to hike a portion of the Appalachian Trail. One of the leaders had proposed the trip, after she saw the trail from a tram that went to the top of one of the highest mountains there. She saw a wide level route encircling the mountain above timberline and she heard about the hut system, the mountain hostels a day's hike apart where you could spend the night and be provided with dinner, breakfast and box lunch. This seemed to be an easy reasonable adventure, and we would only have to carry our sleeping bags and a few necessities. We were not prepared for the strenuous all day hike from the valley below to reach the ridge top trail. By mid afternoon, we were all separated from each other and struggling alone.

The trees were growing shorter and farther apart. More and more this was a world of rock and stone. I was not even sure if I was still on a trail. I climbed up and over a few big boulders, found something that looked like a trail again, and kept going up.

I came abruptly to the mountaintop, the treeless rocky plain of a wide shallow valley with a rise of crumbled rock on either side. I could not hear anyone coming up behind me on the trail or see anyone far ahead where the wavering track melted into the rocks. I was alone, enfolded in a quiet gentleness. This was not my land; there was none of the rawness of the younger mountains in the far West. These were older mountains that had had more time to make peace with the wind, snow, sky, and rain, and they shared their peace with me. I felt complete and at ease. The tall plant with a thick straight stalk and tiny white flowers that stood at the crest of the trail where I entered this barren but kindly land seemed like a friendly guardian as I passed.

36

There may have been a wind, but I felt only the sheltering stillness of rocks that have settled in their place. There may have been a stunning view if I had turned around, but I only wanted to look straight ahead into the tender embrace of the heart of the mountaintop, hidden only from below, wide open and welcoming when you at last arrive. There may have been a monumental vastness, but I felt a generous intimacy, an intimacy from the mountain and from my heart too. I was twelve years old and yet I felt a freedom beyond this life, a feeling seamless with this place, a certainty, I knew how to be here. I walked slowly out into the plain, following the meandering trail that wove gently across the mountaintop like a thin soft stream of breath.

I reached the Lake of the Clouds hut on the far side of the open plain in late afternoon. By dinnertime, we had all gathered there. We had hiked the same trail, but not everyone had arrived on the same mountain.

We were tired the next day, and even some sections of the promised level trail were challenging. As we crossed the slushy surface of an ice-packed slope on the north side of a ridge, the leader who had proposed the trip stumbled and fell. She slid a few feet down from the trail before she caught herself. She was unhurt, but the icy slope dropped off sharply fifty or sixty feet below us into a great shadowy chasm between the flanks of the mountain, bottomless, its true depth hidden from view. Only one person fell, but we were all slipping, and the dark chasm below us was as huge as the mountains themselves, a massive downward darkened space, compelling in its emptiness, pulling our eyes into it, into another face of the mountain.

The leaders and the other adults accompanying us held a conference on the trail. They called off the trip. We took the nearest trail back down to the valley and went home.

Neither of my parents got along well with my father's mother. We seldom went to see her. When she came to see us on a rare visit while I was in junior high, my parents treated her as a visiting dignitary, with cordial reserve and a structured itinerary that left little time just to be with her. I barely knew her.

She was in her early eighties, with long white hair that she wore in two braids wrapped around her head. Each night she would undo the braids, comb out her hair, and braid it up again. I came into her room one night when her hair was down. Thick luminous white hair, rippled and curled from being in tight braids and faintly green from the shampoo that she used, reached down below her hips, a waterfall of hair pouring down her back. She was wearing a sleeveless satin nightgown that was a pale salmon color like her skin, and the sagging flesh of her upper arm swayed as she combed her hair. She had a mesmerizing elemental quality, no longer a grandmother sitting there, but a fluid interplay of texture and color, of satin, skin, and hair, of pale salmon and pale green, all pulling apart and coming together again in the rhythmic motions of the combing of her hair.

She was a Christian Scientist. No one in the family spoke much about it, and I did not really know what it meant. While she was visiting, I had an accident riding my bike. I flew over the handlebars and woke up in the ambulance on the way to the hospital. I felt no pain, my body and the sounds and sensations all around me condensing and dissolving like a mist or a light rain. There was no concussion, there were no broken bones, but I had deep gashes on one side of my face, an elbow, a hand, and a knee. The wounds healed with clotted white scar tissue except on my face. I found out years later, long after my grandmother died, that she came into my room each night after I was asleep and prayed over my face.

How did those fibers of my skin decide to be supple again? In the same way my grandmother combed her hair, with the long strands and the textures and the colors coming apart and pulling together again, through faith in the healing art of prayer, the blessings carried in a believing heart that knows that lines of energy are not fixed, they can be reworked, rewoven and made whole.

Twice a year, in the spring and fall, the church youth group helped raise money for the church by cleaning houses and doing yard work. Members of the congregation would pledge money to the church, and we would send a team of three or four teens to wash windows, rake leaves, or whatever needed to be done.

One year someone anonymously sponsored the cleaning of an elderly woman's house. The job was assigned to our crew. We arrived after lunch on an autumn afternoon at the door of a drab two-story house in a fading neighborhood, on a street lined with similar houses set close together. The yard looked shaggy but not abandoned. A small frail woman with eyes like a cautious bird peering at us from far away opened the door to let us in, and we waved to our ride that they could leave. The old woman seems almost invisible to my memory now, except for her eyes. She was already disappearing even then.

She left us to clean on our own. I do not know where she went while we worked. She may have just moved quietly from room to room to stay out of our way. The house was filthy beyond anything any of us had ever seen. The telephone had a thick yellowish crust on the mouthpiece and around the dial. The stove had an inch thick layer of greasy crusted and congealed food on every surface except where the flames of the gas burners kept it at bay. The toilet was the same, encrusted with organic residue on the seat and inside the bowl. The windows were filmed over with dirt. A dense velvety dust covered everything else. We were horrified and appalled. The only way any of us could deal with the shock was to clean. It took the whole afternoon. When our ride returned to take us to our next job, we told them it was going to take us longer here. When they came back again at the end of the afternoon, they brought us a shopping bag full of fresh-picked apples from the backyard apple tree that would have been our next project.

The frail woman was still elusive, but one of the boys had talked briefly with her and learned that she used to teach piano. We had already cleaned the old upright piano and carefully dusted the keys. It was tremendously out of tune, but we left the bag of apples for the piano teacher near her piano with a note for her whenever she might reappear.

The following spring we were asked to clean her house again. It was almost as filthy as before although the crusts were not as thick, and we found the bag of apples exactly where we had left it. The apples had decayed into a putrefying mass.

In the fall, we had been revolted, but hopeful too. We could clean her place for her, and her life could change. Now looking at the bag of rotting apples, my thoughts were imploding, stalling out; even sadness was not adequate here. We had left the apples near the piano because we thought she loved the music, loved to teach, and so she would find the apples there, but clearly there was a limit to the draw that things you cared about could have on a mind already moving like a ghost on the edges of its own life. What kept her alive, if not those things, those loves, that we felt would be so important to us if we were her? What kept her living alone in the midst of what we were experiencing as filth? Did she care, or was she already like a shadow to herself, her physical world fading in and out, falling away, and not noticing the incrustation day by day of even the most functional things? Someone knew enough about her situation to sponsor the cleaning of her house again, but why was she still allowed to live this way? Perhaps she wanted to. In our brief contact with her at the door, she did not seem demented or afraid, just immensely inward, almost content to be only remotely connected to her world. People lost in the midst of what they love, people who stop living even when they are alive, what is it that binds and blinds us from inside? Face to face with something that had no easy answer, all the lostness and the good intentions intertwined, rotting in that bag of apples, wordless at the end, the piano teacher's gift.

Mr. Grubb's hand moved vigorously, tapping the green chalkboard with the stub of pale yellow chalk at the beginning of each curving line he drew. The big diagram of the leaf was almost complete. He added some wavy lines with arrows for sunlight entering from above, more arrows exiting from the small round pores on the underside of the leaf in the midst of the molecular formulas, then turned to face the class again and continued with his discussion of the mysteries of photosynthesis. We were studying the inner workings of plants in high school biology, and I was fascinated. I had always done well in school, but Mr. Grubb's biology class was the first time that the education I was accumulating began to open into enhanced experience of the naturally arising wonder of this world, this life. I was enthralled.

Mr. Grubb's full name was Marsden Ulysses Grubb, a resonant grand parade of a name that completely redeemed the "Grubb" part, but we would not have made jokes about his name anyway; we liked him, and we respected him. He was from a farm in Iowa or Missouri, and he had a deep soft rumbling voice like ploughed earth with a Midwestern drawl. He was an older man, heavy set, with thick black hair even as he aged, and a weathered face as if he had spent his life outdoors instead of in a classroom. He was a natural teacher. He had a good heart and a sincere passion for the subject of biology, and he led us enthusiastically through a miraculous world of living organisms and living processes.

Air flowed in and out of little sacs in lungs, blood flowed around them from inside; they were like tiny sea shores bathed in small essential tides. Hearts pumped, blood flowed, nerves sent impulses. Bones constantly being reborn from saline mineral waters of interior seas supported huge bodies traveling on land. Tiny one-celled creatures lived singular lives of unimaginable simplicity and strange beauty all around us. Transparent oval bodies of paramecia covered with clear rotating hairs held clusters of internal cellular parts like luminous jewels. Amoebas moved within constantly shifting bulging form, pulsing and amorphous yet inherently unified. Other cells divided and divided again, becoming more and more complexly organized and defined, becoming a person or a cow. A shimmering world of living order supported us at every step, a miraculous net of cellular intent.

My rapture over living energies reached epiphany with the plants in the miracle of photosynthesis, the sacred alchemy of green leaves uniting water, minerals, and light into sweet sap, leaves in silent transpiration breathing out oxygen, leaves weaving molecules together, quietly making sugars out of light. I went outside; the grasses, trees, and bushes up and down the street were all involved in this absolute grace of sunlight becoming life. I have never ceased to be in wonder of the whole effulgent process called plants and their practice of living light, from the tiny roots and first leaves of sprouting seeds, to the glowing colors of the trees in fall. The wonder has only increased for me through the years. We are never apart from a natural radiance in the most fundamental ways.

Opening

Rob

I knew what was coming. I just pretended to read the *Moonstone*. Another day of dread waiting for the teacher to react or toss me my paper covered in red ink. This was the last day of tenth grade in this former Army paraplegic hospital that had been the location for Marlon Brando's first movie. It was a bleak look into my future high school years. However, there was a small ray of hope. My parents were opening an eye and realizing they had to do something about our education. I do not know if they knew that I had yet to read a whole book and that my vocabulary outside of etiquette was very poor. They decided to enroll us in a new school that had just opened down the street, a very small personal guidance school with an open-ended philosophy that had evolved out of the owner's desire to have a better school for her own children.

Cal Prep was then in an old real estate office built to resemble a ranch house. Each class had no more than seven students. The whole atmosphere washed away years of judgment and opened a new dialogue for learning. The faculty was honestly involved in guiding and teaching us. I loved it from the start. My brother and I were born in September, so early on, just new to the school, the students and teachers held a little party for our sixteenth birthday. I was truly moved; everyone freely expressed genuine love for us and joyous heartfelt aspirations along with many hugs. As I walked home that day with my brother, I felt as if a bubble around me had burst, as if I had never seen the street I was walking on though I had walked home countless times before.

There was now a joy in the mere experience of things. It was like being let out of prison after many years in solitary, confronted by this world with a freedom to choose and a resolve not to go back. I began talking and arguing. I was at the beginning of a revolution. I was very enthusiastic about learning. My parents were completely surprised, even shocked, by the utter change in my behavior. I almost made straight A's that year.

During the Christmas vacation whenever the whole family went out shopping I would make a fire in the keeping room fireplace and read *Siddartha* and *The Razor's Edge*. I had just seen the movie version of *The Razor's Edge* on TV. I read the book soon after, and they blended in my experience. I could see myself as the main character Larry Darnell as Tyron Power portrayed him, with the elegant parties and the formal way of his world. It seemed so much like my own life. I saw myself as Larry having returned from a war changed, questioning, reading, and studying on a spiritual search. Then he left his upper class society life and following his heart, he slowly made his way to India, the Guru, and an awakening. These two books made an enormous impact on me. The Buddha, Siddhartha, and Larry left their privileged worlds to wander and seek the truth within their direct experience.

After the holidays, the school moved across the street into a collection of small funky sixties style shops and rooms that once sold dried flower arrangements. On the first day back, before class began, I was sitting outside and a friend came along and gave me a copy of *Be Here Now* by Ram Das. Most of the book was quintessential hippie pop art, which did not touch me at all, but I liked Ram Das's biography detailing his spiritual journey. One sentence affirming intuition as a fundamental process to understanding and knowledge was the most pivotal part of the book for me. I knew intuition was born in my heart and here was a confirmation of its relevance. This was major breakthrough. I felt my earliest memories and experiences were affirmed now. I also followed his guidelines on meditation. I began sitting in full lotus for thirty minutes every day and little by little extending the time. I noticed my mind's activity slowed, my breathing became calm, and a feeling of well-being.

The same day I received the book, the English teacher gave us an assignment to write an essay in class. At the end, she was quickly reading the papers, and when she came to mine, she screamed out, "These are sentences, paragraphs. This is English! What did you do over the vacation?!" This essay showed progress but I had a lot to learn. I knew I had to go to college in order to continue this freedom to study and grow. During the summer that followed, I remained in my room reading constantly, a book on one knee and a dictionary on the other: Hesse, Kafka, Huxley, Maugham, Thoreau, Dostoyevsky, Yogananda, the *Upanishads* and the *Bhagavad Gita*, and the early books of Carlos Castaneda. The *I Ching*, Blake's poetry, and meditation were all great influences, but I was growing up in the early seventies, and so I also began drinking, smoking pot, smoking a pipe, growing my hair long, and becoming a vegetarian, though I was not drawn to heavy drugs.

I stopped attending Mass on Sundays, which was tantamount to heresy not only because of going against the church, but also because it disrupted the fundamental order of my parents and my siblings' lives. For me, Sunday Mass was an empty act of doctrinal obedience that led nowhere. I knew my spiritual life belonged to another path. I also could not understand why most people were confined to a lesser form of spiritual practice. I felt everyone was on a spiritual path; that is why we are here.

I was not only opening to the world, becoming an adult, but I was also opening spiritually in a way that was difficult to comprehend clearly, similar to waking and trying to remember a dream. At times, it was like a stone hitting the calm surface of a lake, the impact sending out waves of influence and sometimes these waves came back, opening me further.

Around this time I began driving; I also took up bread baking. One Saturday morning I was alone in the main house, my brother was in the back near my grandmother's house, everyone else had gone out for the day. There was a knock at the front door. I had just noticed we had no raisins in the house for the Hesuka-Czechoslovakian holiday bread I was making. As I answered the door, I felt a severe chill over my whole body. A large man in his thirties was talking to me, another one was standing just off the porch, and I could see a smaller man at the end of the driveway. I cannot remember what the man was saying, but a force inside me slammed the door shut and threw the bolt home just as he kicked the door so hard the side of the house shuddered. I raced around the house closing and locking all the windows and doors, and then I realized he had stopped yelling and had gone. I went back to my bread baking a bit shaky. There was something ominous within what had just happened, like the early part of a horror movie. Being sixteen I put it aside and decided I needed to go to the store to buy raisins. I called to my brother on the intercom that I was going to the market and I told him about the strange men.

As I drove near the market, one of the first big supermarkets in the area, I could plainly see the three men standing in the large parking lot near a rusted van with no windows. This did not stop me. I knew they were dangerous; why did I continue? As I drove into the parking lot, I was very aware that they saw me. It was as if there was another aspect of myself moving me; nothing I did was rational. I did not hesitate and parked in my favorite spot, the farthest place from the store. I was determined to buy raisins even though I felt danger all around me. I walked toward the store with three sets of predator eyes on me. I was shaky. My legs felt like I had run a mile, but my mind was clear, different.

I continued into the store and bought only a large box of raisins. As I walked back to my car, the large man was walking forcefully to overtake me. I did not see where the other two were. He began shouting at me, getting closer and closer. The world began to drop away, and then something inside me opened up. He was about to grab me. And as everything faded out, "Raisins!!" exploded out of me as I shoved the box right up to his face, with no thought, no memory, no place, no beginning or end. The bubble that is this world shattered and in that opened space I held him with a force, a gesture, and a word. I grabbed him and like a cartoon character, he froze. I turned, walked to my car and drove home, not looking back.

My sister Mary had just broken off her engagement with Eddie, a man she had met in college, a low rider type, a tough guy wanna-be. I was not aware of all that was said between them. One day I was standing alone next to the kitchen table near the kitchen door. I could hear the screech of Eddie's souped-up Cougar coming to an abrupt halt and the sound of running boots. I was eating a peanut butter and jelly sandwich. I was sixteen and my only concern in this life was whether the jelly was spilling out the other side. Boots rushed along the brick breezeway toward the kitchen door. The door burst open, a space emptied and a shape entered. Eddie, neither shock nor horror. He was out of place. This bursting cloud of Eddie leveled a 30'06 deer rifle at my face and pulled the trigger as I stared into the barrel of the gun. Click, he levered another round, click, again click. He went wild. Laughing and crying he fell to the floor. Still laughing, he explained how shocked and dumbfounded I looked. The sandwich did not help. Crying he said over and over, "I just can't believe it, I always reload my gun, I always reload after shooting! I never leave my gun empty, never, never!"

He laughed at my face, my expression, for I had not moved, my eyes never left him. I knew about guns; my dad had taught us to shoot and care for revolvers, rifles, and shotguns. I knew they could kill. I was still held within that moment, unmoving, emptied. I had nothing to say. I just stood there and let him laugh in my shocked openness. He finally came to himself and I went to get my father, who talked to him outside.

I never spoke about this to anyone. It was like waking up from major surgery, your body barely functional, your mind empty yet filling fast like a hose with a kink in it loosening up and then gushing forth to fill a void.

These two events, with Eddie and with the raisins, were dramatic openings for me in this already full year. These moments of aware openness were like sounds vibrating, sometimes loudly sometimes softly, but strangely always there. These were powerful experiences that were drawn to me in this time of my life, expressions of an energy unbound and released.

TAKEN BY THE CURRENT

At the end of twelfth grade, some of the students from Cal Prep went on a river raft trip up in Northern California. For me the most memorable part of the trip was about four minutes long.

The guide of our raft rowed over to a beach after passing a short but intense rapid. He said if we hiked upstream, he would show us how to enter the tube. I did not quite know what he was talking about but it intrigued me. When we had hiked back up the river above the last rapid he said we could swim out one at a time to the middle of the current, keeping our feet in front of us, and let the current take us into the middle of this storm of waves. In the center we would be sucked down and into a tube and shot out the other side.

So one by one, we all tried it. I swam out into the center, the current taking hold of me, my tennis shoes straight out in front, my heart too. I could see this wall of churning waves up ahead but before I could start thinking too clearly the current shot me forward, and in a second I was consumed by an explosive rush of sheer force all around me with no way out. Everything was beyond you; you had to let go. It was like dying, knowing there is no chance to return and carry on with this life as before; you are in the pike, with a force thrusting you beyond your body, beyond your conscious mind. It was so all consuming that your mind was on hold, cut off from ordinary reality. You have lost your ability to act, your body is just a conveyance, a form in which to survive this onslaught of force and energy, in fact you have lost your body, there is nothing, function has no purpose. Sound as if large speakers were on high with liquid static overwhelming, shutting down the mind by sheer overload. Then you are shot back to life swimming for shore. The dream abruptly continues; you are back in your body having to breathe.

On a summer afternoon, some days after returning home, my parents got a call from "Aunt" Francis, a long time friend of my mother's, who they said sounded like she was sloshed. She wanted us to meet her new boyfriend. My mother thought this was a fun idea. Francis was a fat bawdy woman in her late fifties who looked as if she would burst out of her dress at any moment. She had a Mae West character with a similar drawl to her words. A taxicab pulled up in our driveway and I watched through the window, as Francis emerged from the taxi, barely able to stand on her own; then a medium build man in a bright yellow tailored suit appeared.

Francis introduced us to the man. She had her everyday emerald on, the one with a slight flaw, a big green jewel the size of a man's thumbnail. I found myself walking with this brilliant yellow man out to the porch, where we sat and talked. My father brought drinks for him and for me. I had recently begun drinking gin and tonic with a lime. I could feel that my family did not want to be around the man in the yellow suit.

It was a hot day, and we sat together on the wide veranda looking quietly out at the gardens, the lawns surrounded by patios, and my grandmother's house in the back creating a cloister accented by rose bushes and border plants in full bloom. Then he looked at me and said, "I recognized you, you're different from the rest of your family." Before I could say anything, he continued, "Don't leave this beautiful place, don't go out there, it will destroy you like it did me. I know you see things and I know you know this." I agreed that my parents had built a kind of refuge from the rest of the world. There was a strong sense of retreat here. Of course, my parents used it to support their belief in a social life, as a setting for their elaborate parties, but just as easily when alone you could rest within a space it allowed.

I told him I had to leave. It was like being taken into the current and driven by your experience. Even at this age, the events of my life told me that the cloister is no barrier to suffering. It allows you a space to abide in, but your habits, your mind, and your emotions are all there; you cannot run from them. The retreat, the cloister, the cave, are all ovens cooking you, laying bare that which can so easily be covered over by the sheer volume of this experience. I knew he felt that the world had consumed him and he did not want that to happen to me, but I had to follow a rhythm played out within the force of my own blood. It could not be understood logically. Other forces add to this world of experience. It may at times not make sense, some things becoming clear many years later. I knew I had to leave in order to find the cloister which resonated with the rhythm of my own heart, something beyond this life, as it arose naturally again and again.

PASSAGE

My ninety-three year old grandmother lay in her bed breathing heavily as my whole family stood by in the dim light of her room, witnessing her passage from a long and healthy life. We were all waiting, not only for my grandmother to pass, but also within our own passages, my parents into retirement, my uncle Eugene into his old age, my sisters out of the house, and my brother and I into separate rooms in the house and in our hearts.

We all stood there in our own dim light between the ending and beginning of changes in our lives as my grandmother's body tried to continue a rhythm that had been going since her birth; what had been so easy and second nature was now so burdened. We were surrounded by these breaths, to be followed by an emptiness, the quiet filling the room, a space of time beat out by my own heart, and again her body would resume though the sound and feeling were more hollow each time. Finally a definite quiet, an utter stillness unlike any other pervaded the room. We remained unmoving and silent, witness not only to my grandmother's death but also to our own.

While I was at UC Santa Barbara, I was confronted by my clear interest in a spiritual life yet I had absolutely no desire to enter any of the formal religions that were available to me. Yet remaining in a secular world was not happening either; I was not interested in following along with those around me. Beyond the classroom, I would hike the trails that traced along the edge of a cliff above the ocean surf below. Here was all that I loved. The early morning sky with its deep, deep blues of the earliest part of dawn with the stars still visible, Venus and Mars clear and luminous above the ocean's surf, the crisp cold sea air mixing with the scent of sage brush and grass, the stillness within the movement and passage into dawn. These were my loves, but now as I wandered the trails alone, waiting, I walked through this beauty and glory in an unseen embrace, held at low tide, like holding one's breath.

I would get up very early on the weekends. The campus would be deserted. I would walk the concrete pathways, feeling like the beach sand drying out waiting again for the ocean to return, and

51

then wander along the cliff, too restless to sit. I would stand in the sea breeze within the ebbing flow of this dark, waiting at the edge of something as tremendous as this cliff edge against the ocean and the sky. All I could do was wait, listening to the waves come in and crash into a momentary hush until the tide rushed in again. It is here in this passage that awakening comes like the brilliance of knowing that passes into one's limbs and pushes out to the canvas or sculpture, a simple truth uncovered.

I became interested in art as a medium for spiritual growth. I was influenced by William Blake and how he expressed his spiritual life in his poetry and his art. There was something I needed to see and to resurrect out of a depth I had yet touched. I began working on a portfolio to transfer to the art department at UCLA.

I had just finished hanging my drawings and setting up my sculpture for my portfolio review when the whole UCLA art faculty poured into the gallery. They were early! I was not supposed to be there but I was surrounded as they all very intently looked at my work, asking me questions about it. They were interested, encouraging, and helpful. One of the faculty said the work was better than the work of his graduate students.

After I was accepted, I was completely bathed in art classes. I would get to the campus by six o'clock in the morning and sit alone in a studio classroom drinking coffee and writing in my journal. The whole day was before me, all painting and drawing classes. I would usually eat lunch in the sculpture garden and meditate or sketch in my journal before the next four-hour studio class. What a joy! Then I would take the bus back to my parents' house and work late into the night on my artwork.

One class was very special to me. It was Jan Stussey's anatomy and figure drawing. Everyone I spoke with said not to take it, that he was too strict and gave too much homework. His class was four hours long, two days a week with a lot of homework. You could not be late, miss a day or any of the homework or you would fail. He would lock the door until the break though he always provided hot water, coffee and tea. He gave all he had; I think that was what I loved the most, and if you gave all that you had to the work, he was totally with you. He was always open to questions, and he knew if you were following him. He had a creative and inspiring approach to teaching anatomy and drawing together through a wide range of techniques and materials. He was very encouraging to me during my final portfolio review and talked to me about places to visit when I was in Europe.

While I was at UCLA I saw an exhibition of Japanese screen paintings which had an enormous impact on me, spontaneous direct movements of the brush to invoke nature, poignant reflections of life, a cherry tree branch that grew across a portion of the screen, almost hidden by a heavy snowfall. As you moved around a screen, the whole piece changed shape, directing your eye and body, all of it adding together to invoke a tone and space in one's mind.

Another pivotal influence was a recognition that came at the end of a Japanese art history course. The professor gave a one-day lecture on the sculpture and life of Enku. I felt a strong kindred bond with Enku's work. He was a Japanese esoteric Buddhist monk who lived around the 1600's. He left his monastery and walked the countryside of Japan carving Buddhist images with rough expressive strokes. Spontaneous and quick with his axe, he worked with a dynamic blaze of strokes and cuts; the deities looked like they were bursting apart.

I was also beginning to appreciate the Zenga painters of Japan. I knew there was something in the movement within these spontaneous acts of painting and carving, and in the sculptural quality of the space delineated by the screens, an intent that was moving me, shaping me, creating a path to enter the sacred.

It was getting clearer to me that I was not as concerned with the world and life as everyone else was. John had gone to Art Center

School of Design in Pasadena. He had recently moved to New York City and was on his way to a successful career in advertising. For me, being an artist was less defined. I was not concerned with the practical in the ordinary sense. There was something in me that needed to come out, not something emotional or psychological but a spiritual memory that arose in experiences throughout my childhood. These experiences were not within the realm of language; they arose as feelings, open and aware, touching and being touched by this world, a union of two aspects of inner being, one a purely spiritual memory, the other an experience in this life as vision. In order to see into this depth I needed the time and space that art afforded.

My first studio retreat was in a second floor apartment in the back of an aging Spanish-style building in Hollywood. The building looked abandoned. An old bent wrought iron gate opened to an unkempt courtyard with a few shaggy date palms. There were a number of spaces that seemed to be occupied, but I rarely saw anyone. I used the living room with large windows opening to the west as my studio.

I was reading Thomas Merton, Suzuki Roshi, D. T. Suzuki, and the lives of Zen masters of China and Japan. I was also reading St. John of the Cross, a Carmelite and follower of St. Teresa of Avila. During this time, I corresponded with my Aunt Mary; I wrote to her of my enthusiasm for his poetry. I thought that the Zen-like quality I felt within his words would also be of interest to my aunt since she had entered the Carmelite order soon after graduating from college and had spent most of her life in cloistered contemplation. She wrote back and told me to look more deeply into St. Teresa. Although I did, her words never touched me as much as the words of St. John of the Cross. There seemed to be different kinds of mystic experience, and I was certainly drawn to his passion for a knowing emptiness.

I would spend my days meditating, reading, and painting. I rarely went out, saw, or spoke to anyone. I was trying to blend spiritual practice and the light I felt in my heart with the light that plays across my hand. The light was a reminder, a sign, always penetrating whatever was going on in my life.

One afternoon while I was still at UCLA I had visited a friend who had an apartment close to the beach. We were sitting apart, listening to music that meant a great deal to her. My mind, though, moved to the window; the clear afternoon light was bathing this space filled with objects. The light had a special clarity to it, a strange captivating force, as if it would pull the sky and the ocean into the room. This pure veil of light poured through the defused lines of lace curtains, and then a breeze brushed the curtains aside and I was immersed in a soft light, becoming the sky and at the same time the depth of the ocean. My mind was the light, and all the surroundings were the accompaniment of experience played out as a curtain swirling and curling against the cool ocean light. Allowing, adrift yet pulled by the light's current of expression, it wasn't just illuminating space, it was kindling my heart, a kind of intent within the softness and gentleness of an offering that was and remains radiance, open and simple, the breath of a vastness sparked within a tiny seed of light in my heart.

The ephemeral lucid quality of one's heart, the light through a window, and veils of color were all one, but I could not grasp the full significance. In Hollywood I painted abstract color fields in diptych and triptych panels. I would lay down a wash of color and let the pigment settle and dry, and then repeat these washes, producing a haze of color with a sense of depth. I was waiting. As I worked in this way, I realized that my whole experience was part of the paintings and that painting was a spiritual act. The movement of my body as I painted and the paint as it dried were all gestures on this journey.

In the late afternoon, the sun would pour through the windows. I would sit on the window ledge blending with the warmth of the light, looking out over the sun-drenched blur of forms no longer just a city, my mind letting go. I was allowing a process to unfold and just giving in and trusting my heart. Intuition is not a single moment. It unfolds gradually, like a mist slowly burning away, suddenly its all clear. It is an organic function through the good days and bad days, the pulse of one's life.

GROUND ZERO

Rachel

A clear light shimmered on the surface of the lake, and the autumn air was soft and warm. I sat on an old blanket spread out on the sloping earth close to the water's edge and made a shelf of my shoes to keep my books from sliding in. Out in the center of the lake a few windsurfers were gliding back and forth, riding invisible currents in the air. On the far side, golden grassy hills dotted with live oaks flowed smoothly up into a pure blue sky, a sky just as bright and seamless as the sky of my memories.

I had returned to California. I had been accepted at Stanford University, and my parents let me go. I attended classes but the rest of the time, if the sky was blue, I would be outside, happy just to be immersed in the sky, the whole of this and so many afternoons all swallowed up and lifted into the deep blue livingness of the soaring open sky. As a plant starved for water, I drank in the blue. I could not get enough.

It was 1965, ground zero everywhere for an entire generation about to unfold, explode, implode: confrontations over civil rights and war, flower children, student revolutions, sex and drugs and rock and roll, the Haight-Ashbury, the Filmore Auditorium, Ken Keasy's bus, psychodrama, Esalen, Tai Chi, and Zen, coed dorms, group households, teepees, geodesic domes, back to the land, the Whole Earth Catalog, and think tanks in the hills.

Even the ground was unstable here. The San Andreas Fault ran through the hills near the small cabin above the Stanford campus where my parents lived the year I was born, and there was a familiar vibrancy in the land and in the air, a sense of hidden patterns waiting to play out, so many different ways to ride the coming waves, so many more ways in between, so many alternative threads leading through the explosive maze of energies poised imperceptibly in an autumn afternoon.

At the beginning of winter quarter, freshman year, we were studying Medieval European thought in Western Civ., and the instructor for our discussion group set up a field trip to a rural monastery in the northern part of the Central Valley near Red Bluff. The Trappists were establishing a community there on a farm that had belonged to the Stanford family, and they were willing to allow a small group of students to visit.

Pastel winter light spread softly over the flat fields all around us as we turned onto the gravel and dirt driveway to the farm. We parked near a line of tall evergreen trees that were startlingly upright for this level land and formed a windbreak for a small orchard. Long green grass flecked with tiny yellow flowers grew freely all through the orchard and close around the trunks of the bare fruit trees. As I got out of the car and turned to face the orchard, I felt a spacious radiance welling up from my heart, reflected in the winter light on the uncut grass thick with wild mustard, and a feeling of going not just back in time but outside time as well, to a place where even ordinary things are valued and tended in a very different way than in the modern world.

A monk came out of the classic white farmhouse. He was a young man, with tonsured hair and heavy sandals on bare feet. His long robe flapped around his legs as he approached us with an exuberant stride and a big open smile. We had arrived later than we planned, and it was time for lunch. He led us inside the farmhouse to a plain room with rough plank tables. The monks had already eaten or were eating elsewhere, so we talked quietly with each other over the simple meal they had prepared, a hearty soup and round loaves of freshly baked bread. The bowls were all different from each other, so were the spoons. I found an unexpected freedom in the frugal grace of eating from their unmatched spoons and bowls.

After lunch we were given a brief tour of the grounds around the house. The monks were working the land as a farm, but we did not see anyone except the young brother who was our guide. The barns, outbuildings, and farm machinery all looked weathered and worn, but very clean, with a kind of emptiness to their utilitarian presence, as if there was a deeper purpose to their usefulness, an invisible inner life even to the practical.

We came to the chapel, which looked like just another farmhouse at first, with wider lower eaves and a dense hedge of bushes surrounding and protecting it. We were allowed to enter the small area set aside for guests that had a separate entrance. A heavy wooden grill divided us from the main part of the chapel. The openings in the grill were very small and it was hard to see inside, but we could hear the deep voices of men chanting liturgy or murmuring in prayer, and as we sat for a long time in the narrow alcove, just listening, I began to understand the importance and the power of hiddenness. The monks with their cloistered life were not hiding the shadowy things to which so many people cling, but hiding something bright, something so secret and luminous you have to strip your whole life bare and keep it simple and apart, so that this gleaming mystery, sacred, holy beyond time, already residing in your heart, could truly bloom.

We spent the night in Red Bluff, at a rundown motel. The monastery and the simple hidden life of the monks seemed to be a bright island receding in the distance as we moved farther and farther away, but from the first moment of seeing the orchard grass growing long between bare trees in the soft winter light, their way of being had touched my heart and left a silent witness.

Headlights shone on the winding roads that led up into the forested hills on a rainy night. I had been invited to a party off campus. We parked the cars along a bend in the road and walked a narrow trail in the dark in pouring rain without flashlights. Guided only by the shine of the rain and the narrowness of the trail we crossed a small foot bridge over a rushing creek and reached the gate house of an old estate, a small one-room Old English-style cottage with leaded glass windows, a large stone fireplace, and a feeling of being very far away in time. A small group of people I had not met before were talking quietly. I do not remember any liquor or food, just this small group sitting on the floor together, talking in front of the fire. A tape of Japanese music was playing. It was the first time I had heard Koto music, and I was enchanted by the sounds.

I was not comfortable at parties. I once climbed a tree at another party in the hills and spent the evening sheltering in its branches, listening as waves of drunken laughter and the grinding sounds of "Louie Louie" repeatedly flooded a peaceful night. These people gathered around the fire here were different, but I was still a little shy, and I went outside for a while.

In the dark, I found a ladder leaning against the house next to one of the windows. I climbed the ladder to get out of the rain under the eaves, and watched as beads of water fell from the roof through the light shining from the room. The gleaming drops of water merged with the Koto music and the light. Luminous quivering sounds fell drop by tender drop in the darkness and the rain. I stayed on the ladder for a while, suspended with the brilliant tones forming along the roof edge and falling away again, melting into the night, over and over.

When I went back inside, the conversations were also flowing and bright. Communication seemed effortless, and I realized that for the first time in my life I did not have to translate my thoughts into some other form to be understood. I went back to the dorm full of enthusiasm for the amazing openness of these new people that I met, and learned a few days later that everyone at the party had been on acid except for me.

From earliest childhood I had loved to draw, and I used art to clarify my experience in an intuitive way; my choice to major in studio art came naturally. I took as many studio courses as I was allowed, mainly painting and lithography. In all my work, I loved the moments when a line, a color, or an edge shifts imperceptibly from being pencil, paint, or ink and becomes alive evoking three-dimensional form, and I loved the play of light touching gently on opaque surfaces or passing through translucency to reveal the inner light hidden in even the simplest things, a flower petal or candle flame.

One quarter I embarked on a self-guided tour through art history. I had been reading *Letters to a Young Poet* by Rilke, and his eloquent advice about solitude and the creative process touched me deeply. I memorized a long passage about the true nature of sadness and inspired by Rilke's belief that art is more fully experienced through openness rather than through theory or criticism, I went to the undergraduate library and took out a huge armload of big, color photo, art books each week. I began with the Paleolithic and worked my way forward in time, sweeping whole eras from the shelves and then sitting with the books, looking carefully through the images with artist's eyes, with my heart.

It was a thorough egalitarian review, and in unexpected places, in the unusually naturalistic sculptures of the reign of Akhenaton, or the curved space and the magical realism of angels' wings and wildflowers in the Northern Renaissance, or the trusting otherworldly stillness of the *Sleeping Gypsy* by Rousseau, I found clues to something subtle and profound that I felt had been lost from the visual arts ever since the great prehistoric caves of Altamira, Lascaux, Pech Merle, and others: a lyric naturalistic grace, both real and transcendent at the same time, that gave witness of an

61

ancient united heart and mind flowing through reverent hands, touching holy undulating Earth, knowingly part of a fluid whole.

By the spring of 1967, the whole campus was in a ferment of inquiry; everyone was questioning everything. I took a course called Belief and Unbelief with Prof. Michael Novak of the religion department, a thoughtful provocative look at reintroducing a context for believing in a secular doubting world. The reading list included Martin Buber's *I and Thou*, and *homo ludens* by Johann Huizinga. Both books were pivotal for me. Buber's insights into the transforming quality of relating with a holy Other and the possibility that you could resanctify every aspect of your world, including yourself, through the qualities of your relating left a deep and lasting imprint. Huizinga's work was a scholarly study of the history of the play element in culture, but his premise opened out for me into a realization that you could take an aspect of the creative process itself as a spiritual path. There was a way back to the reverence and wholeness of the caves; it was already present in my life, a spontaneous ageless essence accessible directly through the particular kind of openness I felt making art.

In early May, I saw a flyer for a Buddha's Birthday Celebration at the Stanford Memorial Church. I decided to go at the last minute. The interior of the church with its massive round columns, high dome ceiling, and kaleidoscopic mix of frescoes, mosaics, and stained glass was softened by the early evening light. White curtains had been suspended here and there throughout the church and in front of the altar. The audience was small. I sat alone to one side, enfolded in the twilight of the high-ceilinged sanctuary unmoored now from its accustomed solidity and function.

Without any introductory words about the life of the Shakyamuni Buddha, or about Buddhism, multiple slide projectors began to beam images of the Buddha all through the vaulted space. Sculptural Buddhas shining on the columns blended with the massive stones as if carved there of stones turning to light, turning to Buddha forms. Waves of painted images of Buddhas merging effortlessly into other Buddhas dissolved the curtains into translucent glowing veils. There was no other light in the church except the radiance of endless Buddha forms floating in a vast tenderness of their own, embraced by the faint red glow from the tall stained glass windows above the altar illuminated by the lingering twilight outside. I was fascinated, and entranced more than I knew.

The next morning, hurrying, late for class, I took a shortcut down a service road that led behind the church. I was singing a favorite song, a rock ballad, an anthem for peace and brotherhood, a poetic clarion call for people to choose love over fear and come together now. I had heard Jefferson Airplane perform this song in concert and I could still hear the exultant echoes and the soaring harmonies ringing in my mind as I sang. I was getting closer and closer to the church, singing with a deep longing for another part of myself, the timeless inner radiance, to return for me, the same plea carried inside the song along with a lyric reminder of the transience of life. Suddenly my mind opened skyward, gleaming and bright. I stopped, everything stopped, rooted in unknown certainty, rooted in the light, going beyond wonder, going, going home, enveloped in the vastness of an inner brilliance, the intangible substance of light, so high and deep and wide, measureless, secure, nothing left outside, nothing separate in any way, the oneness of a shining whole in which nothing can ever be apart.

Then slowly, returning from this gleaming wholeness, the endless radiance too began to pass, and I was hurrying again, even later now for class. I was hurrying again, but part of me was not going anywhere. The timeless moment lingered in my heart; it was my heart. It was the same moment of absolute blessing I had felt in the little paper chains around the Christmas tree, in the welcoming embrace of the mountaintop, and in the openness of the sky. I knew that more than any of the other kinds of experiences I had ever had in this life, I wanted to stay with this expansive, ephemeral, nameless brightness, more true than anything, and I was willing to wait and remember until it opened again.

I would wonder from time to time, maybe it was in the words of the song and the wisdom there, or maybe in the melody. Years later, deep in retreat, I realized that moment was from the all-encompassing wholeness present everywhere. The splendid brightness on the road behind the church had come through the blessings of witnessing the Buddha forms the night before, and through my singing, and the song, through hurrying and being late, being neither here nor there, being in between, all coming together to allow that shining opening of my heart.

CLOUDS' HANDS

We waited until the headlights disappeared, then ran across the glassy surface of the road. The rain had stopped, the sky was clearing, and light from the full moon shimmered on all the glistening surfaces suddenly revealed inside this gleaming night. We held the lines of barbed wire open and helped each other through the fence, a small group of friends wandering the grassy foothills close above the campus, drawn by the wild beauty of the passing storm. A strong wind drove bright white clouds fast across a starry sky. Someone found a kite and managed to launch it in the air. We could not see the kite against the flowing sky; near and far were shifting back and forth inside the molten light. The wind rolled the grassy hillside like the sea, nothing solid anywhere. We took turns holding the kite string, and when it was my turn, I felt the fine taunt edge of the string pressing against my hand, and the tension of the line as the invisible kite pulled hard against the moving air, an anchor in this fluid world, an anchor to the sky. Finally someone let it go.

The older Asian man turned slowly, arms upraised. I was in the back of the class. I could not see the whole of his movements linked to the enigmatic grace of his accented voice speaking softly their names: golden stork spreads its wings, carry tiger to mountain, needle at sea bottom, clouds' hands.

I missed the first class, I was starting at the second session, and Master Kam Choy Man met with me afterwards to teach me the opening for Tai Chi Chuan. He suggested that I ride my fingers lightly on one of his arms as he moved so I could feel the chi; it would be clearer than explaining in words. His arm was luminous, pale yellow alabaster, no muscles or bones, only flowing sky and clouds, oceans of seas, and a soft fluttering at his fingertips.

The classes were challenging, transposing left to right as you watched. It was easier to find the movements from inside later, remembering his grace with the help of the list he handed out, printed on pale yellow paper like his arm. I loved Tai Chi. I loved the slow movements melting into each other, the soft turns of the wrist, the gentle hands, the rolling shift of weight and breath, a living centering. Master Choy said to keep your steps very small; you should be able to do them in the compartment of a railroad train. I did them everywhere, in parks, front yards, and living rooms, on rooftops and forest paths, daily for the next ten years.

Shortly before I graduated from Stanford, I moved to the same small neighborhood of old summer cabins where my parents had lived the year I was born. I was living in a group household on a few semi-wild acres along a creek, with access to the open hills on the other side.

I was kneeling beside a small flowerbed, trying to coax a few flowers from our dry unruly yard. It was a summer day in August, and everything, the yard, the air, was hot. A group of four or five people walked by, laughing and talking with an Asian man who wore a long dark robe. The Asian man seemed slight or frail perhaps, but buoyant and bright. The people who accompanied him were taller and moving as people move, but the Asian man moved as curves of light, and his laughter was part of the rippling of his curves. He smiled and acknowledged me. I smiled back, enveloped in his presence. He was a river of liquid light flowing through the dusty yard and the brittle air that could not quite be called shade under the canopy of the tall trees. I did not know it then, but he was Shunryu Suzuki-roshi, a few months before his death. A member of our household and some friends of his who were students of the Roshi had brought him to walk the open hills. I never saw him again, but I never forgot his easy, graceful joy.

The next summer at the same time of year, my father died. He was fifty-three. The neighbor who found his body called the police, and I received a call from a detective, who told me, in a classic TV cop's gravelly voice, that my father had committed suicide. The coroner ruled later that it was accidental, but there was a lingering question from the detective's call, and what really is the difference between taking a decisive step yourself and putting yourself in the way of other circumstances that will do it for you.

My father had been in the midst of changes in his life. He and my mother had separated with mutual relief after twenty-five years together. He had had a mild stroke, which affected his work and his golf game. He was taking many different medications. It is hard to say if even he knew how he really felt.

The apartment that he moved to after he and my mother sold their house had belonged to the uncle of a business colleague. The uncle had committed suicide by jumping out of a window in the apartment, seven or eight stories to the ground. I stayed there while we packed up my dad's things. I did not know about the uncle then, but one afternoon when I lay down to take a nap, I did not sleep. I watched the curtain at the window instead, fascinated as it billowed out into the room riding on the hot, humid, summer breeze, and as it was sucked backed again, hard against the screen, over and over, as if trying to get out.

One of the things my father said to me when I saw him for the last time, four months before he died, was that he had spent his whole life behind a desk, and if he could have his life to live over, he would find a way to be outside. I took his ashes to a place outside that I thought he loved. On a summer evening in the Midwest, I opened the package with his name on it and found not ashes but small pieces of chalky bone.

My dad had given me his passion for going outside. It ran in the family. His father had it too, not just going outdoors but also going outside in terms of questioning boundaries, limits, anything that was preset, not always to rebel but to see how they worked. I had inherited that questioning too, along with their love of the outdoors.

At the time of his death, I was painting studies of feathers, stones, and plants, exploring the organic functional beauty inherent in natural things, looking for an aesthetic outside culture, outside art history, a living ordering, a beauty that is sacred, intrinsic, and true. I was looking especially in forms of plants, in their shapes born of waters carried upward in rhythmic curves reaching for light. Now on this hot humid Midwestern night, looking at the little pieces of my father's bones, the broken edges of the actual structure that had supported his life, bones born of fluids also seeking light in another way, it seemed completely natural to me to want to paint pictures of my father's bones. As I spread his "ashes", I put the biggest pieces in my pocket.

My father had vacationed in Florida near the end of his life. He seemed to find a peace and a freedom on the beaches there, and he brought boxes of seashells home from every trip. I had kept some of the shells, and I set each piece of bone I wanted to paint inside a different shell. I was very calm and careful at the start, using the forms and colors of the bones and shells as a way to explore my feelings about his death. The traditional pigments for oil paint are rich in elemental nuance, and I chose two kinds of white: flake white, with a warm translucent fleshy quality, and titanium white, chalky, brittle, opaque, and very bright. I used the two whites as a dialogue about what was living and what was not.

When someone close to you passes from this life, you find out very quickly how you really feel about death. I was certain then that death was like a veil, a doorway, leading to a brightness and a peace, and that it was only here in this life that the shadows and turbulence arise. So I started painting a stark white "dead" bone inside a "living" shell, then a shell and bone that were both alive, with the delicate edges of the bone like lacey edges of a sea tide on a small shore inside the shell.

Then I glanced over at the bones I had not chosen to paint. On some there were spots of clear green stain, on others, crusty formations of dull orange red, and all at once, all the fears of death that had receded so easily swept over me in one engulfing wave. How can you touch these human bones? These are your father's bones; the spots are unburned flesh, your father's flesh. You should bury them right now! I felt that if I left them unexamined they would hover forever at the edges of my mind, and that this was the way you became haunted, from within.

I found a larger shell with faint rainbow ridges around the rim, heaped all those crusted and stained bones in it, and started painting. I could not stand to look at the bones; they made me nauseous with fear. The painting looked just like them; I could not look at it either. I could only focus on the moving tip of the brush tracing every curve.

It was August, and peaches were in season. One day I took a break while painting and ate a fresh ripe peach. I held the fleshy fruit in my hand and took a bite. The juice was dribbling down my chin. I could not taste or feel the sweet flesh in my mouth; I could only feel the bones inside my hand, the bones that held the fruit, the bones just like my father's bones, the bones I was afraid to see. I kept painting, and by the time I finished, the fear had just worn away. I did not conquer death, or move beyond its reach, but now the bones, my hands, the brush, the peach, the shells, the summer heat, the sadness and the questioning, the veils and the light, were all one, simply what is.

I finished three more paintings: a piece of chalky bone like a snowy mountaintop inside a chalky full moon shell, a living bone and living shell placed as if peeling apart to reveal a rainbow spiral on the shell, and then a small piece of bone like a tiny face riding on a wing-shaped shell flying away.

CLOISTERS

Rob

Cool, peaceful, seated at a thick wooden table like an illuminator's desk, the light was pleasant to read by and follow the lines painted where no self abides. Histories of Chinese Chan and Japanese Zen Buddhist paintings spread across my desk, one brush, spontaneous, a moment beyond the hand, beyond the paper, and beyond the brush and ink, an arisen gesture, elemental and fluid, paintings of nature, self-portraits, and calligraphy. I'm not working. I'm not out enjoying this hot summer at the beach. I am following the lines and expressed brilliant moments of past masters who had blended the knowing felt in their hearts as seen throughout their experience. The Romanesque-style Scripps College library was where I spent the summer of 1979, studying these past masters' work and their temples, sculpture, and gardens. I was searching for more clues before my first semester at Claremont Graduate School began, searching a dim memory, the Zen Buddhists, the sacred movement in their elemental space.

I remembered another summer when I was in Rome, in 1975. I went with a guide and a few other people to see a Titian painting in a small cathedral not open to the public, an experience that made a deep impression on me and seemed to have a great relevance to my sense of passage into a sacred space.

70

We met our guide in the middle of a clashing urban storm. We walked engulfed in hot dry clouds of exhaust for a short while and then turned on to a more residential street with less and less traffic as the street narrowed. Suddenly it widened to encircle a modest cathedral, a simple unadorned enclosure of marble. We walked up the marble steps in the glare of the street. Then the door opened and we were ushered into the cool cavernous dark. The door closed and locked with a dank echo. My eyes strained to adjust. I followed the footsteps of the priest, the sound of his leather shoes tapping out a path to follow through the smell of burning candles and the hushed whispers within a sacred space. The footsteps stopped, all of us coming to a halt. A light suddenly illuminated a large Titian painting of Jesus, startling in the cave-like darkness. There was just enough light to see the painting, to see the light that was arising out of Jesus, epiphany's radiance pouring out of a spiritual being. This whole experience for me was all encompassing, a passage along the corridors of one's awakening like a light within me illuminating an unnoticed path. As soon as I began to breathe, the lights were extinguished and we again followed the sounds of our guide. We emerged abruptly into the Roman summer again. One is led to the divine on a sacred journey, out of solidity's grasp, within light, movement, shape, and sound, to a pith of brilliant treasure within.

For me graduate school allowed a sense of openness and the time to see what arises, waiting through the bad days. You cannot force your heart; you have to allow it space and abide patiently being fully aware with faith for that spark to appear.

One night I was sitting in my studio. I looked at a box of dried pigments on the floor next to me. I picked through the box, found deep blues and a bottle of violet, and mixed them together. I also had a perfect square frame which I placed on the floor and dusted the pigment inside it. I lifted the frame to reveal a perfect square field of dark blue seemingly floating off the gray concrete floor, and sat back. There was something special in the rawness of the pigment, the earthiness and the color, and I could walk around it. I could now paint with materials of the Earth and contrast them with synthetic materials, creating a dialogue that evoked spiritual or elemental qualities.

My mind was racing to touch something, trying to remember a dream, red iron oxide, the blood of ancient artists, and clay, dense fabric of Earth, Padua northwest of Venice, and the sky, the blue of the Florentine painter Giotto. I painted a six-foot square of this enchanting blue on the floor of my studio and went and found a shovel. I remembered a place I had seen nearby where red iron oxide clay was exposed by runoff. My poor VW was crushed by the weight of many concrete sacks full of earth. I stretched a sheet of clear plastic over this field of Giotto's sky and covered it with a three-inch-thick layer of wet clay. With the help of some fans, the clay cracked as it dried, exposing rivulets and fissures of blue sky. Here I was, standing around my mind, watching its clay, earthen, blood-soaked density crack and reveal a precious, sky-like truth.

There is movement in the flow of the seasons, impermanent and elemental, revealing, opening, and subsiding again. After allowing others to experience the work, I shoveled and swept it away, impermanence, the inevitable element.

I did a number of smaller installations over the next two years using this new avenue for exploring the spiritual path through materials and space. This series of works culminated in a large installation for my graduate show based on a drawing of an elementary human figure with an aura surrounding the figure. I called the installation *Garden-Variety*, common or ordinary. It was a contrast of materials out of the suburbs of my childhood and the spiritual journey, the ongoing path of return.

The elemental stick figure was "drawn" with screens of corrugated fiberglass, like the fencing around the swimming pools of so many homes in and around Los Angeles, but also reflective of Japanese screens. I liked the translucent green quality of the fiberglass floating a green shadow on the sand and the white dolomite stones marking out rays from the figure's heart center where I had poured a mound of rock salt. Looking down at the figure from above, the image was like the simplified lines of the monumental Earth drawings in Nazco, Peru. I painted the back wall of the gallery a deep dark phthalo blue, and the whole figure was traced around with a clear plastic pathway. I was seeking the sacred in the materials of my world to reflect the natural, organic rhythms that map out the divine.

I began creating larger and more extensive installations in empty warehouses spaces, two thousand to four thousand square feet, using natural and synthetic materials with an eye for the elemental and translucent: stone, salt, coal, sand, asphalt, and grass sod with clear plastic, colored acetate, corrugated fiberglass and colored glass. These installations were drawings you could walk into and around, images of rudimentary human figures delineated by translucent colored screens and curving pathways, a movement through veils of color, with some characteristics of cathedrals and Zen gardens, entrances, passages, and above all a presence of the sacred, a feeling one enters into.

This work ripened into *Cloisters*, my last and most comprehensive installation of this kind, a glimpse of union within the heart, penetrating into an enclosure rarely entered.

I was working at a French bakery from 2:30 a.m. to 10:30 a.m., and during the day I worked on my installations. I found an old carpet showroom and was able to rent this two thousand square feet space for one month. The image was already drawn within my mind, the materials chosen, the screens made, everything ready. After getting off work Friday morning, I rented a truck and hauled literally tons of materials to this storefront.

I opened the door to the space and was shocked to find an enormous table used to cut fabric and carpet. I tried to move it out of the way but it would not budge. I had so little time to create this whole installation before I had to work early Monday morning, I was furious. I grabbed the edge of the table and shoved it as hard as

I could. It moved two inches on an angle. I grabbed the opposite corner and pushed with all my strength, again it moved only two inches. For an hour and a half, I sailed this behemoth through this space and into the next room. Now the space was clear and open. I unloaded the truck and began to work.

Once the installation was complete, I would come down to the space after working and sit while the doors were open to the public. The storefront was all glass and aluminum frame with a double glass door in the middle. As you entered, you were confronted with tall red acetate screens delineating another entry within the space, a doorway, and a path of clear plastic and asphalt to walk on. I used asphalt because it was everywhere, you walked on it, you drove on it. The smell of it was always there, everywhere you went someone was digging into it and patching the hole with fresh asphalt. Asphalt was the ground of this modern world.

As you walked along the asphalt path the red light from the screens surrounded you, and you came to a fetal figure of translucent green glass drawn on a floor of red plaster with a series of green acetate screens encompassing this womb. I used red and green because they are complimentary, they vibrate with one another, and the whole installation was bathed in the interplay of these colors. The embryo was green, the nucleus of awakening. The surrounding red was the intensity, the fire of spiritual practice.

Farther into the body of this cell, the red background turned to white plaster and there was a large male figure, primal and central, drawn in weathered bricks. Screens of red acetate stood beyond the head of this figure. As you continued along the sinuous path of asphalt, you came to the end just past the red screens. Here on a large mound of rock salt was a small figure drawn in shiny black stones reaching down the slope to touch the ground on which this union evolves.

All beings are like bubbles or spheres that are flooding out of essence, coming into existence. The central figure was our personal sphere of influence, our ability to be aware and to choose. The small figure above it reaching down was a blessing, a gesture, a moment, something that touches you and opens you to your heart's luminous nature. The rock salt was elemental, translucent essence shimmering in the light. The whole installation was trying to show a vision of the nature of all phenomena. The figures were spheres of influence, a spiritual union, an intersection within one's being, a movement along the path of return to essence, moments of blessings that move our minds to recognize. They were complex visionary states welling up from my heart, vast dynamic images, which I tried to recreate for others to experience and a mystery I tried to unravel for myself. Most people found them incomprehensible, and I would not fully understand or recognize them until deep into the practice of Tögal.

As I sat with my work, one day a service man came by to fix something. He was surprised to find the installation there and asked if he could walk through it. Afterwards he thanked me, saying that my work had touched him deeply, and he was going to tell his priest to come see it too. He said, "It was like being in church".

I dismantled and hauled it all away at the end of the month, the heavy weight of impermanence.

CUTTING AWAY THE BLIND MAN

In the fall of 1983, I moved my studio to a warehouse in South Central Los Angeles. The main artery out of downtown LA that cut through the warehouse district was a fast drive with many eighteen-wheelers, the road rugged with a crisscrossing of railroad tracks. It was common to see the long arms of the automated crossing guards shattered and obliterated by a racing truck unwilling to stop and wait for the slow trains. At that time, many of the warehouses and steel mills were abandoned, and as you came close to the projects you would see burned out cars and empty lots filled with garbage. A quarter block down from the Plaza del Rio housing project were three nondescript warehouses with a central gated driveway between two of them. This led to a compound walled with cinder block topped with steel fencing, sheet metal, barbed wire and razor wire.

This was my neighborhood, my burning ground, and even though it was in the midst of the Bloods and Crips drug war, from the first moment I stood in the studio I felt I was on the most holy of places. I could feel how this land abided by itself. There was a presence here long before man arrived, a power moving and changing with the fluidity and simplicity of tall grass moving in the wind, embellished by the delicate light of stars.

I was working as a baker for a restaurant in Pasadena. I would wake up at two a.m. and immediately, unconsciously, put on my clothes, stumble through the dark warehouse, throw open the roll up doors then drive fast along darkened streets, passing wild dog packs running across train tracks, abandoned lots where the shadows of men could be seen standing around trash can fires, and glimpses of men darkened by the soot of their past trudging down the long streets moving because movement held some last hope of doing.

When I first moved in, I cleaned out a small pit of toxic chemicals left by a former tenant so I could plant a bougainvillea vine. In the process of digging out these chemicals, I found a four-foot piece of clear cedar. I immediately carved a Japanese Avalokitesvara, a Kannon, inspired by Enku and the German expressionists. I stained it with black ink giving it a feeling of a shadow or a block of coal. This Kannon expressed ongoing indestructible compassion. Though blackened and compressed as coal, he radiates blessings throughout the six realms.

The Kannon that arose out of my heart, the cedar, and the sacred ground marked the beginning of a tremendous outpouring of images. If any word has meaning to express this time in my life, it would be passion, the passion that was the Buddha's search for liberation, the shock of suffering that cracked open his beautiful privileged life, and his extreme asceticism, the intensity, courage, and self reliance to find the truth within his own experience. He went beyond his reasonable world, to venture into the realm of profound direct experience and awakening.

In this holy place, within the burning, dried salt bed of tears, I carved as if taking the last hill, the only hill in a battle waged over lifetimes. I hauled dead trees into my studio, cutting with chainsaws and axes, unleashing clouds of dust and smoke; sections of trees would fall, crashing to the floor. One man said listening to me carve was the most frightening sound he had ever heard. Every cut I made was consumed in the vibration of my spirit crying out to expose, cut out, and lay bare the ultimate essence. Out of this cloud of wood, rubble, and smoke came images questioning the very nature of belief, where holding and grasping to doctrine blind one from the very source of this belief. Life-sized carvings of faith, prophets, priests, worshipers, angels, and monks came out of me.

Friends of mine had to cut down an old walnut tree in their backyard, and they arranged for a man to haul it to my studio. What I did not realize was that the whole tree was going to be hauled to my studio, every leaf, twig, and rotted branch, filling one end of my studio. I began to dig through the old rot of the walnut's past.

I found the trunk buried under its crown. I stood it up and began carving; I knew this old wizened tree. I was working from a large ink painting I had done called *Belief.* A man stands alone enclosed by the night; he holds a long pole that extends into the sky as if affixed to a huge fiery star. An abandoned freeway curves across the painting held aloft on thick pillars lit by this blazing star. A portion of the walnut trunk had rotted at the bottom. I cut it out and exposed the stance of *Belief,* bracing to hold a star, pitched upon the movement of one's inner sea with the pull and the weight of a wind-billowed sail. The face of *Belief* was strained under this pressure, the tension of holding to an affixed brilliance. I carved a hand near his head to hold a long bent rusted pipe and attached a flaming star of rusted corrugated steel, the slow fire of rust, the slow rot of wood, straining to hold the ephemeral and root the transcendent. I then placed a mound of huge chunks of raw coal next to *Belief:* fire, rust and rot, the fixation, density, and strain of holding to a belief.

Again I dug through the debris that was once a walnut tree and found another section, cutting a base so it could stand. I had no paintings to guide me, no sketches, only a sense or feeling about faith. Often in the process of carving, I would stand in the gesture of the piece I was working on. Now as I began carving, knowing myself within the wood and the strokes of my axe, I stood in the posture of a life, a glowing coal. The head falls slightly as the arms embrace. Eyes are closed, held tight, a certainty, a knowing, a pain, and a cry. As I carved to reveal, I yearned to expose the core of the sun, an assurance of something intangible, ephemeral, pulling in your heart. I then bent a glass rod; the figure gently holds this translucent shiny beam of faith.

I confronted issues of holding to a religious structure versus the openness of the mystic man or woman who has left the known order and found an awakening in their own direct experience. The work was called *Hanap'atu and Coalsack*, named after two black cloud constellations in the Milky Way. In Incan cosmology, the black clouds were considered as important as the more familiar groupings of stars. I felt the relationship between these black clouds in the sky as a dialogue between clinging to a doctrine and letting go to find the essence beyond concepts. Within a tall niche of rusted steel, *Hanap'atu,* the toad, crouches on a slab of polished granite. Holding to the security of the enclosure with one hand, he reaches out toward *Coalsack* with the other. *Coalsack* is slouched like a homeless man dying on the sidewalk. His upper body, heavy like a sack of coal, is propped up by his arms, but his face reflects a knowing inner brilliance. This is a question at the point of revelation: to be so close to the shore and yet hold to the raft, to cling to the finger that points at the moon. Though *Hanap'atu* sees the knowing in the eyes of *Coalsack* and wants to reach him, he cannot let go of his structure.

During this time, I continued to do large ink on paper paintings, many of them of the night sky, moments within this eternal apocalypse. I painted angels bursting into flames standing beneath abandoned freeway overpasses as a star in the night sky goes supernova, shadows of men around trash can fires with abandoned freeways arching above them, our contemporary cathedrals with the night sky as their domes, prophets alone amid the rubble of our age, and a stream of Bodhidharmas marching toward a blazing sun.

I carved two life-sized men standing around a trash can fire, one stares up at the night sky, seeing the moment at the end of time, splitting his very being, while his counterpart across the fire holds his hands near the fire, soft and gentle just as it is. These images were questions that released more questions, a trail of snowflakes to the divine.

Elliot was singing to the wild dog pack. Her aria had been going on for over an hour now. "Elliot!" I would say through the window, "Elliot!" "Ahoowoo oohwa woowawoouawoo", as she wagged her tail and licked at the screen. "Elliot!" "Awwoowoowa awoo woowoooowaawoo" I made my way through the studio past explosions of belief and prophecy and rolled the big door up. There was Elliot wagging her tail all excited, "How great you came out to join me," as she dropped her tennis ball at my feet and excitedly waited for me to throw the ball, her eyes fixed on the ball. But I had things to do, like sleep. "Elliot, please!" I said, pleading with her. She would flop on her back, stick out a leg, throw a front paw over her head, turn toward me and smile. A millisecond after petting her tummy she was up and ready to play. "Enough therapy just throw the ball." I went in and rolled down the door. "Awoooooo waawooooowooo waawoooowooo" "Oh, I'm tired."

Then I heard the gate as if someone was climbing and pulling at it. I peered through my window and saw Elliot ripping at the chain link fencing on the gate with her teeth, tearing it, bending it and trying to squeeze through the hole she made. "Elliot, stop that." I said. She began ripping at it in earnest now as she smashed her body into this small hole in the gate. "Elliot!" Wiggling, squirming, and then she was out, prancing about and running off with the wild dogs. This was our guard dog. By the time I drove back from work, she would be asleep in her doghouse.

You never really knew when Elliot would be in the compound or out for the night. Strangely enough, whenever I really needed her she would appear. There were a number of times when I would drive home to the studio late at night, and as I got out of my car to open the gate someone would lunge out of the shadows. As I dodged a blow from something in the shadow's hand, Elliot would appear out of the darkness of the street, exploding into a growling, barking, biting monster. She would be all over the shadow, then chasing him down the street. I would throw the gate open and drive in, and as I went to close the gate Elliot would be prancing back up the driveway looking very cute, and then she would see her ball and run and get it, dropping it at my feet, wagging her tail, "What a great night to play!"

Elliot was already living at the compound when I moved in, and she adopted me. We bonded in a way that was like a partnership.

One Friday evening I was alone in my studio and all my neighbors in this compound were gone as well. I sat writing in my journal and making small sketches, when I realized that there was a dead quiet over the whole area, no dogs barking, no helicopters, no gunshots, no cars were moving; it was completely quiet. There was a coldness to this silence, waiting, listening, like feeling the eyes of a predator on you. My breath was deep and slow within this silence, my heart beat against it. And there was a darkness; it embraced me, freezing me within its ice. All I could do was wait within my own heart listening for the footfalls of my stalker. I remained unmoving like a deer frozen by a snapped twig. The darkness was speaking to me, a chilling acknowledgment that there might not be enough time. Within this darkness, I felt a point of light, they were not separate, they were in cahoots, revealing, pushing, and exposing me. My recent work of angels and prophets arising as visions in the wilderness, they were from this dark brilliance, forcing me to see and remember, to return as a circle is drawn.

I was driving home from Otis Parsons Art Institute finishing work around 9:30 p.m. As I got close to my street, I noticed I was almost out of gas, the gauge on red. At that hour on Friday night I was not about to get gas in South Central. I knew I could get home and worry about gas in the morning, the safest time, mostly.

I was just about to turn onto my street when from the shadows across the street came a woman's scream, "Help me! Help me! Please help me!" Something stopped the car in the middle of hell. A black woman holding a small boy in her arms ran up to my car crying and wailing frantically pleading with me to help her. She said she did not know the area, was lost, could I take her to her boyfriend's house. There was something else that motivated me to unlock the door and take her wherever she wanted to go. There was another agenda working me. I was driving fast, down farther beyond my conscious desire to help, beyond the gas gauge passing red, through the darkened streets, swerving around gangs of men, being totally aware of the night, my life on the line for someone I have never met before. I finally pulled up to a dark ominous house, empty and silent. She again pleaded with me, not to leave her there. Now I was driving to the nearest police station, as I said it, I wondered if in all that area was there a safe place; did any of us have a safe place to go? "No! No! Please take me to my mother's house!" she cried. Back toward the projects. Did we talk? Do I know her? The connection was too hard to confront rationally. The boy in her arms barely moved and never spoke.

As we neared the projects there was a part of me, the one who was on empty, who had been used, and the other who understood and recognized this woman outside of time and had unlocked the car door for her. As I let her out on the corner, she laughed like a wild witch, but somehow I knew she missed something. Afterward I just sat in my studio with a ringing mind, sensing something I could not completely recognize.

I had been chain sawing for an hour working my way through a tangle of eucalyptus branches. I was trying to cut sections of a great tree that had been pushed over by a construction company. I had not realized how heavy each eight-foot section would be, and I nearly crushed my neighbor's truck hauling them back to my studio.

I had been drawing many sketches of priests and monks with long staffs, and I immediately started chain sawing to rough out a log and get it standing. I drew a priest on the log and cut with chain saw and axes. Again I drew the priest on all angles, and as I carved I considered who this priest was and why was I so intent on rendering it.

My thoughts always went to my father. He was in my mind someone who would have been best suited to be on a spiritual path but stayed within the secular world. Even though he remained in that worldview, he never lost his basic underlying goodness. No matter how angry he became, no matter how narrow or rigid his views were this presence never left him. I once painted my father sitting on my window seat at the old house. His face held a true tenderness while his hands held to a character that did not fit him. I remember him telling someone at a party that during World War II when he was promoted to Master Sergeant and was to train his own men, his own Sergeant had to take him into the forest nearby and make him get very angry, teaching him to yell with a force and a command. This is how I remembered him as I was growing up, as if he wore a uniform of authority long since passed. I had painted him, seeing this as an old cloak that he wore, a character that was out of place.

As I continued to carve, thinking of him and the spiritual path, such a long and arduous trail, I also saw myself. Here and there throughout my life, spiritual experiences arose, tearing through my ordinary mind, revealing such a simple radiance yet shocking in contrast. Then it would be gone, the experience fading. I too am a spiritual priest, a monk with no interest in the rule. I follow the tracks of the radiance as if left in the snow, following as fast as I can, before the tracks melt.

I carved the body as if robed, leaving the rough cuts of the chainsaw, and smoothed the simple shape of the head with a chisel but left out all facial form. I painted the whole sculpture with black ink like a shadow at the corner of your eye. The figure held a long staff of rusted pipe. As I sat looking at the piece, I knew something was not there. I grabbed a rag off my table, soaked it in black ink, and tied it around where the eyes of the priest would be.

I could see my father walking through this life as if blindfolding himself to a truth he already possessed; he could see it if he chose to. I saw myself with the same capacity, every step I take, cutting away the blind man.

Throughout the early years at South Central, I would study the night sky. The compound in the back was safe enough standing in the shadows, and with books and star charts, I began to learn the names of the stars making up the constellations. I was also fascinated with traditional views of the stars in Native American, Polynesian, and Chinese cultures. The ancients were less fixed within the narrow confines of reason. For them the night sky was an elemental presence, like the Earth of which I knew almost nothing. The ignorance I felt standing outside in the shadows of the night stunned me. I did not know how to live with the very planet I was born on, and I could not use the stars to navigate my way. The elemental aspects of this world have a presence and an energy that were being denied. Here was the apocalypse, amidst the debris of our civilization, and the beings caught in it. This apocalypse was in a friend's eyes as she drew closer to death, and in my father's holding and denial. The apocalypse was our regret at the moment of our civilized death at not having lived the wholeness of this experience. It is within each fraction of a moment after we exhale and before we inhale again. It is within every moment of our lives.

I lived with a sense of death; it seemed to imbue every action and thought. As I drove home at night, a shadow would move; as I laid down to sleep, a sound; as I made something to eat, a tightness. Standing in a wall's shadow with the wild sounds beyond, looking up at the night sky, I felt a tremendous jolt of energy surging up my spine radiating throughout my body. The shadows, the stars, my own heart beating were all the gentle touch of death endlessly reminding and prodding me to remember.

Every six months or so, my father would be rushed to the emergency room with complications due to heart disease. I would drive down to help my mother and do what I could on the weekends until my father recovered enough to come home. This went on for many years as his system slowly declined. He would spend more and more time alone at the house while my mother was out shopping. He once confided to me that when Mom went out, he would sit in his chair and feel and see a growing darkness moving from across the street, coming toward him. He said it terrified him, but he would quickly change the subject. He refused to see a counselor and did not want to think about death. He was trying to hold onto his routines and habits and my mother, and all the while, his life was fading away.

An artist friend I met during graduate school had been battling Hodgkin's disease for a number of years. I went to see her soon after she told me that her cancer was progressing again after her third remission. She was considerably thinner, with a wan complexion. We talked openly about her health and some of her recent artwork, which was an expression of her fears and nightmares about death. She was opening the door to look at death, but too much of her wounded past would surge up into her mind.

Fear was in her throat within the background of all her words. She asked if I would spend the night. A number of years ago we had had a short relationship, and now as I held her through the night, her skin was covered in a film of cold sweat, her breathing labored but steady. There was a smell that sent chills up my spine. I did not sleep. I could feel death all around her. By morning I felt like I had tried to warm the Earth with the small lamp of my body. I was completely drained and had to leave.

I asked myself what I could do for my family and friends. I could offer them my life but they would still be caught by their hopes and fears. I saw in myself my own ignorance, trying to remember a dream. I found a truth in my friend's eyes before she died and in my father's garbled cry as he passed, a regret at not looking at or living the basic elemental aspects of this life and searching your heart to glimpse a simple radiance. Death abides within this dream upon this Earth, pointing and pushing us beneath the vault of the sky, the sun, the moon, and the touching brilliance of the stars marking out the pattern of our hearts. The mystic journey was laid out before me here in South Central LA, and the challenge was to accept it. This is why we are all here, the only reason we are here, to follow this journey over countless lifetimes, to return to essence.

Five Fathoms

Rachel

White and black wolf dog running in a molten night, running toward the dawn along a ridge top of a grassy hill, grass flowing in the wind, fur rippling from muscles moving inside fur, inside the circling rhythms of his loping stride, big black spots on fur moving, forming shapes of black war horse with powerful arched neck galloping across white dog fur, both bursting now with flowing lines of light, glowing hairs threaded with tiny yellow and gray dots, the luminous shadow shapes of tiny clear spheres.

Bare-skinned woman bathed in yellow light, standing in front of an open doorway filled with the blue-black darkness of a timeless night, bare-skinned woman becoming bear, bones swelling, muscles swelling, legs already rooted deep in lush bear fur, one arm still woman flesh holding heavy skin of bear, other arm reaching down deep inside into bear's skin, woman skin flowing, melting, fusing with bear fur, radiant serene moon woman's face, bear's moon floating in a silent sky, bending over, reaching in, reaching down, diving deep into warm bear's sea, her face inside bear's face now, moon looking through reflection of moon's eyes, lush golden fur and heavy skin of bear rising up and sealing over down her back.

I was immersed in the forgotten remembering encoded in my dreams. Patterns are stored in many ways. Bones hold the traces of a life, the support from within. Dreams hold other traces, an inner support of another kind, and after painting my father's bones, I began to paint my dreams. I wanted to know what was going on while I was asleep.

The world of dreaming touched on multilayered realms of experience, a flowing union of past, present, and future, of heart and mind intertwined, the spacious and the personal, an ageless sea of fertile energies. I went to sleep with open hands, with respect for whatever my dreaming could say to me. I was fascinated. I wanted to listen and learn. I kept a journal. I trained myself to wake up in the night and write in the dark to stay close to the dreaming mind. One morning I woke up to find I had transcribed an entire dream in ballpoint pen on the outside of my thigh.

I began to dream simple events in my daily life four days before they happened. By the time they ripened into my "life", I would already be absorbed in the thoughts and feelings of the next four days ahead. The "present" had become distant, passing by like a memory. I was moving through my life on an angle on several layers at once, and my daily mind seemed to be the last to know; the real decisions were clearly being made somewhere far below. After a month of dreaming in this way, the dreams veered off and opened into a wider range of experience again.

Beautiful rainbow lights flooded out of plants, flowers, and the trunks of trees. Elemental helpers and animal messengers brought healings and teachings, wordless knowings about the unfolding nature of this experience, this life. A recurring dream ran through subtle permutations on its own and finally resolved. I danced, I flew, I traveled the forested lands nearby and returned to my body as if being sipped back through a glowing straw.

Clear precise scenes of plants, animals, and other beings would arise in my dreams fully composed and resolved aesthetically. Dreaming was becoming art. Images that had been cloaked in familiar detail by the inner storyteller that brings the memory of dream across the borders of sleep revealed their truer nature as I painted. My hands had a wisdom of their own, outside the preconceptions of what we presume to call the waking state.

I read the first four books by Carlos Castaneda. I was touched, as were so many of my generation, by the ambience of his books. I was not drawn to the psychotropic approach to alternative states, but to the evocation of the desert landscapes, the dialogue with plants, and the lessons in personal discipline for simplifying your life, for touching your world lightly with respect for its livingness and mystery. I began to find my hands in my dreams. The first time I saw my hands, the dream ignited into a spacious radiance, which burst through the walls between the dream and the room where I slept and the rainy night outside, melting them into a vast luminosity, vividly alive. Subsequent lucid dreams did not open in the same way; they seemed to be just another deeper kind of dream. I was still looking: How to wake the hidden sleeper from inside?

After seven years of intense focus on dreaming and painting dreams, I had a landmark dream, a powerful teaching within a future memory. I saw high ramps and scaffolding of an endless roller coaster ride extending everywhere. People with fixed leering grins and glassy eyes rode standing up in the cars, and I had a definite knowing that the entire Earth had become a prison planet. Then another scene, bonfires in the night on a flat, open area upslope from a river in a narrow valley with mountains on both sides, and an abandoned three-story stucco building built on a rise. Gangs of people roamed from fire to fire, holding their children's feet in the fires and torturing each other. In the forest nearby there was a small monastery with red tile roofs. A large stone basin was overflowing with bright water, filling a courtyard with a fluid brilliance. I looked longingly, but I knew that the monastery was part of the same layer of the dream as the roller coaster and the fires; it was not far enough from the horror. A profound certainty arose in me that even the deepest symbolic aspects of the mind could not set you free. A more fundamental, essential ground, transcending and permeating symbols, cultures, and structures, was where true freedom is. I ran farther up the mountain into a part of the forest with smooth trunks of red-barked trees.

I kept painting, but there was a feeling from this and from other dreams that my real work was still elsewhere and would not start until later in my life.

Throughout most of my dreaming years, I lived in a small town near the coast in northern California, and I was married. My husband and I had dated for a while when we were both freshmen at Stanford. When we ran into each other again by chance six years later, we felt like old friends. We had both traveled alternative paths and seemed to have arrived at the same place, but my husband was ready for an outwardly more conventional life, and I was still listening to a more unpredictable inner call. We built a house together, something he had always wanted to do, and spent some time abroad as part of a business he was hoping to set up. He helped me get started showing my paintings. We tried to help each other with whatever it was we were feeling in our deepest hearts that we needed or wanted to do in this life, but we were heading in different directions.

In the first year of our marriage, I had a major surgery. I entered the hospital the night before and was given a sedative as part of pre-op. I was mushy but awake when it came time for Steve to leave, but instead of leaving, he crawled under the bed. Neither of us said a word. I stayed curled up on my side, with one arm dangling over the far side of the bed while Steve held my hand all night. Afterward he said the floor was heated, and it was actually pretty comfortable.

In the morning, he came out from under the bed, straightened his clothes, and went out to the nurse's station to sign some papers, just as if he had arrived early for visiting hours. Then I was being wheeled down the hallway on a gurney towards the surgery, seeing

Steve standing by the door of my room growing smaller and smaller. The wide hospital corridor was shadowy, but I could still see him standing there as the big steel doors opened. I was whooshed into the glaring lights and shiny chrome of the operating room, feeling how much easier it was to be swept along held within the momentum of your life, and how much harder it must be for Steve then to be the person who was waiting, watching until you emerged from your destiny again. In a way our whole marriage was like that, each of us being carried along by our choices, each of us waiting at opposite ends of a hallway growing longer and longer to see where the other person would emerge. Finally, we divorced. He was a good friend.

I returned to the Bay area and stayed with friends for a while. Then I rented a small day studio and house sat for a year, moving from place to place, a few months at a time, living between the cracks of my own and others' lives: stepping into the abundance of a well cared for vegetable garden in late summer, embracing the solitude of winter at the gatehouse of an empty estate that was for sale, or enjoying the companionship of friendly family dogs whose owners were away.

All the while, something was driving me, between the moments of gentle offering, towards offerings of another kind, driving me toward people and experiences, recognitions not completely recognized, entering situations to absorb, reveal, and heal patterns that extended far past individual lives. There was a reason I was here. The people that I touched or was touched by formed another kind of dream, a web of gestures I did not fully comprehend as they unfolded. I was following my heart through the maze, if for no other reason than to learn to trust that following; there was a deeper intent here.

The ex-con biker guy was charismatic, quick, and mean, and he introduced me to his clotted world of porno motels and semi-retired auto thieves. I was appalled at the opaque sadness of the narrow hallways, the shabby, sometimes ornate but always strangely hollow rooms with the curtains tightly drawn, and the countless sexual acts devoid of any tenderness repeating endlessly on every channel of the cable TV, but I was in love, and I did not judge. Early one summer morning, his body in the hold of yet another drug, wanting sex but unable to stay erect, he began beating me in bed. I did not fight back, I entered a stillness instead, my body going limp as if to save it from a fall, surrendering completely to the open sea that was myself and also this terrible fierce wave towering over me. An unexpected certainty came over me in the first fiery moment of shock that I had been waiting my whole life for this, without knowing it.

I told him later, in another context, that he did not need to keep carrying prison around with him by responding as if he was still there. My words surprised me as I spoke them, and I was afraid I had overstepped his invisible and very twitchy boundaries, but he looked thoughtful and said that was the smartest thing I ever said to him. We parted soon after that; the complex gesture between us was over.

I did not know, when I began a brief affair in the spring of the following year, that every year at Easter time this sensitive well-educated artist from a wealthy family back east entered into a delusion that he was Jesus Christ returning for the Last Judgment. On a warm spring afternoon, as we walked together on the grounds of a seminary nearby, his mind suddenly exploded full-bloom into the wrathful Jehovah Christ. As I listened to the cadence of his words, so ancient and so fierce, so full of judgments over transgressions of the law, the whole of the Judeo-Christian mind-body split opened like a chasm in front of me. An eerie light burned around him, barely visible in the clear sunlight, and who was I to say that at that moment he was not the wrathful Christ come back to slay us all and send us to eternal hell. Where are the boundaries of a mind unmoored and cut off from the heart?

Later his friends warned me about the violence that usually followed on his words. I knew there was nothing I could do to stop the tide; this had only been for witnessing. I ended the relationship that had barely begun, and heard afterward that at the apex of his passion that year, he shoved a street person through the plate glass window of a store.

A few months later, I was visiting a friend who was learning to draw, and as I went out to get a sketchbook from my car, I noticed a small car in the driveway across the street. The engine was running, the car was rolling, the driver's door was open and a large man was pulling a woman from the driver's seat. I heard muffled voices; then the woman cried out louder, "No! Please!" and his first name, the same name as my wrathful Judgment friend.

They were struggling. My heart opened wide. I entered another kind of time, spacious, calm, and bright. All the thoughts that could be there were concentrated into a clear wordless intent: No one should ever do this to anyone or themselves again. I already knew that even the police were reluctant to interfere in domestic violence, so explosive are the bonds that once were kind and now have burst. I did not care if I died; I did not care if I got hurt. For this woman and this man, for the street person a few months before, for my lovers, for my parents, for anyone anywhere caught in ways they could not recognize, I walked quietly across the street. The man and woman were still struggling, as if they were very far away, suspended inside the bright expanse of my heart. They did not see me until I stood beside them. The man let go of the woman briefly. I put my arm around her and held her close to me. She was very small, she fit under my shoulder, and she put her arms around me. The guy was huge, bigger than both of us together. I looked right at the big man's eyes and said very softly, "You cool it now." He turned around and walked away.

The painted textures of the lush bear fur, the glowing doorway and the blue-black night beyond were all cut through with the seam between the two panels set up on my easel, one above the other. I was painting the *Bear Lady* again, life-size this time, and the day I started her I had only two smaller canvases on hand. When I placed them one above the other, the six-foot high space had seemed perfect then, like a door, but as the painting became more detailed and naturalistic in a dreamlike way, I was looking at the seam, wondering what was it doing there?

The dream was about movement, transformation, bending over, reaching down, and standing up again. I got a second easel and two more canvases, and started a second figure beside the first. I had a large square of four panels now, and I adjusted the composition so I could rearrange them as I painted. I could work on a woman beside a standing bear, or on a woman with the hind legs of a bear standing beside a bear with a woman's leg emerging from a swirling bear fur skirt. Woman or bear, no beginning and no end to the moving in between. Wholeness is a verb, so is dance.

I began dancing again. I had taken a short belly dance class after my surgery years before to help heal my abdominal muscles, and I discovered that I loved the undulating circular movements and the elemental quality of the dance. I had had many dreams of belly dancing, and I had studied for a while with Jamila Salimpour in San Francisco, learning her particular style that maintained the dignity and sacred grace of this traditional form.

There was something missing from my carefully rendered paintings, despite the luminous details. The molten livingness so apparent in dreaming never found its way completely onto canvas or paper. In belly dance I found a way to reconsecrate and celebrate the feminine aspects of that livingness directly, outside of paint, through the elemental energies that formed the natural landscape of my body. With the same thoroughness I had for painting and dreaming, seeking the same hidden depths in a way that I could share, I now threw myself into belly dancing, making costumes, rehearsing, and performing.

Belly dancing is a joyful responsive art. You borrow energy from people gathered for an already celebratory event, whirl the energy around and give it back, returning to the audience something of their own even more fluid and alive; your best performances are never fully yours.

The midday summer sun erased all sense of depth in the parched blond hills above Cupertino as I drove through the rolling countryside to the Serbian church. Behind the long low building, a lush canopy of grape vines made a sanctuary of cool shade over an extensive stone patio. A large group, perhaps a hundred family and friends, were gathered for a fiftieth wedding anniversary. I went inside to change into my costume; then one of the grandsons led me through the crowd under the huge arbor.

An area had been cleared away, and a frail, thin, elderly man who looked as if he was going blind was sitting stiffly on an upright chair alone. A row of six or seven older women, ample-bodied, dressed in black with long black shawls, sat shoulder to shoulder nearby looking straight ahead like a breakwater to hold back the sea. They all looked alike to me. I asked the grandson, which one was grandma. He said the third one from the right.

The music started and I began to dance. People were clapping and laughing, some voices calling out jokes about grandpa and the belly dancer. They were passionate exuberant people, and as I danced I could feel that grandma and grandpa were young and juicy once, and very much in love. As I took off my first veil, I went over to grandma. I raised the sequined pink and blue chiffon above her head and arranged it around her shoulders over the black shawl, so that now I would be dancing as her for him, as if they were young again. The crowd was joyful; it was easy to ride the energy, easy to spin it around and give it back. The whole atmosphere was playful, spontaneous. Someone called out, "I've been to Cairo and this dancer is better than any I saw there." At the end when I went over to grandma to retrieve my veil, she smiled and said, "Thank you," with tears in her eyes.

I stood quietly by myself in the crowd around the dance area at the annual Native American Powwow held on the Stanford grounds. It was the first time I had been to a powwow, and I was longingly immersed in the heartbeat rhythms of the big drums, watching fancy dancer braves in elaborate costumes high stepping and spinning with feathered arms outstretched as if soaring in the sky. The drums were suddenly silent. All the dancing stopped. An eagle feather had fallen from a costume, and a prayer was said as it was reverently lifted from the ground. Then the dancing began again.

There was another longer break; then a soft-voiced man spoke into a microphone. You all remember…, and he gave a woman's name. She was in a bad automobile accident the night after powwow two years ago. The best doctors at Stanford Hospital and the medicine men worked on her all night and she lived, but the doctors said she would never walk again. Last year she came to powwow and went around the circle in a wheel chair. She's walking now and this year she's going to dance.

There was a movement in the crowd near me. A young woman was standing less than an arm's length away, with clear eyes and a quiet smile, a pretty woman in a long fringed buckskin dress covered with beads and little folded metal cones. She had colored ribbons braided in her hair, and tall wrapped moccasins. Another woman, close to her age but plainly dressed, her sister perhaps, stood at her side.

The crowd moved apart to let them through. The dance ground was empty now, and she walked slowly supported by her sister's arm. They circled the dance ground once; then the drums started up and her sister let her go.

She began to lift her feet rhythmically higher and higher, still with gentle careful steps. Other dancers came back into the circle, forming a wide line behind her. No one else was dancing. All the costumed fancy dancers were taking small short steps, barely raising their feet. Only the healed woman was dancing and she was spinning now, with quiet awkward grace she led them all around in a long spiral.

I stood in the crowd crying, crying, my tears were pouring down, not only for a woman who could walk and dance again, but for a people exiled in their own land who had managed to sustain a living context for a oneness that the invading cultures forgot, crying for the invaders too.

MOTHERS OF RAIN

The sacred dancing and sense of community at the powwow had touched me deeply. I felt a lingering poignancy and a longing from having witnessed the young woman dance and the respect and reverence of a community expression of belonging to all life. I looked at my life, at what I loved and where that was leading me. I loved belly dance, but I was aware that most people had a different perception of what I considered a sacred art.

A friend had introduced me to the work of movement pioneer, dancer, healer, choreographer Emilie Conrad-Da'Oud. Through her workshops, Emilie's world of micro movements and cellular discovery blended with what I loved most about belly dance, a way to touch a unifying, universal energy directly through my body. The tiny undulating watery movements of Emilie's work, reflecting the natural creativity and fluidity of healing, were offering another way to explore the vast interior dimensions within the mystery of our physical forms.

I had a strong sense that all the divergent forces in my life were ultimately part of one full encircling reach, but some of them were profoundly not of my culture or time and showed no signs of converging yet, and that sense of separation ran counter to the wholeness arising from within. I longed for a situation in which all the aspects of my life could come together to clearly express the oneness living through my world and myself. Art had been my refuge again and again throughout my life, and so I decided to go to graduate school, seeking cloistered time and space to allow another stage of this intangible memory to unfold.

My studio at Mills College was in an older building that also housed the boiler room for the entire campus. The building had a kindly, alive quality. The hallways and the rooms were always very warm day and night, and the walls creaked and gurgled as water flowed through the pipes. When the first-year graduate students in art drew lots for studios, I traded with another woman for a room that was down a dark corridor in the center of the building. It was a small space, ten feet by fourteen feet, with no windows, but the walls were almost twenty feet high and the whole ceiling was a skylight. Coming out of the darkness of the hallway into the brightness of that tall, enclosed space was like entering my heart.

I had been accepted in the MFA program as a painter, so I began to paint again, but I had reached the point at which all the current forms of my life, my dancing, dreaming, or my art were no longer adequate to hold or express the living contents. I took all my unfinished canvases, nailed them together to build a small hut in the middle of my studio, and painted the inside of the hut with black chalkboard paint. I wanted to make a dance of drawing dreams, weaving images together in ephemeral lines of rainbow colors overlapping and erased. I wanted to connect the process of my art, not just the images, to the aliveness and tactile kinesthetic joy I touched in dancing. I turned to my childhood memories, to my spontaneous delight in drawing that was somehow wed to my love of the hills and sky then, and to my great enthusiasm for making mud and grass stews in my mother's cooking pots. I began making simple proto-animal figures of mud and straw as a tangible bridge to the energies stored in those memories. They were life-sized two legged deer, because sifting through the whirl of converging memories, ideas, and dreams, looking for a clue to the emerging wholeness in my life and work, I had remembered the young deer.

While I was living near the coast, I had seen a young deer coming up the narrow path below the house. She saw me on the balcony and stopped, looking peacefully up at me for a while. Then she turned her head to one side, gazing at me out of one eye like a bird. I melted into her eye, her eye growing, becoming everything, the pure deep roundness of her eye all encompassing, no other time, only this spacious moment within her single eye. The trail fell away, the earth beneath her feet and the forest at her side pulled apart in delicate fine shreds. Suddenly she was within a vast soaring field of blue, standing on the pure expanse of an endless sky, a sky beyond all time, a sky arising from her heart.

I do not remember how we each returned, how she walked away, or how I went back inside. The shining gesture held inside her eye had cut through any before or after, any then or now, and although I later tried, I could never get the dimensionless quality of the experience to fit on paper. But I remembered that her hind legs had been hidden from view, and with her head turned to one side, she had seemed even more bird-like then, a two-legged deer.

All the diverse strands of my life came together in the figures of the deer. I tore down the hut. With hands grounded in earth and hay, I overshot my childhood by thousands and thousands of years. I entered a world far older than memory and dream, and found that I was welcome there.

Through the repeated motions of bundling and tying hay and kneading and shaping mud, I felt a kinship with ancient working rhythms and with countless ancient hands that had given shape to the sacred, offering their prayers through the elemental materials that sustained their lives. I felt a kinship with the gestures of the daily lives of early hunter-gatherers, and with countless moments below the threshold of culture, the heat of the day radiating from bare earth at twilight, the coolness of shadow on skin, the rolling motion of a hip as weight is shifted from one leg to another. I felt the presence of innumerable animals, birds, insects and fish, digging, weaving, and secreting nests and homes, cellular lineages carried in the holy fluids of incalculable bodies, timeless oceans transmitted endlessly inside time. I was not alone. The same timeless seas that flowed through countless hands and feet flowed through my hands, all of us shaping and being shaped from within by the fluidity of light, the fertile essence of inner radiance as it takes on apparent solidity. The aura of ancientness that I embraced in my work then was a way to express that unity, a time "before" there was a split between fluidity and form, between matter and light.

A profusion, a celebration, of proto-animal-human figures poured out of me. They were taller, less totemic, more gestural, more alive. I made armatures of branches, borrowing the curving shapes of trees. I tied and wrapped small bundles of hay in layers, golden fibers of hay gradually forming a musculature of light. I coated the hay with papier mâché instead of mud to make a paper skin. The sudden weight of wet paper pulp caused the armatures to turn and shift from inside. The figures dried in gestures of the living weight of materials balancing themselves. They were dancing as I had danced, with the joyful temporary immortality of elemental Earth. I covered the surface of the skins with black tar, the same tar that gardeners use for grafting. I folded bottle caps for "cowry" eyes. I was bridging gaps. I used sequins; I made feathered ladders, towers, flying boats, any way to go across to the bright and timeless now.

Golden bursts of hay came from animal faces and human arms and legs. The figures were living, breathing, light. Seeds in the hay were sprouting in one corner of the studio where the skylight leaked. Everything was alive. I had terrible hay fever; I have had it all my life. I was miserable as I worked, but I was immersed in a tremendous happiness and the hay was the most important part. I had to use these strands of living light.

This great upwelling of energy culminated in the *Mothers of Rain*, tall figures, over nine feet high, that appeared at the radiant edge of sleep, visionary grasslands beings, souls of dryland rain. Their crescent heads blazed with the light of hay flashing from their crowns, their long white curving legs cantilevered from their shoulders like giraffes with shorter necks. Long pale golden manes of plant fibers descended from their chests, manes like my grandmother's hair filled with a living power, manes like virga, the dryland rains that sweep in great long strands across the desert sky. Their wide heart centers, hidden by the hair, were empty space. Light poured through their open hearts from above, illuminating the blessings of their flowing hair from within. We all carry a precious liquid legacy across the drylands of time, a sacred portage from one luminous body of water to another, the secret of interwoven light and form flowing endlessly, light not only in the special brightness, light here now, in everything.

THRESHOLD

I had two shows in Los Angeles of these cycles of elemental figures, and I decided to move to LA. I gave away almost all my personal belongings, books, art supplies, clothes and the few odd pieces of furniture I had acquired, filled the largest rental truck you can drive without a special truckers' license with my work, and drove by myself to Los Angeles, with no plan and very little money.

I found a studio to rent in downtown LA, on the second floor of an old brick building that had housed a seed packing company before it was divided into lofts and galleries. The warehouse was near the labyrinth of elevated roadways and overpasses where the main north south and east west freeways met, a maze of surface streets lined with mostly working warehouses, busier by day, almost deserted at night. It was an area often used for filming movies and TV programs, when directors needed old darkened tunnels under bridges, empty broken streets cut through with abandoned railroad tracks, or a place to stage a fiery end to a chase scene. Driving home at night, you could come across an overturned tanker truck about to burst into flames ringed by actors and all the personnel and equipment of a large film crew, or helicopters circling close around the tops of nearby granaries, with an amplified scripted voice telling someone to stop as beams of camera lights and search lights intersect, a surreal, unreal neighborhood, a hollow space, a gap, a place between. But there were a few weeds growing in the cracks in the sidewalks, and in the evening, thousands of crickets living in the south-facing brick wall of the old seed warehouse sang together, making a rippling wall of sound in the hot urban nights that were never fully dark.

The studio space was large. I had plenty of room to work and live. I kept the slat blinds closed on the high south windows, making a soft twilight in the room. The harshness, on a daily basis, of the chemical air outside and the fast pace of the traffic and the people, was a shock.

The first night in the studio, I heard a rattling metallic sound outside on the street. I climbed up on a box to look from one of the high windows. A young man was pushing a shopping cart that lurched and bounced on the broken pavement. He had only a few possessions with him, a tiny pile of things in one corner of the cart. The clothes he was wearing had distinct colors; they had not yet acquired the uniform tone of earth and age that enveloped the long-term residents of the street. I could not see his face clearly, but he seemed to have some color too, around the edges of a stunned sadness, as if it were his first night on the street, and he still had some bit of energy, some small hope, walking carefully, picking his way slowly through his mind, trying to understand where he found himself in the middle of this empty night just as I was doing then.

I worked part time, days and some nights, painting houses and teaching at universities. I drove a lot; everything was far away from everything else. I had a lot of shows and favorable reviews. I was adding pages to my resume, and wondering now and then if I was losing something from my life. I spent as much time as I could in my studio, seeking refuge in the fertile world I had evoked that was now filling the spacious loft with figures, branches, and hay. I read accounts of the Kung-san people of the Kalahari, and felt a strong resonance with their egalitarian almost extinct way of life that seemed so much saner, kinder, and more balanced than this urban world. I sought refuge in studio time itself, the private sacred space in mind and heart that transcended all the jarring time-bound rhythms of the city that surrounded me.

There were two kinds of studio time that I loved most. The first was sitting in the studio, not doing anything, just being there, the waiting that is not waiting, quieter and gentler than the dawn before sunrise, touching an inner openness, very soft, that imperceptibly begins to flow from you into the room.

I also loved the moment of full engagement with the art. You have wrestled yourself past the inevitable terrible place where you know this piece, this work, is truly a mistake; it will never come out right whatever you do, no matter how many times you have come to this before and know that you broke through, this time it will never work. The time I loved has passed through all of this. It is the moment when whatever you thought you were doing in this piece, whatever question you were asking, whatever material or idea you chose to explore, yields a precious secret, that there is another question there, the answer hidden in the questioning, always moving on; the insight you seek was present all the while, beyond the asking or the searching, no fixed answer anywhere, and you ride that not-knowing, and something fine and grand emerges from your hands, has a life of its own, in hay or sticks or tar, a mirror of the shining question that you asked that has now moved on.

Branches were harder to come by in LA than they had been on the tree-lined campus at Mills. I looked for brush piles left along the streets by gardeners and maintenance crews. I wanted a bumper sticker for my small pickup truck that read, "Caution, I Brake for Natural Materials". I often recycled or reworked pieces, cutting away the papier-mâché skins and the muscle fibers of hay, reusing all the parts, especially the branches of the armatures.

One day, in the midst of dismantling some of my earlier work, surrounded by a pile of arms and legs and heads, flayed paper and tar skins and curving bones of branch, mat knife in my hand, all at once I was not looking at my work anymore; I was looking at my life instead, in a different way. So much leaving, moving on, and going beyond. Sometimes going beyond had been going apart instead, into separateness, into honing identity. My willingness to change and leave behind had also left rawness, furrows, and gaps in my personal life.

I realized that whenever I had spoken of or thought about the hunter-gatherers, I always meant the gatherers alone, evoking the gentle enfolding motions of bundling and tying, of bringing together, of reconciliation, of making whole. All the while, another side, unacknowledged, unquestioned, kept apart but still moving through my life, the energy of forced separation, and the sharpness and finality of those acts. The energy of cutting away, the energy of the hunt, the painful alchemy of separating an animal from its life to sustain other lives and all the interconnections there were part of the inclusive wholeness too.

I knew nothing about hunting, much less the ancient, sacred hunt. I could only sense the shadows of those energies working in our times and in my life, so I drew on Kung-san images, two hunters and an animal. The hunters were in profile; they looked more like animals. The animal was a tall narrow frontal view, more like a human shape. I drew the outlines on big sheets of thin foam core, each eight feet high, and started to cut out the shapes. I wanted edges, harshness, angles, sharp cuts. I wanted flat shadows disappearing into thin lines when seen from the side, slipping through the cracks in our modern world, disappearing at the corner of your eye.

When I removed the cut out shadow shapes, the foam core panels had become magnificent negative space. The Kung-san outlines were openings now, windows, thresholds, doors, passages to the other side, holy portals, burial grounds. I stood them upright lashed to frameworks made of branches and coated them with hay and papier mâché. The foam core and the armatures sagged and turned with the water weight of the paper pulp, and they dried curving and billowing like sails.

I painted one side of each threshold with tar for shadowy black earth, and coated the edges that formed the outlines of the empty hunter and animal shapes with a paste of red oxide pigment: red oxide, blood of the Earth, red oxide, an elemental prayer offered at so many early burial sites for safe passage and rebirth. I poked thin sticks all through this ground from the other side, their cut ends protruding as the broken stubble after harvest, after death. From the back, the long fine tips of the delicate curving sticks were pale roots reaching into air or flowing hair blowing in a timeless wind.

I finished the silhouette shapes that I had originally cut away. They hovered, thin and curving, covered on both sides with black tar, at the periphery of the first installation of the *Thresholds*. The process of discovery that had begun with the Kung-san images had evolved into a multilayered dance, a poetic interplay of questions and answers, of shadows, outlines, and negative space, intuitions in branches, paper, hay, and tar, memories resurfacing, approaching through both past and future time.

In my exploration of edges, flat surfaces, and sharp angles in the sculpture, I had been responding in a visceral way to the harshness and clamor of LA, the fast pace, distances, and freeways, the asphalt and concrete encased Earth, the fouled air, and the striving and preening that were almost mandatory in the art world here. Yet all this abrasiveness resolved instead into the curving space of billowing sails, openings into another dimension, visionary veils; even the harshness and boundaries of this place could open into an expansive, wordless grace beyond questioning.

I had reached a threshold of my own; my work was a mirror of my life, reflecting both the discrete shape of personal identity and the transcendent space embracing the ephemeral nature of that identity, the glowing template through which an openness remembers and witnesses itself again.

HALF-LIFE OF DREAMS

A Shimmer in the Desert

One day in the fall of 1986, I was working in my studio in South Central LA when I got a call from Josine Ianco-Starrels, a museum director who had taken a strong interest in me and my sculpture. She had a deep Romanian accent, a forceful presence, and a good heart. As I picked up the phone, I heard "Robert," sounded out as if the Earth spoke. "Robert, I have a woman for you to meet." This woman was Rachel Dutton, a sculptor who was having a show at a university gallery, and Josine wanted me to go with her to the opening; she thought there was a similar energy in our work.

The show was at the California State University at Los Angeles art gallery, a typical gallery space with a polished concrete floor, white walls, and track lighting, but the sculptures looked like they had arisen from the Earth, the soil enriched with light that brings forth the soul. Rachel used branches and golden straw, covered in layers of paper pulp and fiber, painted with tar. I could feel a resemblance in our work, a presence and a power: the Earth screaming at those assembled, trying to wake them up. The *Thresholds* were large nine-foot-tall freestanding panels curved by the branches that exposed a shape within, a forgotten ancestor, a forgotten aspect of our selves.

We all sat around her sculptures as Rachel spoke about her work and a sacredness that is ancient and indwelling. She then asked for questions. One man said he thought spirituality was more structured and defined, as in Mondrian's paintings, that there was an ordered ideal to it. Josine interrupted him with absolute authority and her indisputable accent, saying, "Spirituality is of the Earth. It has dirt, and hairs, and juice in it!"

Later I experienced Rachel's work at her downtown studio, seeing it within the context of the Earth, not isolated in the glass jar of the contemporary art world. You opened her door into a huge space and a straw-covered floor, the grassland of our ancestors. Large panels of unfolding Earth, fluid human forms, and sticks flowing as if drawn by the wind. Human and animal forms shaped within the freedom of one's heart-mind, the radiance of this heart flowing out of them in bursts of golden grass. I was not in a dream, but experiencing form as fluid as light beyond solidity's grasp, in a dance within one's heart.

Rachel and I recognized each other, but we were not yet ready to explore this understanding. We both had large works we were involved in, things we needed to complete.

Josine introduced me to Rob briefly before they left the gallery, and she invited me to come up to her house after the opening. Josine was my mother bear, my benefactor in the land of LA. She was enthusiastic and supportive of my work. We had a real caring for each other, and we shared a kind of elemental knowing about the Earth that transcended the art world lives in which we met. Rob was still at Josine's when I arrived. She had not told me why she wanted me to come by. She was arranging a meeting between two artists who had more than an affinity in their work, a meeting of deeper connections that may have surprised even her. It was there in his eyes, in the quiet depth and the inner light. The resonance of our work, the gestures and the tar, the essence of light at the core, the spiritual questioning, all came later and just confirmed the presence and the connection between us. There was a feeling in our meeting, a sense that what we shared would sweep away whatever else we were doing in this life, but first we each had a few more things to finish up and release. I was working on a collaborative performance piece involving veils and light, and the performance was coming up soon.

The narrow space between the translucent veils of cloth was glowing with golden yellow light. Small shadow shapes of tiny opaque dots on the cloth in front floated like snowflakes all around me as I moved imperceptibly between the veils. The lights shifted again, coming from behind instead, my shadow floating now in slow undulating motion on the veil in front of me. Then Emilie suggested that I come out from behind the curtain and wrap myself up in it. I rolled up slowly until only my upper body showed. Then she said lean back on it. I arched back farther and farther, surrendering my full weight into the fragile cloth, held completely in the delicate grace of the translucent veil. Yes! Emilie said Eyes! We need eyes. I want slides of close-up photos of your eyes and hands to project with the lights. Then we took a break. I was in the midst of another rehearsal with Emilie Conrad-Da'Oud.

I had been a background performer in another piece of hers the year before, and now she wanted to explore the moment, timeless as water, ancient as rain, the space my sculpture arose from, an inner landscape played out in movement and light. We rehearsed with a lighting designer from the start, and the final piece, *Rachel Raining*, performed at the Japan American Theatre as part of an evening of experimental dance, was a fluid interplay of shifting colored lights, close-ups of my hands and eyes projected momentarily, and the slow fluttering underwater movements characteristic of Emilie's work. I was the solo performer, but it was a collaborative piece, an ensemble of silhouettes, washes of color, and forms of light, held in the quiet watery embrace of the fertile place between the worlds, dissolving, melting into a single eye.

The evening of the performance, Rob had already arranged to go to the desert to photograph some of his work installed in the desert night. He sent me a photo, taken the same night that I danced, of four carved holy men in gestures of entreaty and faith, standing in the darkness equidistant from each other and from a blazing trash can fire as if they were marking the cardinal points on a great wheel with the fire at the center. The photograph expressed a solemn silent dance, layers of moments suspended in time-lapse, light from the fire illuminating the gestures of the challenges of spiritual practice, stars and other travelers in the sky beginning to trace their long slow arcs overhead in the desert night. On the back, he wrote that his work was about "cutting away the blind man."

The day Rachel gave her performance I was driving down a dry sandy riverbed in the Mojave Desert. It was easier than I had thought. The weight of four life-sized wooden sculptures and accessories helped give traction to my rear wheels. The sun had already set when I found a flat open area with a few creosote bushes and low hills in the distance.

I got out of my truck and entered the breath of the desert, a thick field of silence. I was engulfed, standing there alone with a warm dry breeze and the stillness. The desert openness was cutting and slightly dangerous. It tore away the solidity of our world and exposed a living breathing view into the absolute.

The work I had come to the desert to photograph was based on a large ink-on-paper painting I had done of the constellation Crux, the Southern Cross. In the center an arching Milky Way formed a dome above four men standing around a trash can fire. One man kneels, raising both hands up to the sky, praying and entreating. The other three figures stand holding tall staffs, each expressing a different gesture of faith: a monastic, an ascetic, and a mystic. They were all aspects of myself, questioning, confronting, prophets calling out in the wilderness.

A crux is a difficult problem, an essential point requiring resolution. At the apex of the cross is the point where faith, belief, and confidence start to wear away the veils that separate us from pure essential being, just as we are. *Crux* was the desert, its abrasive intensity enshrined under the night sky.

It was full dark by the time I had finished placing the sculptures. I lit a trash can fire and made long-term photographic exposures to capture this mysterious question under a star-trailing arch. I rested at dawn as the desert began to sleep.

My small truck hurtled down Alameda, the main route into South Central LA, bouncing over the uneven pavement and railroad tracks. Huge tractor-trailer rigs churned past me; everyone was driving very fast. Following the directions Rob gave me to his studio, I turned off Alameda onto a side street, then another, passing a housing project, trash-strewn empty lots, a small bleak store, and edgy, wary people on the sidewalks and in the streets. I came to the compound, three small abandoned-looking buildings with a driveway and a gate. Rob was waiting. He unlocked the gate, two panels of chain link fence topped with razor wire, and I drove inside. I entered Rob's world.

A canopy of bougainvillea, heavily laden with deep fuchsia-colored flowers, covered the area in back where I parked next to a high cinder-block wall topped with rusted corrugated steel and more razor wire. Plants in old packing crates and pots were everywhere: roses, philodendrons, lanky pines, mounds of baby tears. I was living on the second floor of a warehouse where the freeways intersect, was grateful just to see a weed growing from a crack in the cement, and here, even with the rusted steel and razor wire, I was in paradise.

As I got out of my truck, there was Rob, with his quietly luminous eyes, and there was Elliot with him: a medium-sized dog, part Doberman, part black Lab, maybe some pit bull. She had a slender grizzled nose, legs a little stiff with age, a barrel chest, and alert, inquisitive eyes. She was definitely more than the sum of her parts; she was herself. She carried her tail upright in a scimitar curve above her back and a tennis ball in her mouth. She was introduced as the compound guard dog, out of respect for her previous calling, but she had clearly adopted Rob as her person, and they seemed to have one of the most mature dog and person relationships I had ever seen, a feeling that they understood and looked out for each other. She dropped the ball at my feet as if she had just offered me the entire world. She took a few small quick steps back from the ball, a charming, endearing gesture, and then she stood looking intently at the ball, glancing briefly up at me with shining expectant eyes: Isn't this ball, this moment, this possibility, just so fine and grand?

Then Rob took me inside to meet his work, powerful life-sized figures of wood, with rich multifaceted surfaces from the carving tools he used. They were elegant gestural studies, alive with the immediacy of his process and his passionate inquiry into the nature of belief: not what you believe, but how, how the holding to the very thing you believe will set you free can bind you from within instead. The room was filled with figures embodying a questioning that did not stop at answers but opened into further questioning, penetrating insistently toward a brilliant core: street people, angels, prophets, priests, a Buddha, all covered with black ink or tar, glowing like burnished coal with an ancient hidden fire. They all looked like Rob. He told me how he stood in the gestures of the figures as he worked, their stance came intuitively from inside, their dialogue was his.

There was an ease between us as we talked effortlessly, as if we already knew each other well, as if we were picking up a conversation started long ago and there had never been any moments in between.

We were sitting on a couch near the open roll-up door as we talked. After a while, Elliot came prancing in. She leapt up on the couch next to me, energetically licked my face and sat beside me,

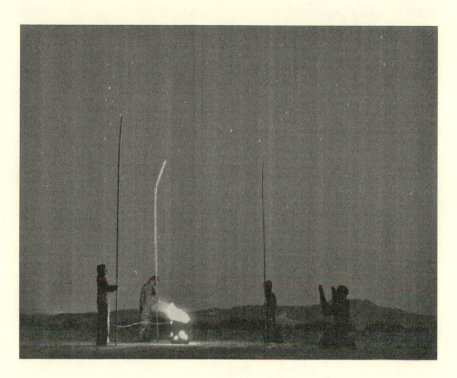

Crux, installation, 1986, Mohave Desert, California

Dubhe and Merek, installation, 1987, Double Rocking G Gallery, Los Angeles, California, and studio view

Hanap'atu and Coalsack, installation 1987, and studio view

Belief, installation, 1987, Double Rocking G Gallery, Los Angeles, California

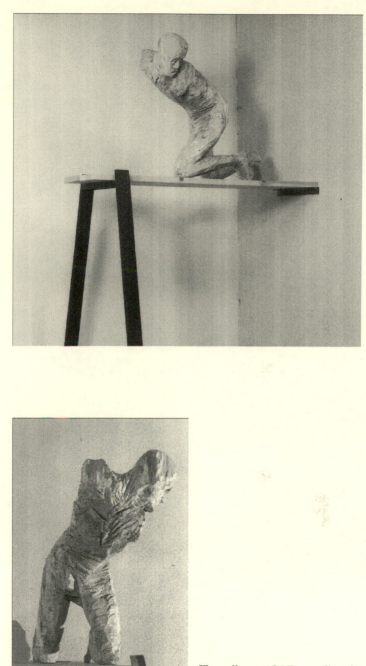

Fomalhaut, 1987, studio view

Thresholds, second installation, 1987, California State University at Hayward, and studio views

Thresholds, 1986, studio view

Mothers of Rain, installation, 1984, Los Angeles Municipal Art Gallery, Barnsdall Park, Los Angeles, California

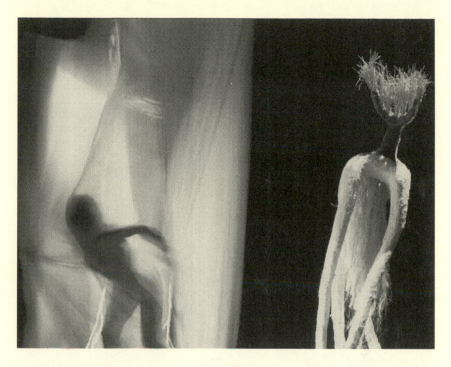

Rachel Raining, performance, 1986, Japan American Theatre, Los Angeles California

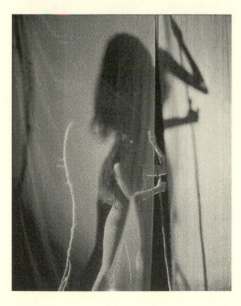

Bear Lady, 1991, Stanley, New Mexico

leaning her weight into me like a chummy woman friend I hadn't seen in years: Let's talk. "Elliot?" Rob said. She was genuinely friendly and affectionate. I felt the same ease bonding with her as I felt with Rob. She did not try to sit between us; she was welcoming me, bonding with me too. She was also very smart; I was the perfect opportunity to establish a beachhead on the couch.

Rachel and I were walking the same path, exploring the same view, knowing the clues, the Earth domed by the blue sky, the light of the sun, the depth of the night with a radiant moon, our forms, our gestures, all one within the same radiance, a fluidity, an understanding beyond this life.

One Sunday evening Rachel called. I had just finished eating three burritos, and when she asked if I wanted to go to a Japanese restaurant for dinner, I said, "Of course." And we began living together, a union out of the soft light deep within our hearts.

We arrived at Joshua Tree National Monument late in the evening. As we entered into the pace of the land, a silence permeated every sound of insect, wind, or the words we spoke, all captured and contained within the vastness of this silence. We slept in the open bed of the truck, enfolded in the night air and the star-drenched desert sky.

We woke early while the desert night was still close around us. We drove through the beginning of first light, along a narrow dirt road winding slowly up through waves of small hills and shadowy Joshua trees to a special place. We reached the crest of the hills and walked a short way. We were on a high mountain ridge that plunged abruptly down to the west. We found a place to sit next to a small Joshua tree on the shoulder of the ridge and faced the east, looking out over the gentle rolling hills that had led so unexpectedly to this high place. We sat within the silence, its tangible embrace sealing us into the fabric of this land, in the company of the little Joshua tree that stood beside us, a kindly witness. The dawn spread slowly through the glowing air that still held some of the moist stillness of the night. And then openness and the silent depth became a union. Our minds were a single sphere with the fading night sky and the reappearance of Earth, a vast simplicity as the sun merged into this sphere. And just as a brilliant ray lit across the desert to our hearts, there was a sudden explosion of sound as two F-16s roared up and over the crest of the ridge streaking close to the ground right above our heads, and we remained, a shimmer in the desert.

We were both finished with the energies of our current studios; our relationships to those places were changing from deep inside. When the studio next door to Rob became vacant, I rented the space and moved in until the next step revealed itself. We opened a wall between; we set up our sculpture together, and added more plants and containers and my pale yellow ceramic garden Buddha to the narrow corridor of urban garden outside the roll-up doors in the back. We sprouted narcissus bulbs in a beautiful bowl filled with stones on the table where we ate; we started cooking Indian food. We were weaving a life together, looking hard at what we wanted that life to be, and we were slowly, surely, leaving LA.

The passionate witness to our inquiry was all around us in our work, the outpouring of life-sized and larger figures that had led us to find each other, the vivid testimony to the questions leading always to more questions and eventually to the moving aliveness beyond questioning. We talked, sharing thoughts, perceptions, memories, dreams, sharing all the insights our art had opened for us, sharing ideas from movies and books, like sleepers slowly wakening, telling in slow soft voices our half-remembered dreams: Where are we going, where do we want to go? Our ageless conversation renewed itself relentlessly, starting always where we begin and end: What do we want to have learned in this life by the time we die?

I taught a few evenings a week at CSULA. Driving home late at night, I took a route that led two blocks south of the projects, through dark narrow abandoned streets, and suddenly one night I was swerving around a burning car. There were no people near, no accident, no movie crew, just a flaming car on fire in the night alone, a silently screaming car blazing with the frustration and the rage all around us. We could leave this place; so many others could not.

I was standing in the shadows along our driveway, holding still, sensing the night. Rachel had called me, letting me know that she had finished teaching and was leaving CSULA. The area was becoming more and more violent since crack hit the streets in '86. The Bloods and the Crips drug war had escalated: gunfire, helicopters, and speeding cars were a constant backdrop to our daily lives. Fires had been set in front of our building and cars were regularly being torched. Every so often, you would see lines of men dressed in black running in a crouch, armed with M-16s and assault shotguns. Then you would hear and feel the waves from concussion grenades as they raided a nearby crack house.

I remained motionless for a long time aware of movement in the shadows across the street, listening for Rachel's truck through the simmering sounds of South Central. Finally, I heard her truck with its distinctive throaty small engine; I moved to the gate and quietly unlocked the chain. As she drove up I threw the gates open to let her drive in, and quickly chained and locked the gates closed.

After Rachel had moved in and we opened up the common wall, our sculpture blended in a dance of intent. Our conversations also became a blending and as we talked about our lives and what each of us had discovered, we found a common ground that we had not yet encountered with anyone else.

On weekends we would drive to a state park near the coast, where the moist ocean air would mix with the dry chaparral and sage. We would walk quietly, our hikes becoming another dialogue with ourselves in the silence, an expression of our shared respect and reverence for the Earth. We walked slowly, pausing to look at anything that caught our eye, just witnessing.

Sometimes Rob and I walked the pathways surrounding a small lake at the Self-Realization Fellowship grounds, a quiet world of green lawns and flower gardens, with the houseboat where Yogananda once lived still anchored to the calm surface of the little lake, and a square arch marking a grotto that held some of Gandhi's relics. There was a another kind of silence here, and in the well tended gardens, a sense of the commitment and steady cultivation needed to allow one's spiritual path to unfold in any context.

One day after we had circled the lake, we stood on a small deck close above the water. Two white swans floated by, with intent eyes and curved beaks suspended gracefully at the tops of long straight necks. They were a beautiful sculptural gesture, precise and clean, and they brought a moment of simple grace for me as I realized that both Rob and I would see the subtle curve, the tilt, the balance, and the weight of those long white necks and heads in exactly the same way.

As Rachel and I offered each other all our experiences and influences, we realized that we were moving toward something we could not quite see, knowing ourselves to be the clues, all our experiences slowly guiding us, and in the next step, taking chances to uncover more and more. We spoke of death, the passing of our friends and family, the increasing danger we felt in our immediate world, and the confounding blind motivation fueling the destruction of our age. We went to see Andre Tarkovsky's film *The Sacrifice* a number of times and recognized a quality in our lives in the beautifully rendered scenes, like stanzas of a poem, blending and juxtaposing images to evoke a decisive moment. The camera lingers with the hands of a scholarly man touching tenderly and pausing over photos of Russian icon paintings, the luminous burning eyes of the icons calling up in him a personal sacrifice at the onset of a nuclear holocaust off screen, a mystic's act to reverse this horror, through an offering of all that he loved.

We were both feeling a sense of apocalypse within our world caused by a collective denial of the sacred aspects of this life. We knew there was something we had to learn in the wisdom of traditional societies that had lived closer to the Earth, the Earth that was elemental experience, a foundation and ground from which all spiritual growth comes. We spoke of its mystery and how we listened with our hearts through feelings and signs.

We heard about a wildflower that had disappeared from the English countryside for over a hundred years and then bloomed again in the bomb craters in London during World War II. The flower had no name; the story was about the wonder that something could reappear after so long a time. Then we learned about the fireweed, a hardy plant used by many traditional peoples for cordage, medicine, and fiber. Fireweed seeds apparently thrive or perhaps depend on strenuous circumstances to unleash the life inside. They can remain dormant but viable for many years, to reappear and grow profusely in disturbed areas, especially in the aftermath of fire. We looked around our studio at our work installed together, the seed, the fire, the root, rivers of grass and blazing exploding stars, the gleaming cores already burning through their casings of wood or paper and tar. We asked what does it take to grow a blade of grass or a life of faith, what does it take to germinate the fireweed seed in our time once the heart has cracked open? Healing seed, luminous essence, present in everything and everyone even when they do not know, how do you get that seed to grow in everyone? Fire opens the seeds, but they do not grow in the fire. There was another step beyond opening.

Suzi Gablik, an art critic and writer who was interested in our work, visited with us in our studio. Suzi was also on a journey of questioning, working on her book *The Reenchantment of Art*, which would include Rachel's work. We talked with her about our dialogue together, the sacred, the Earth, and that we were living a quiet cloistered life as much as we could, even in South Central Los Angeles. She asked us why we were still living here.

We knew we had to leave Los Angeles soon. We needed a simpler life, an open space, to touch the common heart of life on this shared Earth, to see it clearly, to let it grow unobstructed through us. We were remembering together, a direction, a path. It was already opening, whether we saw it fully yet or not, it had a momentum of its own. We had some connections to the art world in Santa Fe, New Mexico, and so we drove out there to see how it felt.

Rachel's truck died outside of Winslow, Arizona. Everything stopped, the car was completely dead, the engine melted, there was no hope, all was lost, nothing could be done. But no stars exploded, the Earth remained as before, the trucks kept rushing by as I opened the Toyota fix-it psychology book and realized it was just our minds: calm down, breathe, and check the fuses.

We had traveled all over New Mexico with no real sign. We were a bit discouraged when we called a friend of a friend. She was very sweet and open; she said, "Come over, stay at our place." We needed a place to rent that allowed dogs. They were moving, "Rent this place, your dog will love it." We needed wilderness. "We're right on a trail to a Rio Grande wildlife refuge."

Everything that we came looking for was being offered to us. Rachel and I walked the trail to the wildlife refuge to think things over. The old cottonwoods were all twisted and curving in a dance of wind and water as we stood beneath them at the bank, watching the Rio Grande move across the shallow sandy plain. A definite knowing came to me that I would never carve again, a sadness, but a certainty that this passionate wave had ended. We were passing into a new pool on our way to the sea.

Our new friend said that her husband would walk around the stupa in Santa Fe whenever he had a big decision to make. She said the Buddhist shrine was easy to see; it was on the road to the airport. We drove up to Santa Fe and found the stupa on a wide straight road on the newer west side of town. The tall golden spire and white bell-shaped roof were clearly visible above an adobe wall that marked out the stupa grounds on a long narrow lot next to a trailer park.

The stupa was three or four stories high with double doors facing a small garden. The doors were closed so we walked along the gravel path, circling the sacred shrine and praying. A Tibetan monk came up to us and asked if we would like to sit inside, then he unlocked the doors and left. Removing our shoes, we entered the small shrine room inside the stupa.

We sat under the tall curving sky-blue ceiling with small Buddhas and deities painted all through the sky. We sat for a long time within the blessings there, and knew these unfamiliar paintings somehow, but not quite why they were depicted in these specific details. We felt the blessings in the shrine room, the well-kept shrine, the stillness of the water bowls and the warmth of the butter lamps, but we also sensed a formality, a protocol that was outside our hearts' path. It was clear to us though, that we would move to New Mexico, rent the house in Corrales, and begin again.

We drove home as fast as we could, knowing we had been gone too long but feeling happy about our new adventure about to unfold. It was late in the afternoon when we turned onto our street in South Central. We could hear Elliot barking; some kids ran back toward the projects as we drove up. Elliot looked half-crazed and let out a wailing cry when she saw us; she cried like no animal I have ever heard cry, an utterly lost heartbroken cry. She thought we had abandoned her. We held her as she slowly calmed down. From then on, we tried not to leave her.

A curator from the LA County Museum of Art visited our studio with members of an acquisition committee, the first step in a ritual dance of yearly visits. We had reviews and dates for future shows. We were willing to leave the art world here, we had already made that choice, but places have their own energies for staying or leaving. The artist who had previously rented Rob's studio had moved to southern New Mexico when he left. Now the elemental heart of this small piece of land hidden under three small dilapidated warehouses encircled by razor wire did not want to let us go, especially Rob, who had been here for five years and had connected this secret Earth to the timeless night sky again through the witness of his eyes.

A man stood out front with a thirty-eight revolver. As suddenly as he appeared, he was gone. I picked up Elliot and put her in Rachel's rental truck. As we drove the trucks out the gate, there was a feeling of an elastic band of energy holding us, stretching tauter and tauter, until finally it broke. Then we fastened our seat belts and adjusted the side view mirrors again. We were on the road, with two large rental trucks loaded with sculpture, books, tools, furniture, household goods, and flat files of our early works, each large truck pulling a smaller Toyota pickup truck filled with plants. We had given away a lot. We still had a lot to give up.

We reached the first big uphill grade, on the border of Arizona, and made the long climb up onto the Southwestern high desert plateau in low gear.

We stopped in the night, parking on a large open dirt area next to a gas station. Rachel and Elliot were in one truck, and I was in the other trying to get some rest. The sound of Elliot barking drew me out of my sleep. I looked up to see a man on a horse riding slowly through the dim circular area of the gas station light to the other side where he was absorbed back into the night. Elliot was beside herself; this must have been the largest dog she had ever seen. I went over to talk to her. She was still barking, standing on

Rachel's lap. By the time Elliot calmed down, it was dawn, so we just got back on the road.

High desert lands flowed by endlessly up and down as we drove east, squinting in the early morning sun, rolling the windows down in the midday heat, then many miles ahead, the next long grade, down into Albuquerque. Gravity was with us this time, as we sailed down toward the wide valley of the Rio Grande, the end of one long road, the beginning of another.

CIRCLING AND CIRCLING

We were exhausted when we arrived, but the high desert atmosphere had an exhilarating crystalline quality. Everything seen through the lens of this bright air seemed heightened, vivid, and alive. We had gone from the urban wilderness of South Central LA to the ancient bosque lands of the Rio Grande, a big jump for all three of us, especially Elliot.

We took her for a walk to the river, and she stayed close to us as she entered an outdoors without fences, walls, and trash. We were following a narrow trail winding between the furrowed trunks of huge cottonwood trees, when she saw a wide flat surface up ahead, shining and immense. Rob grabbed her just as she was about to jump off the bank onto the biggest roadway she had ever seen. He held her while she stared at it. Then we found a little cove nearby where we could stand close to the water's edge. Rob patted the shimmering surface with his hand, splashing a little each time, saying, "This is water, Elliot, not a road." She drank a little, and stared again. Of course dogs can walk on water.

The house was a rambling two-story owner-built cinder block addition to a small vintage adobe. We were renting the rambling side, with a high ceiling, a loft, a woodstove for heat, and very little insulation. It was warmer inside the refrigerator in the morning than it was in the room. We set up our artwork and bought fresh roasted chilies. We walked the levee road to the nearby Corrales Bosque wildlife refuge several times a day, crossing the acequias, the straight canals of precise rushing waters with dangerous hidden undertows, and entered the timeless place of water moving freely in its own way, meandering gently across the wide bottomlands of the Rio Grande. To the east across the river there were Pueblo lands held in trust, undeveloped, untouched by modern times, with the great wave of the Sandia mountain crest rising up behind, blue in the early mornings, pink in late afternoons.

Aged cottonwood trees lined the river on both sides. Their dancing gnarled shapes arched over all the trails. This was their world; it had been their world for a long time. Translucent amber-colored husks of cicada shells clung to the furled bark and twigs long after the cicadas had transformed themselves into the buzzing whirring sound that vibrated overhead. There was no beginning and no end to the lush fertility of this ageless river plain, and like the braided shoals and sandbars already covered with young willows and wild grass, we were slowly weaving ourselves into the rhythms of this place, into the river's song.

We rested and nourished ourselves in the soul of the river, and in the colors of New Mexico, the deep yellows of autumn cottonwood leaves, the dark red of dried chili ristras, and the faded blues and greens of the doors and window frames. One day at midmorning there was a sound, a call gathering in the sky, a call that stopped us, primal, reaching deep within our bones to extract a memory, now a longing, a musical rattling call raining down from the sky all around us. We looked up to see Sandhill cranes circling and circling, rising higher and higher becoming specks among the tones of passage, a movement to an awakening on an ancient journey, streaming across the sky, moving south to live the winter there. Now in New Mexico Rachel and I also circled and circled.

In December, we were married formally in a simple ceremony with the justice of the peace in Corrales, a very kindly, gentle man.

In many ways, our life together was a series of tossing stones from our hearts into the lake of our world, watching the waves move out across the surface. Sometimes the Rio Grande seemed to be more a lake than a great river flowing south. There were times when we would sit in a light rain watching the drops hit this placid water, the expanding waves overlapping, bigger drops and their waves of influence absorbing smaller ones in their wake. As we watched the rain continue to fall, the circles both large and small would create a fabric of more spheres, endlessly peppering this liquid clarity. There is a choice and an intent within the action of tossing a stone, to create a sphere of influence. The gift, the sacrifice, the offering, the action of one's life, freely given, let loose as a stone is tossed, a sphere touching another sphere simply, continuously, wave after wave; slowly over the course of endless lives the effect is made, the sand castle dissolves, the sand is made smooth. It is a timeless reverent movement, toward a single sphere that pops within one's heart.

As the waves gently lapped along the shore, in the soft mud and wet sands at the water's edge, another web of patterning and influence endlessly reappeared in the interwoven tracks of the many other beings drawn to the river. We found traces of their passage melting in watery earth or frozen in the perfect stillness of a winter dawn: skinny trident feet of ravens pausing as they stride, oval toes and lobed heels of coyote and dog drifting here and there, the fainter careful steps of a fox, like a line of flowers pressed into the sand. We saw imprints of the tiny star-shaped hands of small rodents, agile fingers of raccoons, graceful swirling curves and clusters of toads' tracks, delicate tracings of a lizard's tail, and the rhythmic stitches of the marks of beetles and grasshoppers.

We had read *Nature Observation and Tracking* by Tom Brown, Jr. before we left LA. We discovered his book after finding a series of fine-lined curving tracks in the soft sand we had spread under some of our pieces in the South Central studio. We were curious then, and had gone to a bookstore to find more information about animal tracks. We liked Brown's suggestions for ways of entering more deeply into direct experience of nature, including ways of looking with the eyes that were familiar to us, looking with artists' eyes from within your heart, not labeling as you draw.

Now in Corrales we began to read some of Brown's other books about his experiences as a tracker, wilderness skills, and the sense of oneness that comes naturally through living close to the Earth. The idea of being able to go into the wilderness and live in a simple unencumbered way as an aspect of a spiritual path touched us deeply. Brown's descriptions of the Pine Barrens in New Jersey, with its wild mix of wilderness, badlands, danger, and majestic spiritual grace, tapped a primal root in both of us. The charnel ground, the burning ground of so many yogis in the past who found in those sacred places a spiritual opening, was part of the shared memory we were beginning to remember.

We had been following clues in our art, our lives, our memories, and our dreams, clues leading us toward an ageless path we sensed but did not yet fully see. Here at the Rio Grande, we delighted in touching with our eyes the lines and curves that traced the movements of so many other lives intersecting and overlaid at the water's edge, looking there for more clues to our hearts' trail.

We were still between worlds. Our plan was to buy land in some secluded area and build a small passive solar adobe house and two barns to use as studios. We drove around a lot exploring. We went up into the piñon and sage foothills of the blue mountains that rimmed this land on all sides, the Sangre de Cristos, the Manzanos, the Sandias, and the Jemez. We drove on small winding roads through cliffs of pure artists' pigments and dry rocky draws that opened out into grand vistas of pastel light.

In remote or unexpected places we found many religious and spiritual groups already drawn to these lands where time was measured in an abiding stillness: white robed Benedictines, black

136

robed Benedictines, Sufis, Sikhs, Catholic Sisters, Catholic Priests, devotees of Amachi, Baptist summer camps, the Lama Foundation, and a Zen hot springs, all nestled in between the living Pueblos and the ruins of the ancient ones. And there was the heavy presence of Los Alamos, the Lab, hidden away on a high plateau, seldom seen, so near the enduring ruins and the other holy sites, the birthplace of a different god.

When we began to look for land, we saw yet another New Mexico, the one in our price range that was mostly made of unfinished or abandoned owner-built homes. We found ourselves looking at the transience of others' hopes and possibly our own, the half-life of dreams.

David, the real estate agent who was our guide, was a tall, strong, conservative-looking man from Minnesota who liked to talk and consider new ideas. He had an open independent outlook, and he was taken by our story and our desire for a simple, secluded life. He had two loves in this life: Arabian horses and the stories of very intelligent people he had met who lived strange lives. Our strongest memory of him would always be of David astride one of his beloved Arabians with his long legs dangling low as he set out onto the prairie engulfed by clouds of swirling snow. He would reappear as the sun and sky briefly cleared, and finally his form would fade away again into the distance and the mist.

We would arrange to meet in towns or at crossroads, and Rachel, Elliot, and I would then ride in the front seat of his large four-wheel-drive truck. He would drive us through the foothills north of the Sandias, the piñon-juniper, chamisa and sage rolling hills and dry washes, dreamlike scenes arising and vanishing with the slow tide and cadence of David telling of another fascinating character with a brilliant mind, and as we edged up out of a dry wash, we would rise onto a flat bench with a sea of dead cars marked out clearly by a barbed wire fence. As we curved along the dirt road and the flow of the land, the apparition would fade behind, with a new vista opening up to the river valley far below. And there we would come across another lost dream, an unfinished split-level adobe home built in an arroyo, eroding now like a Pueblo ruin, driveway completely washed away, with a small flower bed of irises surrounded by an ornamental garden fence safely uphill from the house, and in this experience, another tale of a brilliant man at Los Alamos who lives in a shack not far from there. We would meet him on the plains to the east, in bosque to the south, and the mountains and foothills to the north. And if we passed an Arabian in a field, David would talk fervently of riding one of his desert horses swiftly across the crest of the Sandia Mountains on full moon nights, racing until the dawn.

David had driven us down a long straight dirt road into open prairie ranch land, and just past a cattle guard, we stopped. The landscape flowed gently down to the east. We sat in his truck in silence, listening to the wind. Rachel and I got out and stepped through a barbed wire fence. We walked the land, walking into our dream, the land reaching to the east with no one in sight, and our hearts opened like the sky.

There were no signs telling of property for sale and David knew of no listing, but he said he would look up the owner's name and call him. The land belonged to an older man in his late sixties who had been born not far from this forty-acre parcel. He agreed to our offer and soon after the sale, he and his brother came out to see us on the land and we loved them both. They had grown up here; they loved the land deeply and charmed us with their stories of living in a sod house in the years before the dust bowl. Whenever they drove out from Albuquerque, they would stop by and we would talk together about the land, the weather, anything that held the spirit of our shared love.

DILIGENCE OF MUD

Elliot wandered the land with her nose high, catching all the unfamiliar scents carried on the wind, as Rachel and I bathed ourselves in the sky and the grassland that flowed gently down to meet it. We were held in the quiet, the newness, the unknowness of it all. The electricity had been hooked up to our drop pole, and we decided to sleep in the back of our truck and enjoy our first night on the prairie. The sun had already set. The sky held a lingering brightness, and the land was in a dim shadow when we noticed a small rattlesnake not more than three feet from us. We stood quietly looking, touching the snake with our eyes, watching as the snake slowly moved away.

We met David at the land a few days later, and we mentioned how we had watched the rattlesnake. He thought that we were very foolish. He was open to our life story and our opinions but not about rattlesnakes. We were completely unprepared for his reaction. He felt that rattlesnakes in general and especially the western prairie diamondback, which was the rattlesnake in our area, were the most dangerous, aggressive, and evil creatures you could come across in this life. We were shocked. We had hit a fence in his otherwise open mind.

Before, our process of asking questions had been within the context of making art. Now the questions were arising in a new environment and in trying to make a life. Living on the high desert prairie was now the art, and all experiences were aspects of it, but the elements of this experience had to come to know us, and we had to come to know them in a deeper way. The land itself, the heart of it, was welcoming, and we loved the land; we felt a kinship, but it had its own past and character. We were a bit nervous, and the land was nervous too. The elemental aspects of this world are not just scientific compounds known only through analysis. They are alive within a vast and naturally arising simplicity. We were not going to try to force them into a new shape, like planting a lawn with border plants. Our first experiences on the land were sometimes abrupt introductions to the wholeness of this place, the Earth as it was here, the atmosphere, animals, plants, and the ranchers and others, and their beliefs about the land and how to use it.

As we began living here, it became quite clear that prairie rattlesnakes were very excitable and touchy, especially the young ones. At first, they were surprised by our studio barns and we would find them motionless in the grass as if staring at the barns transfixed by this strange apparition. The snakes were very hard to see, their light reddish brown with indistinct diamond markings blending into the color of the earth. Every day we encountered at least one on our walks around the property and the adjoining ranch land.

When we began building our adobe house, a woman rancher stopped by and when she heard us speak of letting the land be, she said prophetically, "Your land will go bad if you don't graze it." She drove off leaving a cloud of dust and an eerie feeling. In her own way, she was saying that if you allow the grass to grow without grazing it, rodents become more numerous and so do the predators, including the rattlesnakes.

I was still coming down from living in South Central, always on guard for an attack. I was very aware of not having a phone, living more than an hour away from the nearest medical help. I ended up killing a few rattlesnakes. I did not like doing it but felt trapped by the snakes and the circumstances. I always prayed for them, and for all snakes. Then we tried catching them and moving them farther away, but stopped when we realized the dangers for everyone involved, of putting rattlesnakes on someone else's ranch land.

As we lived with the land, it came to know our hearts and we made peace with it. The grama grass grew far taller than grass had grown here in ninety years. The mice, trader rats, jackrabbits, cottontails, meadow larks, horned larks, antelope, coyotes, foxes, hawks, ravens, eagles, and vultures all became our neighbors, and especially the rattlesnakes. There was no animosity, no fear on either side, and so the snakes calmed down. They knew us and we knew them. On any given day, we would come across our friends, as we called them. We came to know a number of older rattlesnakes to the point where we could shoo them into the bushes if a rancher was walking up the driveway. They seemed to know our hearts, and they would sail by our feet with hardly a sign. We became part of the land and walked among friends.

Spring in New Mexico is engulfed in wind, wind that seems to have no end, always a relentless driving force. We moved onto the prairie blown by the wind and the upwelling of violent weather. The spin-off from a tornado two miles to the southeast pulled some of the corrugated tin off the barns that day. We also moved onto the land without water; the well rig generator had died, and the drilling had to wait for a replacement. We had a strong faith that we would hit water, but we had to live for a time with an uncertainty that was profoundly uncomfortable. It was similar to waiting for an artwork to unfold, having nothing that guaranteed a future moment of success, just an emptiness in the waiting. Now the emptiness was heightened by a fundamental need. It was very disturbing to have the whole context of your life pivot on this one thing and being forced to wait. This is truly the essence of the spiritual path. It is abrasive openness.

The wind was intense as we hauled water in our truck from the house of some friends about twenty miles away to cook, clean, and keep a few native trees that we had planted alive. We made a comfortable camp in one barn, with our artwork in the other. We tried to settle into the prairie and feel at home under this cloud of uncertainty. We used this time to go over the plans for our house, a very small passive solar adobe with a greenhouse porch. We worked on details of the construction plan, studied for the homeowners' electrical test, and bought and hauled building materials.

It was not until the middle of June that we finally hit water at three hundred and sixty feet, and within minutes, a rancher who owned most of the land for miles around us drove up. He said we had hit one of the best strata for water you can get in that area, as he slowly fingered the yellowish sandy soil brought up by the well rig.

Rachel and I had just laid three concrete blocks, the beginning of the stem wall of our foundation, when we realized the mortar mix was wrong. Instead of calmly thinking things through, we immediately jumped into our truck to drive to a local pay phone twenty-five miles away to ask someone what to do. Halfway down the driveway, when two barn swallows began circling the truck, forcing me to stop so that I would not hit them, we started to get our answer. Having stopped us, the barn swallows disappeared. I started down the driveway again; the swallows reappeared, circling the truck, stopping us. We knew this was out of the ordinary, especially when we could not see the birds after stopping. I tried again, and we were instantly circled and stopped. Swallows are great builders of mud homes, with a taste for just the right mud, and we honored these diligent little masters. Suddenly we knew that the mortar needed more sand. We got out of the truck, left it in the middle of the driveway, walked back to the foundation and began again.

Our days of building started early, before sunrise, and ended late as we looked over texts and manuals, trying to decipher the building codes. We generally had good weather for laying adobe block and mud. Rachel and I worked well together except for a day here and there when neither of us could communicate or understand anything. Sometimes you just can't. These were miserable days, but we would come together again, taking time to calm down, and within a short time our minds would be flowing in the same stream.

By midsummer the walls were rising. We had survived the levels of rebar and direct burial electrical cable and the days when the simple word for the tool you desperately needed right now refused to appear in your mind. We had propped the rough bucks for the window openings in place, the squares and rectangles that would frame our views of this open land once we lived inside.

One afternoon as we laid more block around the window openings, Rob and I noticed some kestrels and shrikes sitting on the electrical lines along the road. Even from a distance, we could feel their intense focus as they stared at our barns. A pair of Say's phoebes had nested on the far side of the barn where we stored our sculpture, away from the commotion of our small construction site. We thought perhaps their babies had fledged by now, and we hoped the babies would survive.

The phoebe parents had appeared in the spring, right after the well rig broke. They were small friendly birds and the motionless well rig, a monument to our uncertainty then, had seemed perfect to them. They had started a nest right on the rig, on a concealed shelf inside a wheel well behind one of the big wheels. We enjoyed the company of these cheerful little neighbors who were so utterly at home close to people. We became very fond of their short whirring trilling call, their alert profile with a slight crest on their heads, the rhythmic dipping of their tails as they sat on the wires, and especially, their translucent angel's wings that glowed when outspread and backlit by the high desert sun. We had built some shelves under the eaves of both barns to give them other options, but they had continued to work on the nest behind the wheel. They did not begin their new place on the barn until the well drillers fixed the rig and we began building. We had all gotten a late start this year.

After we finished laying more block around the windows and cleaned up, we went back to our camp in the nearer barn and found that the phoebes had brought their fledglings inside the barn. Four babies were sitting close together in a row on one of the trusses, high up in the rafters. The babies looked huge for flycatchers. Their fluffy feathers made them seem larger than the adults, and their puffy shapes were crumpled like dented pillows as if they could still fit easily back together in the nest. They must have been old enough to fly, at least far enough to reach the barn, but they looked a little stunned at the sudden change in their world.

The kestrels and shrikes were gone; we left the big barn doors open so the phoebes could leave while we made dinner. They did not leave. Rob tried to shoo them out, both of us telling them as best we could that we would be shutting the doors for the night. They did not budge. Finally, we shut the doors. The phoebe family stayed right where they were, high up near the doors, while we slept in our usual place at the other end of the barn.

Light comes early to the plains in the summertime, and the next morning, before we were fully awake, the parents flew over to our part of the barn, circling overhead, singing for us to open the doors. They flew out, but the babies stayed inside all day. The barn was their new nest. Even later, after they began flying out on their own, they all came back each night, and we would wait to shut the doors until the whole family had returned. In the mornings, they would fly above our heads, calling to wake us up.

The big doors opened due east, and as we swung them wide each day, the light from the endless brightness of sky and plains outside would flood the whole interior of the barn. The phoebes would fly out into the dawn, their wings glowing in the light, and we would get ready for another day. Laying adobe is hard grueling work. The sweetness of the phoebes and their gentle trust lightened our hearts.

In late July, Rachel left to teach a sculpture workshop in the Los Angeles area for two weeks, and Elliot and I continued laying adobe and setting the roof beams. It was a slow process getting a shovel full of mud, climbing up the ladder and dumping it, troweling it, and setting the blocks I had ready. Then down the ladder again, repeating myself, slowly working around the house under a hot, brilliant blue sky. It was hard not having a phone with Rachel in California, but Elliot and I survived. On the day she was to come home, I watched the road and waited to see a dust cloud rising behind our truck. I told Elliot Rachel was coming, and she immediately perked up, scanning the distance with her nose and scimitar tail. Then she saw the truck and stiffly raced up the driveway to follow Rachel and the truck, barking and woowoowooing a welcome.

Late in the afternoon, clouds started to form, and by evening there was a thick cover. We were grateful that no thunderstorm had grown that day, for we had just finished the plywood on the roof. We were proud of a good job, the plywood slightly pitched to eight inches below the canales to allow for the height of the insulation and final roofing. It was going to work out fine.

During the night, we were jarred awake by the crashing of thunder all around us and a torrential downpour. We stumbled into our work clothes as fast as we could and ran into the charcoal night with flashes of lightning illuminating our way to the house. The prairie and the night were all water, all concussive sound.

Inside the house, we could see by the light of the close lightning strikes that water from the carefully pitched flat roof was pouring down the walls in several places like muddy waterfalls eroding the adobe mortar and blocks. All we could do was try to slap more mud into the joints before deeper grooves wore the walls down. For over an hour Rachel and I worked, digging with our bare hands, not able to run to the barn to get a shovel. We had to stay ahead of the breach in the dike, trying to keep it from growing beyond what our hands could fill. As the storm slowly moved off, we knew the house was saved, but we kept working away in the dark and the cold air, the thunder more a drumming rumble now. At last, we stood under the roof, covered in mud, drenched to the skin, enveloped in the smell of the prairie, the grasses and the high desert earth, a vibrant intoxicating scent of life, and then a nighthawk sounded.

We let the roof and walls dry out for a few days, which gave us a much-needed rest. I think we spent a whole day in bed, reading mystery stories my mother had sent us. The days dried out under the intense blue of a sky so immense it seemed to have grown since before the storm, and with this good weather, we finished the roof. As we stood on the roof looking out over the land, we turned to the sound of something hitting the top of one of the barns. In awe we stared at two great blue herons who had landed on the roof looking startled themselves, having thought the shining tin to be a pool of water. They rose back up into the air with wing beats like our drumming hearts, deep and slow, grand like the sky. They flew over our heads so close we could feel the breath of their wings. What a soaring feeling, with the blessing of their wings, our roof was finished; it was mid-September.

We were thankful for the clear skies of fall, but the temperatures were falling as we kept building, finishing the plumbing, electricity, bathroom tile, kitchen, and greenhouse. The phoebes had gone south. We were working very hard and had not noticed that Elliot was staying to her bed more and more. The nights in the barn were much colder. We would wake up to find the water frozen solid in our teakettle. We had just installed the woodstove in our almost finished house, and we were heating it to dry the adobe floor. That evening when we went back to the barn, Elliot was on the couch as if asleep, but her eyes were open and she was looking at me. I knew she was very sick. I petted her and was shocked to find a small pool of blood near her tail. We immediately wrapped her in a blanket, and I carried her out to the truck. Night was falling; Elliot was so very quiet in Rachel's arms as we drove up the long dirt road and the highways to Albuquerque and the pet hospital.

The veterinarians were able to nurse her back on her feet within a few days, and they enjoyed having Elliot sing to them. We started sleeping in our house now, providing a warm place for Elliot to recuperate. By the winter solstice, we had passed our final inspection and had completely moved in. We had finished the house just before the first snowfall. We settled in, exhausted, slowly melting into the land.

Elliot had recovered, but she was showing her age. The high desert sun, winter or summer, was hard on her with her passive solar black fur. She sought the shade. She slept with us as she always did with her head on our pillow or our shoulder, and she still ran the prairie in her sleep, but not so vigorously. She did not kick the covers off so much, and she often slept the sound sleep of a puppy or a small child.

One night in the middle of winter, a strong wind was blowing rain against the windows to the west as Rob and I went to sleep. That night I had a vivid dream of spirit animals gathered on the prairie just north and west of our house, luminous translucent buffalo, wolves, and bear, glowing in the same dark rainy winter night in which I dreamed. I felt they were Elliot's dream. They were here for her; perhaps it was her time to go and run with them. Then Elliot woke me up, she had to pee, she wanted me to open the door for her. Rob was still asleep; there did not seem time to wake him up to say goodbye, and she had wakened me instead. We usually let her out by herself at night, but this time I clipped the leash to her collar and went out in the rain with her. The wet wind blew strongly from the northwest now, and Elliot pulled just as hard heading into it, into the northwest, where I had seen the spirit animals. She pulled me far from the house almost to the corner of our land. I was crying, I did not want to let her go into that shining windswept darkness. Please Elliot, I am sorry. We are not ready to let you go.

Finally, Elliot stopped surging on the leash, and we walked quietly back to the house and went to sleep. I knew she would stay as long as she had to, until we were ready for her to go; that was her offering to us. I felt relieved and sad at the same time, to have held her back from wherever she could have gone that night.

AWAKENING SCENT

We loved the prairie passionately, but in many ways, it was a harsh, tough place. Gravity was reckoned horizontally here; you could measure the force of the moving air directly on your body each time you stepped out of the lee side of the house or barns into the full burden of the wind. Especially, but not only, in the long dry season nominally called spring, this was a land completely defined by wind. In the early mornings and maybe one evening a week, the wind would die down. We could walk the land upright, enfolded in the sudden stillness without having to lean into the air to balance ourselves against a familiar strength. The rest of the time the land and everything on it, including ourselves, were in the relentless care of strong wind, wind that crashed against the side of the house and bowed the window glass in toward the room in the storms, wind that was always pushing on you, reminding you of its greater force. We had reached a stage on our invisible path, growing more visible day by day, where the path itself was also pushing, pulling, and prodding us, and we had picked this restless, prodding, fluid place of molten sky and air to wear away all the outlines and the contents of our dreams because that wearing away matched our hearts.

The prairie was also a place of simple unexpected moments of wonder and grace. As we walked the land on an early morning in spring, warm sunlight flooded the sparsely grassy plain, but the earth and air were still cold from the desert night. Pearlescent pink flowers of low-lying cactus hidden in the short grass were opening again to the light, and as the petals began to unfold, we saw green bees like small jewels sleeping curled up beside the yellow pollen hearts of the flowers. The bees had taken shelter inside the petals that had closed so gently over them the night before.

148

We walked the land again on another morning in spring, inside a heavy fog that enveloped everything. The dense moisture that filled the air left little room for any other sights or sounds, only this motionless suspension of tiny waters surrounding us. Occasionally a cholla bush or a small stand of wolfberry would appear. The light was a soft coastal gray; there must have been clouds on the eastern horizon as well as fog. Then suddenly the sun rose somewhere overhead, high and far away. The fog was resplendent now, a golden gleaming mist, and in front of us inside the fog was a high curving arc, a perfect rainbow shape with no colors except pure white. The brilliant arc seemed close enough to walk under, but as we approached, the white rainbow hovered always the same distance away, neither near or far, staying with us inside the heavy radiance of the fog.

The days were hot by midmorning in the summertime. We stood in the shadow of one of the barns, listening to a group of young meadowlarks sitting high up on the electrical line near our power pole. It was a large group, and they made a strangely discordant sound as they sang all together. Then they were quiet for a moment. An elder meadowlark sitting with them on the wire gave a clear familiar melodious call; then the young birds started up again, no flute-like tones, no liquid rippling song, just a goofy arrhythmic enthusiastic raucous din of wheezes, blats, and beeps, and a few cracking trial notes, like a whole congregation of free jazz musicians soloing exuberantly all at once. Then they stopped. The elder sang, and the young birds went into their free space again and again. We were laughing so hard we had to hold our sides at the jubilant, wild display of young meadowlarks practicing to learn the lyric grace of their ancestral song.

Later in the summer, a huge flock of starlings appeared suddenly in the midday sky. They were flying close together, so close they could barely move their wings, flying in perfect synchronicity as if they were a single bird. A small falcon dove repeatedly at the flock. The starlings moved even tighter together; there was no leader, only one mind flying, one life. The falcon could not get at any individual bird; they were a splendid, undulating, almost terrifying whole, and their wings made a strange whooshing sound in unison as the flock wheeled and turned, rolling and pulsing like a giant dark amoeba in the sky. Finally, the falcon gave up and flew away.

A little bee taking refuge in a cactus flower, the consecrating grace of a white rainbow in the fog, the diligent praise of young meadowlarks, the protection circle of a flock of starlings: so many stages of the spiritual path arose naturally here, and for us, this flowing unity of instinctive practice became above all else a place of renunciation.

We had no phone. Mail was delivered three days a week. When we went to the tiny relic of a pre-dust bowl town fifteen miles away to get our new rural route address at the small post office on the front porch of an old weathered house there, we asked the post office lady if she wanted us to let her know when we put our mail box up on the road so that we could start receiving mail. She had simply said, "I 'spect I'll see it." We saw her too, coming from miles away, a streaming plume of dust, racing down the narrow dirt road that connected east and west and little else. The nearest pay phones were twenty-five or thirty miles away, depending on whether you wanted to stand on an empty lot beside a gas station and a fast food place off the interstate or on a sidewalk between two rural stores for more protection from the weather.

Elliot could not stand to be alone; we took her everywhere, or one or both of us stayed home. We did not go to movies or restaurants. We knew many of the parking lots in Santa Fe and Albuquerque by heart, as one of us would sit with Elliot while the other went inside to get whatever it was that we were there for, groceries, building supplies, library books. We were functionally in retreat, less and less involved with the "outer" world. Our practice was our life with the land. Our families were not pleased; neither were our friends. Few people wanted to correspond by mail or through sporadic telephone calls that they could not return.

Little by little we cut back everywhere. We ate simple food. We called it being "budgetarians," but something much deeper than saving money was also driving us to simplify, to see how much we could do without. We were touching a reverence buried by the overconsumption of the modern world, reactivating a basic respectful trust in the generosity of life that does not need or want so much, that is content with just enough, and we were looking at what that "enough" was coming to be for us. We read Tom Brown, Jr., Masanobu Fukuoka, and Wendell Berry, each deeply concerned about the destruction of the world, and taking actions in different ways to save the Earth, starting with choices they were making in their own lives with a compelling sense of time running out. We were feeling the destruction of our world as a spiritual crisis and looking at a simple life as a support for a spiritual path, hidden or revealed in the daily choices that we made. We turned off the hot water heater; we took cold showers and stood outside afterward in the cold to dry off. We sat outside naked in the cold at dawn to feel the elemental quality of coldness itself, the purity and directness of its touch, waiting with the soft brightness of first light seeping through the sky and the sharper brilliance of the cold seeping steadily into our bones as the day returned from night.

We grew vegetables in the narrow greenhouse room that also helped to heat the house. It took a while to learn what thrived there. We had an eclectic menu, mostly Japanese eggplant, tomatoes, green beans, and kale, not always well timed at first. One month we ate a lot of green tomatoes; they are quite good in curry dishes. We opened the refrigerator one day and realized it was almost empty; there was only a stick of butter and a partial can of dog food. We decided to make ghee for ourselves and give Elliot the reconstituted dry form of her special food for older dogs. We gave the refrigerator to a friend who had a small hostel up near Taos. We had disembarked from a major aspect of the modern world; how did people survive for thousands and thousands of years without refrigeration? Somehow, in the twentieth century, it had become implied that they did not; without modern technology they just died. We ground whole grain to make fresh bread, made jerky, sprouted and dried wheat kernels and ground them to make sweet panoche flour. We dried berries and rendered fat. We were reinventing wheels.

We made simple tools of stone and bone, and spindles, fireboards, and tinder bundles for making fires. We pounded yucca leaves and made cordage from the fine strong fibers that were released. We made pemmican, the ultimate ancient survival food. We were having purposeful interactions, gestures, with ourselves and with each other, with the land and with our times, with assumptions stored everywhere, to effect a spiritual change. We were willing to try, willing to make mistakes, willing to fail, because we knew in our hearts that all the hints, clues, and half-forgotten memories would come together. We opened doors. Like sleepers entering a familiar dream on a slight rise above the sea, we stepped into our changes, becoming eventually transformed.

There would be a feeling of expectancy within the long period of waiting that precedes the creation of a work of art. The whole atmosphere would be charged, yet no visible sign in the studio would foretell of anything different. One might start by getting out some drawing paper, a canvas or other materials, looking through them, touching them, feeling a format, a shape to come, helping to create, to generate a charge that had been growing throughout this long gestation. It is an exciting electrical web reaching out from one's heart and hands and embracing materials, followed by the wave of knowing without knowing, and the expression pouring through one's hands, the heart reverberating until one has a confirmation of an expression having arrived. Then one could settle into resolution and again wait the long wait.

One day in late summer, it was dry and the sky was clear, but there was a scent of moisture. We would scan the sky especially toward the mountains to the west and north, but always a perfect immense blue. The sun had reached its zenith as we looked to the west again. High above the mountains was a small white cloud, a cloud that was not just itself; it was a seed, a point of growth with an expectant tone, a feeling, a sense, a pull within one's bones communicating a transformation, a knowing of a birth to come. We felt so small beneath the blue dome watching this cloud become a movement and an expression of life. It encircled, stretched, multiplied, and became a wash of gray, steely, magnetic. A moist breeze refreshed the hot summer dryness. Soon the sun was eclipsed behind this simmering, gray cloud mass. The whole atmosphere had changed; the prairie was quiet with an inner calling to hunker down. Huge drops of rain fell here and there, heavy and out of place. A long distant rumble of thunder sounded, just as an expression arises through one's hands, after such an exhausting wait, a rolling, boiling brilliance.

We were held by an extraordinary spectacle unfolding to the north, a black cloud as big as the north itself, moving, growing, and coming our way. Flashes and streaks of lightning, the fire of water, the rumble of a distant thunderous crash. Rain drops became larger, beating a rhythm into a curtain of black rain and clouds lit into shape and distance by bolts of charged fire. A wall of black water engulfed the prairie. Arcs of brilliant light created shapes through this ocean of violent life, a lake where there was Earth, an ocean where there was sky. A lull, just a moment, a stillness, and then a chest-cracking explosion as a fall of golf-ball-sized hail drummed the land like a herd of buffalo stampeding across the open plains. The black receded, the water became Earth, the landscape reappeared, and the meadowlarks called out their joy. There was a calm, open, cleansed atmosphere, alive with the perfume of the high desert grasses, wet earth, and sage. The birds were calling as the storm moved beyond the horizon, and we walked the land refreshed within this vibrancy of life and growth, witnessing, looking, being with the nighthawks diving in whirring arcs as a far-off flash of lightning revealed a Himalayan-sized cloud, titanium white against a deep cobalt blue.

In the summer of 1987 while Rachel and I were still living in South Central, I had begun working on a figure called *Fomalhaut*. Fomalhaut is a solitary star low on the horizon in the southern sky and I saw it as a crawling man reaching out ahead of himself yet looking over his shoulder at where he had come from. I had wanted the figure to reflect a sense of westernized global humanity rushing to consume in order to gain a shortsighted fantasy while the Earth becomes more and more diseased. His self-obsessed view is blind even to his own fall, denying the sacredness of all things, and like the star, humanity is at its nadir, the end of a long cycle.

I had just finished carving. But something wasn't right. I painted the surface with a thin white varnish, making the figure a ghostly white, and yet something was still not right about it. I wandered around the studio. I went outside and looked at the plants, listened to the wild sounds of South Central, and thought about the work. I thought over my feelings about humanity's destruction of the Earth, the ignorance of the sacred, the increasing anger and desire with grave consequences for future generations, basic goodness and decent behavior buried and suffocated. Suddenly I knew what to do. I understood *Fomalhaut* alone with his ego, holding to his desires, crawling out on a plank six feet off the ground. Seeing him in my mind in this precarious position, I walked back into the studio, picked up my carving ax, and lopped off his arms and cleaved off a portion of his head. Now armless, mindless, he crawled in this wrenching posture to the brink of an uncertain end.

A few months after we finished the adobe, my sculptures *Hanap'atu and Coalsack,* the dialogue between holding and allowing, and *Fomalhaut* were part of a group show at the Santa Fe Art Museum. I was still holding to an idea of myself as an artist despite my profound knowing that I would never make art again. Even after finishing our adobe, I felt nothing in my heart arising to be expressed in that way. I already knew what my path was, and I was nervous about accepting it. I was hoping for some sign or insight at this opening.

The opening was packed as we moved through the throng of artists and patrons. Rachel and I were taking turns checking on Elliot in the car. I watched people standing beneath the anguished figure of *Fomalhaut,* holding their sacramental wine, talking over their cheese and bread, people enmeshed in their lives, not really looking, not really willing to see. Watching the people come and go, I wondered if Jeremiah would do any better or anyone who calls out on a street corner the Coming and the Judgment. An owner of one of the largest galleries in Santa Fe came up to me and said that he didn't handle this kind of work himself, but this was the best sculpture he had seen. This was the sign I had been waiting for. I felt that my career as an artist was truly over. I had wanted my art to change people, to effect a change in the world. I was not creating these images to be ensnared by concepts of art and value. Art had been a way to look at my innermost being, to reveal the questions and unfold the mystic. Rachel and I were becoming aware that for us art had mainly been a cover that was understandable to society and our families. It allowed us the time to ask and express our hearts. The art world wanted to show our work, but that kind of dialogue was not enough to keep pace with how we were changing from inside. Our hearts were now in the prayer, and the prayer was the land we loved and the openness, accessible to all who let go. We would pray an enduring prayer of a spiritual life. No need to make ourselves hoarse on the street corner with placards of doom, but to recognize and be the prayer, becoming the awakened scent after a thunderstorm, permeating all.

One morning Rachel and I were reading and Elliot was sound asleep beside us. It was midsummer and the winds had lost their intensity in the heat, but there was an uneasy peace in us, a rest before the next ascent. Suddenly I felt strongly compelled to go get a steer hide, stretch it, clean it, and tan it. There was something in cleaning a hide that had to be done. It was like a skyrocket bursting in my mind. Our land was now a distinct forty-acre square of tall grass surrounded by overgrazed, abused land and animals and there was a power in a prayer that viscerally takes on this whole experience, drawing to one's heart the problems, the pain, and the ignorance.

I drove off with a powerful force pulling me to call slaughterhouses in our area for a hide I could buy. A half hour later I was standing at a phone booth near an old fast food stop and an empty dirt lot with broken beer bottles and paper trash clinging to a fence near an on-ramp to I-40. "Yeah, we have a steer hide. Just finished yesterday." I drove east about forty miles and got off at a town built around the off-ramp. I soon found the small slaughterhouse in an overgrazed part of town. I stopped and talked to a man out front of a non-descript beige building. He said to pull around back. I parked near a corral where a number of animals were penned together with their heads tied close to the fence. They were moaning and bleating, with foam at their mouths. It was a hot day with no shade or water, and their only view was of the large roll-up door where they watched as the next animals were dragged to their deaths. There were two or three steers and a couple of goats waiting in their horror, dying in their fear. The butcher picked up a bloody mass that was once a steer off the red-stained concrete floor. The air was heavy with the stench of blood and bleach. He dumped the hide in the back of our truck. I drove home with blood dripping off the bumper and the dust of men's hearts.

Rachel and I wrestled this mass of flesh off the truck bed. We could barely move it around as we struggled to stretch it out, viewing this immense hide with huge chunks of rotting muscle and fat and maggots. Where it was cut clean, the hide itself had been slashed deep by the butcher's knife. So much careless waste in our world, the butcher, the oil rig, the trash dump, and our benumbed television minds. The hide was so unwieldy that we were forced to cut it in half. Soaking the two halves just made them heavier. We scrapped off a lot of rotted meat. We pulled the hair of our confusion and scraped away our ignorance for days. We were healing this overgrazed land and ourselves.

We were still scraping, standing in our rubber barn boots with plastic trash bags over our clothes, enveloped in the stench of rotted fat and flesh, when all of a sudden I started running around saying we had to clean up. We had to put everything away and wash everything clean. I'm running about in these ridiculous barn boots with a plastic bag ensemble, and Rachel is saying "Okay, dear, okay, no problem," while wondering what is going to happen next. We put everything away; the hides were soaking in Rachel's studio. We had just removed our plastic bags covered with rotted scum, when I looked up the driveway to see the governor of New Mexico and his brother walking toward us; they had climbed our gate, seeing that we were home. They were both ranchers and owned most of the land for miles around us. We had met the brother, who managed the ranching operation. He had stopped by a number of times in a proprietary way beginning with the day that we hit water. He introduced us to the governor and asked if they could see our artwork. We did not really feel they wanted to see our work, but we took them to Rachel's studio. We opened the door, and they just stood there, looking with wide eyes. I think they were hoping for some cowboy, Western kind of thing, not a mystic's cry from beyond time. They backed away and said they had to go. They were practically running for the gate, all the time talking to each other about how tall the grass was on our land.

The pulling, the scraping, and the witness were stones freely tossed in the lake of our lives and the waves had touched our neighbors. They were the patrónes of the prevailing world view that was all around us, and they were drawn to us at this moment, while we tried to cut through the ignorance and the waste, to heal.

Rob was working outside as I finished some kitchen chores in the house. The winter sky was clearing to the west in the late afternoon, and pale yellow sunlight suddenly streamed through the window. Moisture from the greenhouse had built up in the room, condensing on the windowpane in delicate drops and rippling streaks, with a wide border of frost along the metal frame. The low-angled sun projected an image of the window into the room and onto the plain curtain hanging in front of our closet. The glowing oblong of light was like an ancient map. I was entranced by the clusters of circular shapes ringed in gleaming light, the luminous meandering rivers and trails and radiant seas, all spread out on the golden vellum of winter light. I went outside to get Rob, but the light was passing quickly and there were only a few more minutes left when we returned.

The glowing map had opened into a multilayered but simple wonder, poised between light and water, metaphor and inherent grace. Of all the aspects of our experience here, the mysterious transformations of water came to evoke for me the moments of fluid spaciousness that revealed an undefined goodness already present in everything just as it is.

We were deep in the wet part of winter. The land was saturated, frozen hard at night and a sea of thick mud by day. The same tenacious gooey stuff that built our walls and endured in the ruins of the ancient ones now clung enthusiastically to our feet when we went outside, and made our road impassable until it froze again. There is a gloriously unstable solidity to mud. Mud is the epitome of the true nature of whatever we take to be solid and real, utterly tactile and giving way all at once. I loved the mud.

As the temperature began to drop in the evenings, the mud would turn firm, with an elastic quality like rubbery flesh at first, gradually becoming leathery and hard. Waters inside the clay no longer slid past each other easily; they were slowing down, settling together, and remembering themselves as ice. The squishy exuberance of mud turned crystalline. A hidden rhythmic ordering, a shimmering inside the Earth, finally appeared in lacey edges of frost on all the surfaces of this waterlogged land: on thin leaves of dried grass, on tops of fence posts, in the shadows of small rocks. Dreams of sleeping waters made delicate patterns held carefully in the ringing stillness of the cold that allowed us to walk on water temporarily again until the mud returned.

The snow had melted back from the great curving windswept drifts left by the winter storm. Now the banks of snow were floating on a thawing watery land. They rose and fell across the prairie like white-capped waves in the distance or the backs of giant whales nearby. The sky was heavy with low gray clouds. Earth and sky were pressed close together, and the flat seam in between was timeless, primordial, a level sea spreading endlessly to the horizons on all sides. The temperature hovered near freezing. Within the massive weight of the gray clouds, the thick moisture-laden air, and the floating Earth, waters everywhere were approaching stillness, remembering a mystery, one substance, many forms, a brightness fluid and supple, or crystalline delicate and hard, balanced at the fulcrum of the worlds.

We sat on the lee side of a curving drift and placed thin sticks of wood in a tapered shape around a small bundle of finely shredded tinder. Rob knelt on one knee, set another tinder bundle under the notched socket in the fire board, fit the spindle into the socket, wrapped the bow string around the spindle, and began the ageless sacred motions for making fire, pulling the bow back and forth with steady rhythmic strokes until a thin curl of smoke appeared. Then he laid the bow and spindle aside and carefully lifted the smoldering tinder, folding it around the tiny coal. Holding them close in front of his face with cupped hands, he blew, gently breathing life into fire. He put the flaming tinder bundle inside the small cage of sticks and blew again. Small red and yellow flames curled upward, wrapping around the sticks.

The small heat grew stronger, flames rose higher in the air. We added more wood as a light rain began to fall. The drops hissed in the flames and made spots of true color on the rocks around the fire. Clear orange rolling tongues of heat reached upward in the rippling air; then snow began to fall in delicate fluffy clumps all around us, pulling softly toward the Earth and vanishing in the liquid flames. I held out my hand, snow landing gently on my open palm, melting and disappearing into my skin. Pale and luminous, outstretched in the fertile freezing air, my hand was another kind of fire.

We would wake up long before dawn, letting Elliot sleep curled up with her blanket, and go outside to meditate with the Earth in the dark of a brilliant high desert resplendent with stars. There was a long silent waiting around us, waiting as the depth of the night passed. In the summer, there was the crickets' chorus; the nighthawks and the coyotes sang the call of their lives, but in this clear winter night, there were only the soft touching sounds of dry grasses in the breeze, and we were alone within our own night. Though Rachel was sitting beside me and we walked the same path together, she and I were alone together. We could not dwell within each other's experience; we were sitting with our own night as we sat with our own inevitable death, waiting in the hush of grass against grass; embraced by the night, we sat stunned by its power. We waited, with the animals and plants holding their breath, to see if the night would be broken and the sun rise again. Slowly the dark pulled back and revealed all the shapes, creating the world anew. Alone in the dawn, alone with the world all around us and the dawn's advance, the dark receded, until a piercing brilliant arc of light broke upon the horizon.

We were living on the prairie to witness it and be enfolded by it, and then somehow find the courage to let it go.

It took me much longer to realize that my art making was over than it had taken Rob. When we were sculptors, we had worked in very different ways. As Rob carved he cut away to reveal the essence of a hidden core. When I fleshed out the essential gesture of an armature, I added to reveal. It took me a while to flesh out the recognition that the energy for making art was quietly passing away.

In Corrales I had made a series of landscape elements called *Ghost Roots*, clusters of curving twigs wrapped around and around with fine white threads, each cluster with a white curving branch trailing below it, like a long thin root. I was weaving river songs, weaving prayers, weaving myself into this new land. By the time we moved to the prairie, I had several dozen of these delicate woven clouds, and when I hung them up high in the barn, they swayed gently in the wind that worked its way into everything here. The river songs had become part of the ocean of the sky. The wind still pushed and pulled and claimed anything that might resist, but for the eyes and heart, more and more the land belonged to the sky.

Laying adobe block that first summer, or digging in our small garden beds later on, or walking up the driveway to get the mail, a slight shift of the eyes and you were enfolded in a flowing alive expanse. We lived within the vast tides of an ocean of endlessly changing sky: pearl gray dawns in the monsoon season with hollow arching clouds tinged orange and pink like the insides of vast sea shells, the relentless blazing blue of early summer, light snow falling out of nowhere on a clear, paler blue afternoon in midwinter, long gray strands of virga sweeping overhead, never reaching Earth, falling on another land in the sky instead, huge anvil-topped thunderheads suddenly lit up from inside at night along the eastern horizon.

The land was part of the sky. The scale of their union was inconceivable. An instinctive spacious knowing that balked at measuring the immensity of this place in any way witnessed the openness offered here with an endless full embrace. There were fences in this land, and roads, and there were other assumptions overlaid on the patient generosity of the Earth here, but the timeless sky-like freedom of the land was not held back by the boundaries. It was like the pronghorn antelope we saw running together, flowing like a river or the wind across the land, lowering heads and necks gracefully as they approached a fence, never breaking stride, slipping in between the harsh strands of barbed wire as if no wires were there.

I had postponed a show of work in Los Angeles while we built the house, and after we moved in I slowly began to consider how to put some of our experience here into a formal expression as art, how to bring the whole of the prairie into a gallery space. I planned a landscape of *Ghost Roots* with a river of curving cow bones, bones bleached white by the high desert sun interwoven with bones dyed deep blue-green like turquoise stone. I would put a few figures here and there, the final pieces from a series called *Pray/Prey*, a crouching hunter with arms and legs of slender bones and a curving sacrum head, and an antelope-deer drawn from a Kung-san rock painting, an enigmatic side view with the top half of the animal erased. I filled the level cut-off body with bursts of hay like grasses growing from inside, as if the animal was the grassland itself running free.

Then I made the bear. I needed a witness, a vantage point from which to view this prairie dream; it was time to do the *Bear Lady* in 3-D. The first time I had drawn her in pastel fifteen years before, she had been the last piece I finished in that smaller-size format, and the larger version on canvas six years later had been the last painting that I did. I could see it coming; this was going to be the last sculpture.

I felt a sense of nostalgic completeness in the physical tilt of the bear's head, the heavy sagging paper and hay pelt and the weight of a two-legged woman poised on one hip inside four legs. I found four gnarled piñon roots for bear's feet. I mixed yellow ochre pigment into the paper mâché and laid it thinly so the golden strands of hay showed through for bear's fur when it dried.

The woman was less familiar now. How do you transform into something else? By melting down, by letting go of the form you already are. She was more like a column of steam rising in cold air or fluid shapes of bone instead of human form. She had strange, triple-jointed arms, four breasts, and a slender animal face and arched neck. Her whole body was white like the windswept drifts of snow melting all across the prairieland. She was the essence of the simple moments of grace that opened into the inner spaciousness here.

We loaded the work in a rental truck and I drove to LA but I never left the land. We had moved so far away in heart and mind from the world of urbanized culture that I was not completely there as I set up the show. The show was not there in another way. The gallery had not listed the show in the LA Times Art Calendar and the show dates were one day too short to be eligible for review. My career that had always seemed to have a vigorous life of its own was clearly winding down.

There was a surprisingly large crowd at the opening. Josine brought a group of art patrons, and other people had heard about the show in other ways. A slender young man with glowing eyes came up to speak with me. He shook my hand and thanked me, saying he was an artist and a Yaqui from Sonora and that my work had touched him deeply; it reminded him of his home and the spiritual images he had grown up with there. He was inspired to use his own experience and the materials and images from his culture in his art now. I thanked him too; I was very moved by what he said.

The Bear Lady had one more appearance to make; she was going to be in a show at the Santa Fe Art Museum called Singular Visions. In the artist's statement requested for the catalog, I wrote about living on the prairie, outside boundaries, seeking images that witness but do not block the light, and about the bear and her transformations as part of that process.

The Bear Lady was dramatic displayed as a single piece, as were other works in the show, but they were all safely rendered into unique objects by their dissimilarity and the context of the museum, and when the catalog came, the part of my statement about the land and boundaries and witness had been left out. I finally stopped there. I felt that what had touched the young man's Yaqui heart in LA was the elemental energy of the land itself, and something subtler growing from within, a timeless grace beyond the reach of images and words. Rob and I were already touching another way to witness with the gesture of our lives from within the oceanic wholeness of a flowing land and sky already in the heart, but first we had to let go, and let go again.

RELEASING

Rachel and I were facing another turning point. We no longer needed art to form the questions that would touch an openness in our world and our path within it. It was an organic change, not just an intellectual refutation; we no longer needed art, its expression, and its revelation. We had built a comfortable place; our greenhouse provided fresh organic vegetables and helped to heat our house. We had a summer garden and a root cellar. We had immense peace, and a blue sky beyond imagining. It would have been so easy living this beautiful life, building walls and gardens, watching the trees grow tall, living as part of the seasons and the cycles of the Earth. There was a prayer here too.

And we owned it. We had built this dream. It would have been easy to get a part-time job that would maintain this beautiful life-style. We would have had enough and could have remained on this expanse where are hearts had grown and become part of the land. We were living a mystic life cloistered on the prairie, a simple life close to the Earth but we felt the pain and the destruction of the planet even here. There was an urgency, a sense of impending catastrophe that was both global and individual, and there was also a feeling of incompleteness, something that could not be fulfilled here. We felt we could no longer hunker down and enjoy our little piece of paradise just for ourselves. There was an aspect of our spiritual journey that we had not yet connected with, a feeling of something missing, and a recognition that remaining in a pattern too early where the form would become habitual would lock us down, blinding us to the path. There was a growing certainty that to keep going we had to leave our home and all that we had come to love. We had a deep heartfelt knowing that if we held to anything it would hold us in return. What was now for us an epiphany could become a solid mass refusing to move, incapable of change, keeping us from the ultimate goal of one's spirit. We had to leave the security of the known, to answer the call of so many mystics and yogis who had ventured into an unknown, a wilderness. But why was this call growing so imperative now? We did not know; we trusted that the timing of our lives would bring us to where we needed to go.

Letting go has no ties, and when you truly let go even of your heart, the light will manifest. We were artists living a simple life on the prairie; this was a context we were holding to and were held by. To cut our way out, we began burning our drawings. Years and years of work, our success held for the future, a file and a testament holding us. This was our farewell even to the path we had just walked to get this far. Gratefully we burned our offerings to the wind and the early morning, in a trash can fire alone in the desert. Late in the afternoon I suddenly began retching and vomiting with intense gastric pains. Then we heard on the radio that Los Angeles was on fire. The Rodney King riots had broken out close to where we had lived in South Central, our last connection letting go in the flames and smoke, three years and seven hundred miles apart, the path, our prayer, becoming our life swirling out of this fire and into the sky.

We had begun to release the energies bound up in our work, insights held in paper, paint, chalk, and ink, scenes of abandoned freeways, exploding stars, visionary cellular landscapes in the hearts of flowers, studies of bones and prophetic dreams. Rob and I offered them freely on the prairie at the same time they could have been offered forcibly for us in another place, a confirmation of the complex interplay of destiny and choices in our own lives and in our times. We put our house, studios, and land up for sale. I canceled an upcoming show. We wrote a manifesto about our decision and our understanding at the heart of this act. We ended with these words and hoped that people would understand:

> "In many ways, this is more of a continuation of our work than a severance. We have simply put together Rachel's sense of ancient nature living in us all beneath the veneer of civilization, and Rob's sense of apocalyptic awakening as that civilization cracks away, to empower a life based on the compassion hidden at the core, a life of simple acts offered as a prayer."

We sent copies of our statement to Josine, to artist friends, and to several art critics who had written about and appreciated our work. Then we started to destroy our sculpture.

One of the art critics we had contacted lived in Santa Fe. Simone Ellis had been to our studios before, and when she received our letter, she drove out to the land with a large rental truck to see if she could rescue some of our work. We filled the truck with large sculptures. As we loaded the *Bear Lady,* I told Simone that I would be happy if she kept that piece because she liked it so much. Rob gave a smaller piece called the *Prophet* to the woman who accompanied her. It was in the front seat as they drove off.

We had given away so many other kinds of things in our lives, but rarely our work. We began giving other pieces that were left to friends, and friends of friends, and to people we did not know.

When I went to a gallery in Santa Fe to retrieve one of my pieces, I literally bumped into the son of the owner as I was backing out the door. I was carrying *Wind Woman,* a life-sized figure of a woman sitting with her legs outstretched, leaning forward from the waist, her upper body opening into a fanning burst of hay. He said, "I always liked that piece." I said, "Here!" and handed him the sculpture. I heard later that he quit his job at the gallery the next day. Catalyst or converging mirror, forms returning to energy had a momentum even in release.

Rachel and I had given away or destroyed most of our work, but I still needed to find a home for *Faith,* and we wondered if the Benedictine Monastery in the Pecos mountains would like it. We had driven by the monastery many times and had always liked the feeling there. I also wanted to make an offering to a Catholic order to honor my family connection. I called Sister Ann and described the work, and she said they would love it. I also asked if they would like an antique iron farm bell and a large tile plaque of Our Lady of Guadalupe that my grandmother had purchased at the turn of the century. She said, "Do you know the name of our monastery?" I said, "No I don't." She said, "It's the Abbey of Guadalupe!"

Elliot's health was failing again, and we had signed up for a class with Tom Brown, Jr. quite a while ago. Elliot had had a tumor removed earlier in the year, and the vet, who knew her fairly well by now, thought she would die while we were gone. We knew we could not take her with us. We remembered how she had cried when we came back from our first trip to New Mexico. Now she could never be left alone even for a short while in the car without trying to dig her way out. As the time for the class approached, it seemed to come down to leaving her to die, anguished and abandoned even with good care, or to die in our arms.

Our hearts were demanding that we go to Tom's class. There was an urgency, as if there may not be enough time; patterns were unfolding, moments connecting with other moments in unknown ways. There was an appointment calling us, a memory of something not yet arisen, yet moving toward a certainty inside. The spiritual path is not easy; we were working with a mix of inner certainty, confusion, and faith. When we had received confirmation in the mail for the dates of the class, Rachel and I had looked up to see two golden eagles soaring above us in a tight circle, slowly moving east.

One of the brothers who had grown up on the land was a veterinarian. We asked his advice and he said Elliot would die with a broken heart if we left her. He said he could drive to our land and put her to sleep. We made a difficult decision. We waited until the day before we were to leave.

It was pitch black in the sweat lodge at Tom's farm. You could see only dim shapes from the red glowing rocks. The heat and steam and the scent of sweetgrass and sage pulled rivulets of water from our pores. I felt Elliot was there with us knowing she knew of our deepest heart's intent. I cried and prayed to her. Oh Elliot, how we miss you, alone in this crazy insane world. Elliot, I know you couldn't come with us, but we'll see you at the end, standing on that shore at the edge of the last passage, there you'll be, racing along the lucid waters, greeting us with a kiss, to at last cross that open water into an embrace beyond time, a knowing oneness yet still a goodbye.

We drove east across the country to Tom's class stunned by our actions, having given up our art careers, issued a public manifesto, destroyed or given away all our artwork, put our house and land up for sale, and put our beloved dog to sleep.

We drove across an America completely strange to us, and somewhere in eastern Pennsylvania, we stopped at yet another campground for the night. Rachel and I set up our tent on a perfect green lawn, at the farthest area of the camp set aside for tents, right next to a roadway. It was like a nightmare out of my parents' backyard, everything manicured and trimmed with not a leaf on the ground and people in ironed Bermuda shorts and clean white tennis shoes. We walked through the park to find most of it used for large trailers. People hauled huge reflections of their homes and parked them in tight rows with patio awnings over artificial grass, white plastic picket fences, and plastic owl or squirrel night lights. A bug zapper lantern hung inside every screened patio. At the bath house there were signs about the upcoming barbecue night and square dance, Bingo on Thursdays and don't miss Pancake Day. We were heartsick; we had left so much of what we loved, and now we were wandering in a foreign land.

The next day we camped at the Delaware Water Gap and felt more at home among the beautiful old tulip trees. We calmed ourselves looking at the lush plants around us and being with the soothing presence of the river. The following day we landed at Tom Brown's farm in northern New Jersey and set up our tent on a grassy area near the barn. We were early, and the only other people there were some muscle beach guys playing with a tiny football in front of their new striped catalog tent and a couple of young skin heads in heavy boots with long knives strapped to their thighs. We looked at each other in anguish and shock, asking, "What have we done?" Eventually the class would also include teenage girls, Sierra Club grandmothers, science teachers, urban shamans, National Guardsmen, and some very nice people whose labels we never knew but who seemed to have good hearts. And then there was Tom.

Tom Brown was a tall, gaunt, broad-shouldered man who was recovering from a recent illness. Later we would see him at his full weight, muscular and vigorous, but now, even though he looked ill, he was intense, chain-smoking and delivering a barrage of information as if trying to mow down the class. His manner was unexpected, but the traditional ways of living with the Earth that he presented touched a deep memory in us.

One day, along with another round of detailed information about tracking, Tom demonstrated the basic movements of stalking, the slow-motion careful walk used to get close to and touch animals that can also bring you to a state of oneness. The class broke for lunch and since we did not have a job to do, we decided to practice stalking. We found a flattish area to the side of the lunchtime activities of people splitting firewood, cooking, and trying to get their first bow drill fires. I was in front with Rachel right behind me, and as we began our slow flowing movements, we entered a rhythm that was like the openness of the desert. Then suddenly the world and ourselves dissolved into light. There was no form, no thought, just brilliant light in a sphere of light tinted in rainbow colors. As we became this light I knew Rachel was part of it, and I knew how to get there, I felt a knowing within this sphere of having been there many times before.

Rob was a few feet in front of me as we both resolved into light. He was an open brightness suspended over a wide circle of liquid shimmering light. "I" was also light, the same brightness somehow recognizing his. It was a familiar brightness, organic, all-encompassing; all else had vanished. Within the timeless light, it seemed so natural, effortless, and simple being there, and then just as simply, we changed back again.

A woman who was taking the class came up to us. She said she had been watching us stalking, thinking our movements together were so beautiful and then suddenly we disappeared. She looked stunned, paused for a moment, then walked away.

We had given up everything and in that devastating open space there was only light. Within the light, there was no time, no beginning or end, a true knowing though it was not quite the complete return either. It was like abiding in the corona of a blue-black star, the radiance blazing forth naturally, and all that arises beyond the light is this world, the reflection of this light and its intent. The corona is the gap between this life and ultimate essence, and we knew we had experienced this before. Yet afterward, again surrounded by the Tracker school activities, we were also Rob and Rachel living in this dream. This experience of the light was a dramatic sign reminding us that this was our path, and that it had been our path since birth. We were moving toward something we came in to fulfill once again in this life. We knew enough to wait, knowing that this intent would propel us in the right direction if we remained open to this allowing heart of inner radiance.

LETTING GO

On the Road

For each of us our artwork had been a mystic's way in, allowing what is so ephemeral and illusive to become form and image, giving us time to catch up, to recognize. It had been a honing, molding, cutting, and binding process until we were capable of walking the path together to reach resolution. Even now, our path was not always clear. It had been clear enough to get us to our first class with Tom Brown, but we still had a long way to go.

Tom abruptly concluded the class on an apocalyptic note and as we all prepared to leave the farm with a heavy sense of time running out for the planet, Rachel and I were entering a new phase of our life, an unfolding dream, an odyssey guided by our hearts, our memory of the light, and our concern for the Earth.

When we had decided to give up our artwork and our careers, we had written to Suzi Gablik, the art critic who had talked with us in our studios in LA. She lived in Virginia now, and she had invited us to stay with her overnight on our way home from the Tracker class. Suzi was gracious and friendly when we arrived, and genuinely interested in hearing about our experiences. She said she was starting a new project, a series of consecutive interviews, and she gave us a transcript of the first conversation, a dialogue with an anthropologist about early cultures and the sacred. After we read it over, she turned on a tape recorder. She asked us to comment on some of the anthropologist's ideas first. Then we talked about our enthusiasm for learning the traditional skills of living close to the Earth and our sense of global peril if people do not begin to simplify their lives. While we alluded at times to mystical experience as a context for our actions, we did not talk about the light; it was part of a process ripening slowly deep within us that was still beyond the reach of language.

Soon after returning to New Mexico, we received a full price offer for our land, contingent on an appraisal. The prospective buyers' appraiser valued it at three-quarters of our asking price. The buyers loved the land, and we hoped they would be able care for it. This was our last chance to back out and stay, but the inner call was begging us to accept their new, lower offer.

It was only a few days before we were to leave for Arkansas. Some friends who had just purchased a cabin in the mountains of Arkansas and would not be moving there right away had written unexpectedly to ask if we would like to live there for five years. Everything was offered; we needed only to load the trailer and our truck.

The last day we wandered the land, postponing the inevitable as long as possible. That afternoon we saw the two brothers who had sold us this land. They were fixing their fence line along the road, and we walked down to talk. They were always glad to see us, but today we were all subdued. Clouds formed in the sky above us as we talked and they worked tightening the barbed wire. The brothers looked as sad as they must have felt so many years ago when they were forced to leave their home and get jobs in the city. We had been their dream to return to this land. Now these two older men with their past and their loss were tightening the line of fence, feeling exiled from their home, and we were leaving too but for reasons they did not understand. Heavy plops of rain fell, bringing up tiny clouds of dust. James looked up to the sky and in his slow thoughtful way said, "It might rain." Tears welled up in our eyes; we knew we would never see this land or them again. They sincerely wished us well as we all slowly moved apart, the chance of rain having passed.

Even though you know what needs to be done, and have come to a point of letting go, there are subtle hidden ties so deep, so demanding, that even in the process of moving we just could not sever them. We just could not see what was so obvious. We had rented a moving trailer and hauled it out to the land. We loaded it unconsciously with our last possessions and our heartache. We knew the trailer was too heavy but the weight of our holding blinded us to our actions. Nearing the end, the ties unsevered can be the most tenacious; you can cling in such foolish ways.

Our small truck took a long slow first-gear lurch; we barely pulled out of the driveway. We felt as if Elliot sat beside us at the beginning of this journey, but the whole of the land, the sounding of grasses in the wind, no more. Stretching the binding ties so slowly, we drove on, still wandering among our friends, still in wonder of all the wonders. There were no tears large enough to cry our longing as if we were driving out from under the sky, away from the Earth or beyond the vital air.

Rachel and I saw nothing of New Mexico as we drove east, and little of Texas and Oklahoma, a dense cover of loss seemingly heavier as we moved farther from home. The grade slowly began to rise and then finally, inevitably, in eastern Oklahoma a sharp bang and a drag, screeching steel and sparks, the trailer on an angle coming at the back of the truck. I just barely steered the truck off the highway and stopped with the tongue of the trailer an inch from crashing into our rear axle. We were shocked out of our loss.

The trailer was so heavy that the weight had cracked off the bumper mounting brackets. I could not lift the tongue. I was able to unbolt the bumper. We left it with the trailer and drove to a pay phone to call the moving company for help. Within an hour, a kind man in a large truck pulled up. He was shocked at how heavy the trailer was. He called to a friend of his who was working on the opposite side of the highway to come over and help lift the tongue onto his truck hitch.

Then we followed him, rented a small moving truck, and he and his crew helped us unload the trailer and pack the truck, all the while talking about our possessions. We had given up so much that was precious to us in an intangible way and kept truly useless things. They loved our antique furniture, but wondered about all the boxes of garden hoses. Wow, you have nice stuff, but what's this? Whatever was left of our life was all over the parking lot like some strange yard sale with everyone judging our taste in furniture, file cabinets, and trash cans. They finally got us loaded, and we began again, feeling more sober and aware.

We met the real estate agent outside his office in a small town in the mountains of northwest Arkansas. We followed his truck up the steep mountain roads through dense forest with brief openings near cabins and small homes, and onto a narrow dirt track that led back down the mountain deeper and deeper into thick deciduous woods, shadowy downhill turns taking us farther and farther from the paved road. We drove right through the front yard of a small gray cabin on a barren creek side, and then the trees closed in again. We made a sharp turn onto an even narrower dirt driveway lined with trees girdled by barbed wire, and came at last to a sunny clearing and the house. Part hundred-year-old cabin, part refurbished dream, it sat on a knoll in the center of the clearing facing east. The wide front porch, the tall oaks nearby shading a stone well, the vegetable garden to one side, and the small pond out back were charming in a way, but there was a heaviness pulling down on the slope of the roof line, a heaviness that seemed to be reaching up from the Earth here, and we had an uneasy feeling.

We got out of our trucks and stood quietly waiting for the previous owner to arrive and give us the keys. We did not talk much with the agent; he seemed to be from somewhere else too, a city man perhaps, selling country real estate to other city folks with country dreams, like the people who had offered us their future retirement home for the next five years. An old beige pickup truck lurched over the ruts in the driveway faster than it should. "Here's Johnny," the real estate man said. Rob and I could see an older man with a heavy round face and a stubble beard at the wheel, and an older woman beside him with a pinched sour face. We had heard that Johnny had sold the place only because his wife did not like living in the country, and we both said, "Looks like he brought his wife." The real estate man looked surprised. The truck pulled sharply through the turnaround in the drive and stopped abruptly close to us. An overweight man in his late sixties rolled out of the door on the driver's side, saying in a deep Southern drawl, "I shoot trespassers." We all laughed nervously. There was no passenger in the truck. The old woman had vanished.

Johnny was hot and sweaty. His big belly showed plainly in the ample gap between his dirty work pants and his stained tee shirt as he stood in front of us with his feet wide apart, rocking forward and back on his heels. He was telling us about the well, the hundred-year-old barn, and the riding lawn mower, but the rhythmic shifting of his weight and his wide stance were those of an animal defending territory; he did not want to give up this place. The old woman we both saw clearly in the truck was holding to it too. It had been so very hard for us to leave our prairie land; now we were plunged into the complex ties of other lives desperate not to let go, even after they had left, a feeling all around us in the hot humid air, of another kind of heat, the heat of damaged hearts that had never cooled.

Johnny showed us around, and we ended up at the barn. The heat did not seem so oppressive there. The real estate agent began telling Rachel about the construction of the barn, and Johnny turned to me and started talking about his past. For whatever reason, there in the mountains of Arkansas, I stood listening to him tell the dark story of his hatred and prejudice detailed in abusive language. He told me the brutal things he had done to blacks, and then he went on to his disdain for hillbillies. It was as if he was making a confession to me. Then he said accusingly, "I know you don't believe in this. You're one of those yuppies." I looked into his eyes, talking to a part of Johnny I felt I could reach. I told him you could not generalize about people; you have to see the individual for we all have pain. I then told him of my love and great respect for Elena, and that I had always felt she was one of my mothers. He looked at me as if he were seeing me for the first time. He said he liked us both. Then the opening closed and a darkness drew over his eyes as we walked back to his truck. He got into his truck as gruff as he came. The sun had set, the keys were ours, a gloom hung from the trees as he and the real estate agent quickly drove away. There was something not right about this hill, the cabin, Johnny, and the pond, an old horror lying heavy in the woods, as we unloaded the truck.

The Ozarks were a paradise for wild native plants, especially the edible and medicinal ones, and we had arrived in autumn; the flowers, fruits, pods, seeds, and falling leaves of the unfamiliar abundance of the plant world here were fascinating. We spent a lot of time outside learning new plants, the mitten-shaped leaves of sassafras, the pointy knobby bark of Southern prickly ash. We were always trying to stay away from the house, but the feeling of deep disquiet was almost everywhere, a steady undertone.

When we walked up the driveway to get the mail, there were the trees choked and girdled by barbed wire on either side, and we would pass through a place on the driveway that was always freezing cold no matter how warm the day. While looking at plants, we had found a few small areas deeper in the woods that had an even more chilling feel. Closer to the house, the small pond out back was filled with shattered glass; for years Johnny had been breaking bottles and throwing the shards into the pond.

In our daily activities, Rachel and I would feel the heavy quality of old habits from angry, bitter lives, and a number of old spirits were clinging to the house. There was the shade of a man near an old flat stone by the front porch, and whenever I tried splitting kindling there, the wood exploded and hit me below my left eye. I spoke to this man shadow but felt it to be beyond words, too old to listen. I moved to another area to split wood. The cabin itself never harmed us, but it was always unnaturally cold inside, and the windows in the bathroom would fog up and condense on the outside. Making a fire in the fireplace was always a struggle, and it never warmed the house. There was a feeling that the people who had lived in this cabin brought more negativity to an already negative spot and that the area would be happier without the cabin.

We had no interference from this elemental force or the spirits in our meditation. In fact, it seemed that all the negativity would stand down, not looking, not seeking, just there with no intent. We would enter a bright wordless state; we knew the darkness was there, but we were untouched by it, and we would feel nourished and refreshed afterwards.

One day a few months after we had moved in, we were driving along the highway to the nearest town when we saw Johnny in a new sedan. He saw us too and waved, so we pulled off onto the shoulder and he came up alongside. He looked transformed. He was clean-shaven, his hair was trimmed and combed, and he was well dressed. His eyes were clear and open. He was very happy to see us, genuinely interested in how we were getting along. He remembered that Rachel was hard of hearing and spoke up asking her how she was. He had a good sense of humor, and we enjoyed bumping into him. We told him how good he looked and he said he was feeling very well now. His obsessive heaviness had fallen away, and he looked like he had been reborn. We said goodbye; he wished us well and we never saw him again.

We found a spot with good energy in front of the old barn where we would sit each morning, not wanting to go back up to the house. It was warmer there than inside. We talked about the place, sifting through the clues, looking up at the shadowy cabin on the knoll, looking at the beautiful gentle surface of the pond filled with broken glass. There was an old darkness here that preceded the actions of the people who had lived here; it had been here a long time. It was ancient. It lived here as naturally as the rocks, the trees, the sky, the animals, the plants, and all that arises with this dream. It too had a place.

One day we tried to find good spots to sit and meditate on the back porch of the house. It was a cold morning with a storm passing as we settled in looking out at the pond. There was a chill, a presence, pushing us without malice. It was elemental force and now we were driven in this moment into a luminous vision and a dance, a dance between what drives one outward and what pulls one inward. The storm was breaking up, and the winds increased, a churning mix of brilliant blue and rushing clouds. The light was rhythmically playing over the surface of the pond, a surface no longer still but rippling with the wind's breath, shimmering in the glinting sunlight. Then a blue bird appeared, and another and another, until a whole flock was swirling through the changing air, like bright bits of clear blue sky, circling round and round the clearing, inside the shifting veils of shadow and light coming in waves from beside the barn and over the small pond, blue birds everywhere in a timeless union with the shadows and the light, a dance in an ancient embrace. We were part of this dance of elemental presence, witnessing its natural delight coming together, a union, molten and brilliant within a blue-black depth, blue jewels singing, making chains and beading over the fields of luminous veils of light. This was a place of power, sacred, unfathomable, not to be taken for granted. You could come and be a part of this union, and then move on. It was corroding only if you tried to hold or tame, revealing a dynamic energy and grace if you let it go. The darkness has its place too as a teacher in this world. To halt, remain, solidify, and hold only enslaves you within one aspect of this great elemental dance.

The message of the bluebirds was clear: we knew we could not live in the cabin in Arkansas much longer. When a friend we had met at the Tracker School invited us to stay with her and her family in a farmhouse in Vermont, we gratefully accepted. It was mid winter when Rob and I arrived in Vermont. The temperature was below zero in the mornings in our room above the breezeway, and a few weeks into our stay, I came down with a serious case of the flu.

Rob was building a fire; his movements were occurring somewhere far away on the outskirts of my senses. I was buried deep inside every warm piece of clothing that I had, under layers of blankets and sleeping bags. I was beyond hot or cold. It no longer mattered if the room was freezing or not. The fever had a heat of its own. My body was already dissolving; it was a circle, a protective sphere filled with little flickering dots of light. The sphere somehow contained and preserved a collection of energies that still held memories of being a body, but I was entering simultaneous multiple worlds.

An elder's face appeared in the darkness in front of me. Her earthen skin was deeply lined like an old riverbed, and her white hair floated out around her face, moving, wild, and alive. She told me it was time to receive women's teachings, and part of me rose upward and went away with her. Another part of my energy wandered downward, along a small creek choked with garbage. I was searching for something there, pushing through the layers of trash, reaching into the mud, not knowing what I was looking for, sifting through finer and finer bits of refuse, digging deeper with my hands in the wet mud. The residual body inside the protective sphere was dissolving more, the shimmering dots were pulling apart, but the flu had a fierce coherence of its own. I was sweating heavily now, drenched inside the warm clothes, coughing uncontrollably, and peeing in the bed with each convulsive cough. The body's fluids were each going their own way, entering a kind of infancy. Another me began to relive every moment of my life, even thoughts unsaid, a detailed vivid and compelling remembering but also strangely remote, with the uniform texture of a dream.

I was certain that it was very important to be as present as I could with each level of experience that had opened up for me. The women's teachings, the trash-clogged creek, the progress of the flu, and the slow life review continued together in the same overlapping time for four days. I could not eat. I drank water from a metal cup, holding the coolness of the cup in both hands like a blessing. The living brightness of the water was my link to life. As I drank, I touched part of the women's teachings, that my mind is naturally fluid and free like water, with no corners and no edge.

On the third day, still sifting through the mud in the creek, still moving through the personal memories, seeing the recurring rhythms of my life: so many near misses and sudden escapes from situations that could easily have become traps. I could see a purpose threaded through the risks, to understand how and what to heal, not just in my own life but in the life of my times as well. Then another glimpse from the elder woman's world, a white shape like two half spheres or bowls joined back to back by their curved sides. My body was slowly returning to familiar form. I went into the bathroom to pee and had a spontaneous certainty that there was no reserve of pee stored anywhere; the pee and the sensations of peeing were arising together only in this moment. There is nowhere else but now.

By the third night, I was engulfed in mucus, mucus rolling down my throat, mucus pouring continuously from my nose. I sat up all night in a chair. The room was very cold. I could feel it again. I sat wrapped up in all my clothes, blankets, and sleeping bags and held a pile of pillows to my chest to prop up my head.

I kept sitting all the next day. My ears were completely clogged by then; I could not hear anything. In the afternoon the me that had been searching in the mud of the creek bed found a hideous long dark root and set it free. The root floated in the air and then dissolved. The me that was unraveling personal history found missing fragments of my childhood, and the spreading patterns of my life returned to a new wholeness

I was utterly at peace, immersed in an ocean of forgiving and forgiveness, a kindliness so deep and wide, supporting and suffusing everything. The teachings I received in the elder woman's world were sealed, but I knew they would open at the right time. I felt whole and utterly free. It was Valentine's Day. Rob brought our friend's kids up to see me. The kids had made a Valentine for me, and they wanted to give me a hug.

I was back, but I was still on the shore of an immense wonder. I sat for days near the dormer window in our attic room, just being with the soft winter light filled with the brightness of the snow outside and the coldness of the crystal air, feeling the tangible perfection in everything as it is, a wholeness thorough beyond imagining. I was saturated with a simplicity and wordless peace that I did not leave for weeks, and even when I went downstairs for dinner again, it was hard for me to speak.

Rob, our friend, her husband, and the kids were all sitting around the table. The little girl had saved the chair next to her; she wanted me to sit beside her. I saw as if in an overlay that they were all bodies of light. They had small shadowy angular patterns here and there clinging to their luminous forms, but the shadowy bits were not who they really were. They were radiant beings, and very beautiful. I could not find the words to tell them this.

And I could not hear. I still had mucus in my ears, but I had a strong feeling that when they cleared I would find I had lost more of my hearing. I had touched a blessed silence at the heart of everything, and even when that silence began to fade, a part of me did not want to come back all the way.

We had taken a number of classes from Tom Brown while we were still living in Arkansas, and now as Rachel slowly regained her strength we prepared to go back to Tom's for another series of classes at his camp in the Pine Barrens. We had been drawn to his spiritual classes, which focused on deeper and deeper levels of awareness experienced in the wilderness: long night sits and night walks, moving through or staying in different areas and energies both good and bad, visualization practices interwoven with direct encounters with nature and yourself alone in the woods. As we followed these practices, we touched at times the fluidity we had experienced with the bluebirds in Arkansas and an increasing sense of our yogic past. We were always trying to get back to the light we had resolved into so suddenly at his first class. We had connected it with Tom at first, but it was deep within ourselves, and had arisen dramatically at a precise moment in our lives when everything else had fallen away. We kept going back to Tom's classes. We had not found another avenue, and we were hoping the light would open again. Even though the light was still unexplained in terms of what Tom was offering, we knew that these experiences in the wilderness were crucial to our path.

Thunder and lightning crashed all around me as I sat late at night in the middle of the Pine Barrens. Tom had guided our group into the woods and placed us individually. Now we were each sitting alone preparing to do a lengthy meditation, the culmination of a long four weeks of practice. Hail pelted me but I was warm and dry wearing the wool capote Rachel helped me make and a $1.95 rain poncho. Before following the meditation I thought over my purpose, and I could still hear the voice of one of the instructors yelling out into the dark woods, "Do you love it enough to give it up?!" These words were echoing in my mind so loudly that the crashing thunder and downpour seemed to melt away. Rachel and I had been rushing along within a purifying fire of choices in our lives. Now what seemed so solid and primary was ripping from me as if I were standing at the confluence of the solar winds; my arms were pulled from me, my legs and torso severed and blown away, and my face and head breaking apart in the sudden impact. I was left with a visionary radiance suddenly mapping out for me a lucid path, and then just as suddenly, I found myself alone in the woods again.

We were heading back to New Mexico. Realizing that the money from the sale of our land would not last long if we continued renting moving vans, we began jettisoning more of our belongings. We gave our friend in Vermont our antique furniture, gave books to the grade school, and took other things to the local thrift store. We boxed up our remaining possessions and shipped them to a friend in Santa Fe.

Rachel and I were so happy to be under the New Mexican skies again. We were heartened by this familiar blue praise above us, and the friend we had sent our boxes to was going to be out of town for a few weeks, so we were able to stay at his place. Our friend was eclectic and he liked accumulating odd objects from nature, but the pile of trash beside his house surprised us. We knew of his ardent environmental beliefs, and we could not connect him with this pile of stuff. We had been waiting for our boxes to arrive, and when we finally called the shipping company, we were surprised to hear they had been delivered. While we waited for the company to double check, we took a short walk outside. We were passing by the side of the house when I turned to look at the pile of trash and noticed a box with our names on it. That garbage is our garbage! It had been dumped on the side of the house close to the street, and no one had wanted to have anything to do with it. Neither did we really. I guess there were some important things in this tumbled mass of ripped cardboard and plastic bubble wrap, so we worked our way into the pile, and found we had shipped several boxes of garden hoses, and they were not even good ones. They were our affirmation to have a garden again someday, but it helps to have a sense of humor when you are living a wandering life as a prayer.

THE WATERS

We still had a month to go before our vision quest, and we decided to spend some time in the Gila wilderness of southern New Mexico in preparation.

We found a peaceful campground set among tall old trees near the south fork of the Gila River. We were more interested in meditating than backpacking or wilderness skills, but as the Fourth of July approached, the quiet campground was becoming crowded and noisy, so we decided to go into the backcountry to escape the holiday.

The canyon was narrow. The trail and the river crossed each other repeatedly. We waded through the water so many times that we stopped changing back into our boots and hiked in our lightweight beach shoes instead. Cactus and yucca perched on the high rims of the nearly vertical red rock walls of the canyon, but along the canyon floor there were lush plants growing everywhere, and vines and massive deciduous trees with huge trunks. We had entered a secret watery world hidden deep in this mountain desert land.

We hiked for most of the day at a gentle pace. The canyon widened and narrowed, following the river's wanderings. In one place where the trail ran parallel to the river, we passed through a dense stand of horsetail. As we pushed through the hollow stalks at every step, they made a melodious rattling sound like the calls of ancient birds. We were moving away from time, into timelessness.

We found a campsite in a small meadow shaded by tall trees near a slow bend in the river. It was a good spot, peaceful and welcoming, and we spent the rest of our stay there, exploring this island between the river and the trail. We picked tender tops of stinging nettles and added them to our stew of ramen noodles and instant black beans. We stood motionless in clear still pools at the river's edge as golden brown Gila trout swam close around our legs like placid dreams.

We stalked slowly upstream in a faster part of the river, blending with the rhythms of the rushing water as it flowed in complex patterns over and around the rocks. We were disappearing into the patterning, becoming breath and air. Small birds in a thicket of bushes on the bank behind us and to our left began to fly around excitedly, giving alarm calls; then they were quiet again. Suddenly Rob shouted out to me, "Rachel, a rattlesnake!" I looked to my left and saw a large diamondback rattlesnake hurling itself across the river toward me, rattle tail clearly visible as it tried to cling to the moving shapes of water curving over the rocks. I stumbled a few feet back towards Rob, and the snake also changed course; it was still heading right towards me. I stopped, holding very still. The snake flung itself forward in loops and coils, closer and closer to me. Then it careened past my legs as if I were not there, gained the bank, and quickly disappeared into the undergrowth.

A few moments later, we saw horses coming up the trail on the opposite side of the river. The rider on the lead horse of the pack train waved as they passed by. We stood in the river within the overlapping rings of energies spreading all around us: the panicked snake feeling vibrations of the approaching horses' hooves, the alarm cries of the birds startled by the fleeing snake, the heroic effort of the snake as it threw itself headlong across the water to safety, the heavy weight of the horses' packs, the rider's wave, the flowing braided waters, the rocks, and ourselves, all woven together, part of this timeless river's life.

Fourth of July had passed. We went back to the main campground again and spent a few more days there before going up to Albuquerque. The last evening we walked a short way into the wilderness and reached a meadowland. We were talking as we so often did now, not as two people in dialogue but from the softness between us, more like the river's single voice of interwoven sounds talking to itself. We noticed a deer walking calmly towards us as we talked. She seemed completely unafraid. We paused and gazed at her. She came closer, ten feet away; then she knelt down, folded her front legs gracefully under her, and settled in. Gazing peacefully back at us, she began to chew her cud.

As we drove north out of Socorro to Albuquerque, we heard on the radio that the Mississippi River was still above flood stage. We decided to fly to the vision quest in New Jersey.

Rachel and I found our way through the Newark Airport and got on a bus for Grand Central Station. We were going to spend the weekend with my brother John and his partner Joseph. John by now was a successful advertising executive, and he had graciously invited us to stay with them at their Manhattan apartment. Our lives had grown in dramatically different directions, and we had not seen each other much over the years, but there was still a bond between us.

John and Joseph showed us around New York the next day. That evening they invited a few of their close friends over, and we sat around chatting. Then we all walked to a restaurant in Soho, where the waiters seemed to know my brother quite well. They ushered us to the back into an open courtyard with large trees. During the course of dinner, one of their friends asked Rachel and me what we were going to do this week, and as if on cue, everyone quieted down. We said that we were going to take a vision quest. "A vision quest, what's that?" We said you spend four days and nights naked and alone in the wilderness, and you don't eat, you only drink water. They seemed surprised. "You don't eat! You don't see anyone!" Joseph asked what the significance of such an experience was; he seemed sincerely interested. We explained that it is a simple yet profound entrance into a circle of time leaving everything outside, even your spiritual practice. You expose and open yourself, and allow and witness all that arises. The conversation was quieter after this.

The next day John and Joseph refused to let us take a bus into New Jersey as if it were a dangerous foreign land. They drove us to the arranged pickup spot, the bus station at the small coastal town of Tom's River, but my brother and Joseph were worried about leaving us alone in this strange parking lot in New Jersey. We told them that we would be fine and not to worry, just as a loud boom box started playing, and we all turned to see three shirtless fat men in their late twenties sort of dancing to the electronically amplified beat of someone's heart in spasm. John and Joseph looked horrified, and we had to really convince them now that we would be safe and that we would call them after we left the quest. We waved goodbye, feeling their worry and relief.

Rob and I had picked our individual sites in a downpour. Now on the first day of the quest, the sky was clearing and I found out where the shade at my site was; it was not where or how I had expected it to be. The splintered sunlight and the dappled shade, the cold night air on my skin and the calls of the whip-poor-wills were simple gestures, expressions moving me beyond other expectations, towards a naked, soft, open mind. There was nothing else to do for four days and nights but simply be here, no food to make, no firewood, no prayers, surrendering, with a tremendous effortless force, an intent quietly opening our hearts, allowing blessings to unfold.

We sat by the pond in the cedar swamp. All around us the grand columns of the cedars held up the vaulted sky of this majestic cathedral, and the cool air moved with the same constant soft rippling as the tannin waters. Rachel and I quietly wrote notes about our quests, trying to remember all the subtle and not so subtle experiences laid upon four days and nights. We rested within the protection of these natural giants and the cool waters, just being with all that had happened and all that was to come.

Vision quest experiences are traditionally seldom spoken about. They are a direct personal knowing, a sacred encounter, sometimes enigmatic, sometimes startlingly vivid in their detail, a transcendent guide to the rest of your life. Slowly, over time we began to share our visions with each other, we were already so thoroughly one life, but today we were letting the experiences settle, allowing the patterns to coalesce.

This had been a long year. We had taken four wilderness skills classes, four shamanic skills classes, a vision quest, and driven or flown back and forth across various parts of the country numerous times, with or without our belongings, and now we were looking for a quiet place to spend the winter.

As we drove into the archetypal western town of Pagosa Springs, we could see a big cloud of steam rising from the spring near the San Juan River. We turned off the main street and parked near a sloping walkway with handrails that led to the heart of the spring enclosed by a tall rusted fence and barbed wire. Even surrounded as it was by fencing, motels, a post office, and a spa, it was still a holy place, a radiant offering, an ageless upwelling of primordial goodness, heat and light, water and fire, pulsing with the energy of molten rock and liquid sky. The blue of this pool, encompassing the very depths from which it came, was not just a vivid vibrant blue; it was a presence as ancient as what we had felt in Arkansas, but the dynamic force of the energy here was to heal. We rented a small cabin west of town for the winter, and the healing spring became our guide. We came often to stand at the railing just being with this presence. There was a shimmering essence here as in our meditation, of light and color penetrating to an experience familiar like an old friend yet still undefined.

SANCTUARY

As we drove east from Pagosa Springs in early May, the passes were still covered with snow. When we arrived in the Pine Barrens a week later, we plunged directly into the moist heat of an East Coast summer that had started early this year, and the first week of a two-week wilderness skills Tracker class. We set up our tent away from all the activity, helped out as needed, and wandered through the area looking for places to build a shelter, getting a good look at the relics of other caretakers' dreams.

After the class left, we got down to building a shelter. We had come across resourceful and sometimes incongruous variations of shelters in our explorations of the area: above ground, below ground, and split-level, a hybrid mix of natural materials, planks, and tarps. We decided to build an underground shelter, and we looked for a site that would drain on all four sides.

Our shelter was completely below ground with a circular area about six feet across with a fire pit, a ledge on one side for storage, and a raised alcove on the other side just large enough for the two of us to sleep. We used fire-killed trees for our roof beams and bark plank mill ends of cedar for the first layer of the roof. For the next layer we heaped debris in a mound with more bark planks over that, and then we buried and contoured the whole area. Because the only way this kind of shelter could really work required a much bigger mound of debris and larger sheets of cedar bark than we could find here, we included a tarp near the upper layer before the final contour of the hill.

There were two openings, one over the fire pit and one over the bed, with a small ladder that could be moved to either one. You could not quite stand up in the main area. The sandy soil was surprisingly damp, and many of our things began to mold, but the airflow was very good, and the earth was cool. We had finished building just before a high-pressure ridge built up over this part of

New Jersey. The temperatures stayed in the upper nineties with ninety-five percent humidity day and night. We were not used to moist heat, and we were happy with the shelter; it was always cool inside. Frogs, toads, lizards, and mice liked it too; we had many visitors.

Early on, we had given up trying to explain to people in the West, or elsewhere, why we were drawn to New Jersey for wilderness experience; you had to be there yourself. Even with the moisture here, the sandy soil and the short gnarled scrub oaks and pitch pines had the look of a dry land. Scattered swamps, creeks, and springs were hidden between random waves of sandy hillocks and knolls, with few real vantage points anywhere. The largest hill, referred to as a mountain because of its unexpected size, was about three hundred feet above sea level, and all you could see from there was an endless ocean of the tops of trees.

It was easy to get lost. Everywhere looked the same, and yet not quite, in a discomforting way. You felt you should be able to recognize where you were, where you had been, and yet there was no easy logic to this land, except in the meandering of waters across the nearly level sands. There were a few straight highways cutting through connecting knowable worlds, but there was an almost desperate quality in the straightness of those roads, in their reliance on an alien order to insure that you could not possibly get lost.

Between the few paved highways, an endless maze of sandy rutted roads and fire breaks wove a no man's land of beer party areas littered with trash, illegal toxic waste sites, abandoned rusted cars, hunters' stands, and surreal landscapes of industrial schemes abandoned and overgrown, sewage disposal beds that were carved out and never used and a vast rectangular area cleared for a dump that had closed down. Off-road vehicles came frequently, sometimes to drain their radiator fluid or oil on the shores of the creeks, sometimes to leave huge bonfires burning out of control as they left. Police came seldom, if at all. You were pretty much on your own. At night, the sky had an eerie glow from the lights at the nuclear power plant nearby, and in the daytime, you could sometimes hear the big guns practicing at Fort Dix. The rawness was in its own way exhilarating, because even with all of this, there was still a pristine presence here, in the remaining cedar groves, cathedrals outside time, in the traces of the grandfathers and grandmothers who walked these lands long ago, in the tannin waters and the medicinal plants, in the animals and the birds that still sought shelter in the natural remoteness of a place that for most people was unnavigable. There was a freedom, outside the boundaries of civilized uses of land, outside concepts of untouched wilderness. The Pine Barrens were just what they were, outside. They were a lot like Tom.

We melted gradually into quiet rhythms for our days, mostly meditating: sitting meditation in our shelter, at the pond, or in the cedar swamp, and slow walking meditation blindfolded. We had experienced in one of Tom's early classes how stalking blindfolded toward the sound of a drum could heighten your natural awareness, your sense of being within this dream fabric of our world. It had been one exercise among many, and now we wanted to focus more on the kind of opening it allowed. We decided to stalk blindfolded along the fire breaks, the narrow sandy ditches used as trails throughout the camp. By relying on their deep slanted sides to guide us instead of a drum, we could both move freely, surrendering to the flowing movements of the slow walk, surrendering to the timelessness hidden behind our eyes.

We mapped out a route that led us to the pond in the cedar swamp, blocking off a few side trails with string so we would not get lost. We would begin after lunch, starting fifteen minutes apart, blindfolding ourselves, and then slowly stalking down the trail. It would usually take about three hours to go all the way to the pond. It was a beautiful way to place your mind. Without the ordinary boundaries maintained by your eyes, you perceived the world in a very different way. Walking blindfolded and moving so slowly shut down all concepts of motion. Flowing and continuous, with no coming or going, no here or there, you became one with all of your experience arising moment by moment. Eventually, moving in this non-moving way, we would feel the moist cool air of the swamp. We would remove our blindfolds, and keeping our eyes in wide-angle vision, we allowed ourselves down to the pond, our minds as vast as space, a knowing that was form in movement, nothing more.

Rachel and I knew that all we wanted to do in this life was spiritual practice, so we had immersed ourselves in a daily schedule of different forms of meditation within the direct experience of the wilderness. It was now the summer of 1994, and we had been wandering for some time. Our families were more and more puzzled by our choices, and we made an effort to both look normal and explain ourselves to people, especially our mothers, in an understandable, relevant, and responsible way. I usually kept my hair and beard well trimmed, and we put on nice clean clothes when we went to town.

I washed down the truck as best I could, and then we made our way along the sand roads out of camp toward the main highway. It was a non-stop undulating, sometimes roller-coaster type of ride. Driving quickly, avoiding deep pits filled with water, trying not to stop on the soft sand, we reached the highway and drove to a nearby park, a very clean and orderly parking lot, a bathroom and pay phone, and a perfectly manicured lawn. It was a strange place, and there was usually no one there. I called my mother first, and while I was involved in making the odd and strange seem responsible and normal to my mother, Rachel was getting nervous, covertly watching the security guard slowly drive through the parking lot eyeing our truck and us. Being a pit dweller in New Jersey on a spiritual journey and trying not to be noticed, I got off the phone, and Rachel told me about the security guard who had been watching us, coming by several times. As Rachel called her mom, I nervously tried to act normal.

The security guard drove up again, but this time he got out of his patrol car and started walking toward us. He seemed old for this kind of job, and there was a cloud over him. He wandered around the bathroom area but then came up to me. I looked at him and he said, "Are you a priest?" I said, "No I'm not, but I pray." He began telling me all about a great sadness that had befallen him. His wife had suddenly left him and was going to divorce him, and his children had stopped talking to him. He had also lost his job of many years and had recently become a security guard.

I could sense he was not an alcoholic, and I could not see anything that had made his wife and children leave him. He actually seemed to be a very sensitive man. I spoke to him in a way I thought he might understand, saying that God is not neutral, he may want you to begin a new life, a spiritual life. His actions may seem harsh, but it pushes us into new spiritual territory that can benefit others. He listened to me and was thinking over what I said. He finally asked if we would pray for him. I said we would, and he smiled and walked away. Rachel had finished talking to her mom, and we drove back to our camp.

The high-pressure ridge held for most of the summer. The days and nights were always hot. We sat in meditation in the mornings; we walked blindfolded in the afternoons, always moving toward the blessings of the cool tannin waters.

Blueberries were in season all around the swamp. Every bush had berries with a slightly different flavor. We had favorite bushes, favorite vintages. We ate blueberries right off the bush, and we cooked them in pancakes. We walked, we sat, we swam, we ate blueberries, moving within a summertime that was innocent and generous like the summer days of a child.

Now the summer was subtly turning to autumn. Maybe it was the angle of the light and sensing the birds and animals preparing for winter, or maybe it was the deciduous plants turning slightly less green, but we knew we had to do something for the winter ourselves. We continued practicing and waited for a sign.

In only a few days, people would start showing up at the camp to prepare for another class. We walked down to the cedar creek without blindfolds, along the familiar trail to the water, into the cool atmosphere of the cedar swamp and onto the raised walkway. We slowly entered what was always here, a holiness, and we were just another aspect of the presence of this sacred spot. We came to the end of the small dock at the place where the creek widened out into the pond and started across the narrow walkway to the other side. We stopped on this small bridge close above the water, immersed in the ageless quality of the cedars, the moist air, and the clear, amber tannin creek flowing imperceptibly.

We saw a painted turtle swimming downstream underwater on the far side of the pond. As we touched the turtle with our eyes, the turtle seemed to become aware of us, turned around and began swimming very slowly toward us, coming closer and closer. We were held motionless in the steady approach of this wonder that finally came directly beneath us. We looked down on the other side of the bridge to see the turtle emerge, and right below our feet, in a shaft of sunlight, the turtle stopped, holding upright inside the water as if standing erect, stretching arms and legs and head far out beyond the shell. We could see the pale soft golden color of the under shell and the bright red and yellow lines on the upper shell and the outspread arms and legs and the head. Ever so slowly, suspended in a primal grace of pure reverence, the turtle's head began to lift, cutting softly through the surface of the water, and with closed eyes in full sunlight, the turtle took a single breath. It was a timeless gesture of rapture, the passion of surrendering, of being water, breath, and air, of being holy radiance and sunlight, of being communion itself simply as you are. Then the turtle slowly slid beneath the surface and swam upstream, as we watched with tears in our eyes.

CAUTERY

We headed west again; we had no sense of place yet, for where we needed or wanted to be. We stayed with friends and house sat. We were wandering and camping, following our hearts. A buffalo stood a few inches from our truck, with steamy breath condensing in the early morning air. The buffalo's head filled the window on the driver's side, his huge eye like a deep opening into space. From the grand overlook at Island of the Sky, Utah, we fell with our eyes through an immensity of distance, a sheer drop, miles high, miles wide, toward the Green River meandering across a surface as far away as the moon. We sat quietly with the lush autumn growth of water plants in a small forgotten campground at the end of a long dirt road beside a rushing creek. We listened entranced to the shimmering tapping sounds of yellow cottonwoods along the Yellowstone River. The temperature dropped below freezing that night, and as we walked around the empty campground the next morning, the sun rose above the mountains to the east, filling the cottonwood canopy. The trees were enormous yellow globes of light dazzling in the cold autumn air. Then a few yellow leaves fell, then a few more, again and again, until the sun released a cascade of gold, golden cottonwood leaves fluttering and flickering all around us. There was nothing anywhere but these yellow gold pieces of grace filling the air.

The turtle swam upstream after taking its reverent surrendering breath, that was clearly how and where we were to go, but which breath, and which way, leads us upstream?

Francesco throws bolts of his father's very expensive silks and brocades out the window of a medieval tower to the crowds below, yelling to them to give everything away as the streams of cloth unfurl in the air.

A thin line of hot wax entered the fabric defining the turtle drawn on the front of a tee shirt. The pot of wax simmered on the floor between us as we dipped our hollow tools into the clear liquid and continued a line. The reservoir on the tube held not quite enough each time; we were picking up where we left off again, it was part of the charm, the look of batik. Our money was running out. We were making hand-painted, hand-dyed, batik tee shirts as a way to sustain our simple searching life.

Two tortured bare feet step along a path of rock and snow and up a rough scaffolding. Francesco carries another stone to build the wall of his church. A crusader, an old friend of his, stands beneath him, speaking of his dissatisfaction with war and life, wishing for a life that had meaning and purpose. Francesco looks at him and says that he once believed in words.

The turtle came alive as we painted the rainbow colors held within the channels of cool wax. The turtle's shell was like a stained glass window, alive and opening into another life. The blue butterfly on the turtle's back was inseparable from the shell, the sky blue wings of the butterfly were an illuminated bodily form of radiance itself.

We painted a two-legged deer with tiny dots of light pouring from her heart, two rainbow trout forming a circle together, a buffalo with ascending rays and rainbows, eagles, hawks, ravens, mice and spirit tracks. We worked through the winter creating these expressions of spiritual union in nature, having given it all away and needing to offer again another gesture. The snow and the freezing temperatures outside enclosed us in the farmhouse we were house sitting, enfolding us in another step on our trail, another dynamic revealing and expressing to us and to those who would eventually receive a shirt.

Francesco moves slowly in anguished rapture through layers and layers of newly dyed cloth hanging all around him at his father's dye works. Slashes of red, blue, green, and yellow stains cover his clothes, his face, and his hair as he moves through the veils.

Spring weather burst open for a while inside wintertime. The sunlit air was suddenly warm and vibrant. Bright-colored shirts hanging in long lines outside rippled in the wind, rows and rows of offerings, the rainbow images, the deep reds, blues, and greens of the shirts and the flashing, spinning air woven together as a single prayer.

"Look at the birds. They neither sow, nor reap, nor store in barns, yet our Heavenly Father feedeth them." Francesco entreats the Pope, having suffered in his own passion, a passion asking and crying to the world around him, why? Why can't we be as the birds and be content with this sacred unfolding wonder, why do we confound the offering with demands for more, denying the sacred and accumulating, storing, hoarding, and controlling beyond the simple offering of this sacred vision?

We have made hundreds of offerings, boxes of prayers.

A large flock of rosy finches appeared at our birdfeeder outside the kitchen window. The reddish pink, golden brown, and gray brocade of their feathers made a rich tapestry of birds fluttering, hovering, and feeding everywhere. We had just emptied out our last big bag of birdseed on the ground beneath the feeder as we packed up to move again, and the first birds to find our offering were these rosy jewels, whose other life was in the arctic or above timberline on mountaintops.

We drove into town to return the video of the life of Saint Francis, *Brother Sun, Sister Moon*, for the last time. Then we packed up another trailer and pulled another load of our hearts back to New Mexico, to wait, to pray to embody what we longed for.

It was a hot, dusty imprisoned day. We had been parked near the beginning of a long line of venders waiting in their vehicles for the flea market manager to open the gates so we could pay our booth fee and set up our tent. This was the peak season at the Santa Fe flea market, and you had to arrive early before the parking lot gate opened. At eight a.m. the manager would open the gates and you again lined up, a rag-tag bunch of trucks, hippie buses, moving vans, old school buses, flatbed trucks and campers, with a sprinkling of sedans and top of the line RV's. Here we waited until maybe four p.m. or maybe later in the hot sun and dust. We had brought our books, food, and water; we had covered the windows with reflective survival blankets; we made ourselves as comfortable as possible and waited.

By four o'clock the line had grown and snaked around the parking lot and out again onto the highway. In some animal kind of way, you knew he had opened up and was selling booth tickets, but it was like being stuck in traffic on an LA freeway; you would drive five feet and stop, then two feet, always watching the engine getting hotter. By the time you got to the manager, you would be completely grateful and so happy to receive your colored ribbons that represented the days you had rented. You were free to go beyond one mile an hour; it was almost more than you could handle, so exhilarating driving down the long empty lines that would be filled with venders and shoppers the following day.

We would head for our favorite row and set up our booth next to a nice retired couple from Albuquerque. We were all happy to see each other as we busily set up our tent. It was now about six p.m. We had been at this for twelve hours. The next morning we would arrive early, set up our rack, and display our tee shirts all around our booth, and after everything was arranged, we would sit down and wait.

The Santa Fe flea market was on a dry plateau just north of town, a barren plain, very windy in the afternoon. It was an upscale event, with expensive jewelry in glass front display cases, boutiques of designer clothing with full-length mirrors, galleries with work by contemporary artists and craftsmen, antiques and fine oriental rugs, all in tents. For added ambience, there was also a diverse assortment of dream catchers, batiks, beads, garden statuary, sunglasses, hats, hand tools, household appliances that need some repair, couches, tables, silverware, handmade leather moccasins, photographs, reprints of cowboy art, used books, polished rocks, stained glass, beds, potted plants, wrought iron, roasted nuts, buttons, old shoes, objects from nature, whatever else people had found in the back of their closet or garage that weekend that they decided to sell, and tee shirts. And of all the vendors, the tee shirt people and their wares, either hand-painted or machine-screened, were the lowest of the low.

We had worked hard all winter; we had hundreds of tee shirts. Why did we do this? Do we remember now? Everyone wears tee shirts; we had placed our offerings on shirts for people to wear close to their hearts, a reminder of the sacredness of this entire dream, but as the weekends pass, we are realizing we are here in this hot dry dusty place simply because we are. There are easier ways to make a marginal income.

The flea market was the last big grinding stop along our odyssey, the place where we would wear down, for once and for all, any last hope of resuming any kind of identity congruent with normal life. We had a vision, an experience, and we were trying to bring it into our life as best we could. We did not really know yet what the turtle in the Pine Barrens had been showing us, but we knew it was important and specific, and we were waiting for the meaning to unfold.

There were several distinct neighborhoods at the flea market. The vendors with large permanent booths, the jewelers and the boutiques with mirrors, were all in the front near the entrance. In the middle of the long rows leading out across the plain, temporary vendors set up small single or double booths each week. It was a hassle, but at least we all had shade. The far end of each row was like a parking lot, open to the sun and wind, with people selling their wares from the tailgate of a truck, or the backseat of a car, or a blanket on the ground. Everyone had a favorite row and a different strategy about the best places to be, in the middle, to the left or right, closer to or farther away from certain other categories of merchandise.

Over the weeks, we always seemed to set up near the same vendors. We all liked each other, and were happy to see each other, chatting as we assembled our booths. The friendliness helped offset the inevitable weekly uncertainty of our financial situations, and sometimes when the pace was very slow, we went around to each other's booths to commiserate.

People passed before us coming from both directions. The little tents lined up next to each other precluded our view; we only saw a twenty-foot strip of people but we were hearing a crowd of thousands. We were sitting, we had been sitting since early this morning, and we would continue to sit. We each had books to read, comforting in the hand, but we had settled into our meditation and only occasionally read. We would read a few lines from Rumi or Ramakrishna, or *Mysticism* or *The Philokalia,* and then we would lay the book down. We were sitting with humanity pouring by in a strange flood moving both ways. We could not get stuck on any one person or group for they flowed by too quickly. We would nod a bit and bring ourselves back, gripping our books tighter. We could not hold to the sounds; it was all the crowd. No one was stopping by so the idea we were selling tee shirts fell away. We just sat; we could not allow ourselves to react to our aching butts for there were still another four hours to go. We sat waiting; we sat forgotten and forgetting. We sat hot, we sat cold, we sat hungry, and we sat crabby. Sometimes we looked at each other and just started laughing, it was so ludicrous, and sometimes we sat and looked at each other and wanted to cry. Is today Rumi's poem about the winemaker, the grapes surrendering to the trampling, or is it the passage from the *Bhagavad Gita* about burning with the bliss and sorrows of all beings within your heart, or is it the nothingness at the top of the mountain of Saint John of the Cross? Rachel and I could find ourselves selling a shirt and being asked for change, and we could not count. Once I just couldn't; I just wanted to sit, and a woman made me give her change. I was going to round it off or let her have the shirt, but she made me count. I sat back down. Sometimes you can have a headache too. The sun was setting; it was the end of our third day of sitting in waiting.

Occasionally a few people would emerge out of the flow, come inside our booth and become particular: skinny people, fat people, wealthy people looking for deals, less affluent people just looking, teenage kids in love walking hip to hip with their hands in each other's back pockets, or tourists with sunglasses and cameras with only a few hours before their bus goes on to Albuquerque. They all looked around and then they left. A few people would buy, sometimes enthusiastically, sometimes more than one shirt. A woman who had bought a shirt with a fish on it a week ago returned. She wore her shirt in her yoga class, it was the best shirt she had ever found for yoga, and she wanted two more. A husband and wife stopped by. They had seen someone wearing one of our shirts in a sweat lodge in the Pecos. They liked the images, but they left without buying.

Other people came by just to talk. We had never seen them before, but they would tell us their lives: their boyfriend left or they were going to leave their wife, they wanted a new career, or their mother was ill. They were not asking for advice. We were just there, witnessing, listening as they found their own way through their feelings and their thoughts. Then they left, sometimes with a shirt, more often not.

We had made equal numbers of dark green, dark blue, and dark red shirts. The green ones sold out first, then many of the blue. We had a lot of red shirts left. A woman with two small kids went through almost every shirt on the rack, then said, "You have too many red shirts," as she left. A few hours later, another woman came into the booth. She was looking for red shirts, to send to a friend who was a Tibetan monk. She liked the turtle with the blue butterfly on the shell, and the deer with the fan of tiny white dots radiating from her heart. She bought them both, in red. She came back in a few weeks. She had sent the shirts express to her Tibetan friend while he was in Switzerland at the peace talks there. He and the others in his group had loved the shirts.

In a small gap between two of the shirts hanging on the side of the booth, I could see part of a man wearing a dark red robe coming rapidly up the row. I motioned to Rob, and suddenly a middle-aged Tibetan lama with an angular face was standing in front of our booth. Rob spontaneously made a praying gesture with his hands and nodded. The lama returned the gesture and apparently, with wordless signs, asked if he could cut through the booth to the next row. We said yes, and then he walked through our booth, out the back and disappeared. We had pulled our truck up to the back of the booth leaving a walkway only on one side, but the lama had gone out on the other side into a narrow crack too small to pass through. He left a kind of vibrating energy, a tangible trace, and we sat there quietly in his wake. It was a sign; we were getting closer to an opening, but it was not quite time yet.

Sometimes the weekends at the flea market had a strange stillness. We had found ourselves in our own desert trying to survive, and as we sat waiting as we had done so many weekends now, we knew we needed to be here, we knew we were waiting, and we knew our hearts called us to remain. But the day wore on and on; no one had bought a shirt. We had a few dollars in our wallets and just enough in the bank to cover the rent. Why did we abide in this nightmare of uncertainty? We had never intended to wander for almost four years. Why did we leave our careers and land? The hours ticked by, the wind picked up. In the late afternoon, there would sometimes be the threat of a thunderstorm, but most of the time the dust blew along the feet walking by. People came in, looked through the shirts, praised them and blamed them and moved on, leaving us to the constant flood of feet. Were we waiting for people to make us a success, our hearts said no. We remained watching the crowds and our hearts. We had to wait through the days and weeks with no knowing left. We had to abide in our uncertainty, or we were lost. We knew where to search and how to find certainty, but we remained as the hours became days. We would pack and resume our vigil the next day, driving, eating, sleeping, driving back again. We sat, or did time stand still? The feet kept moving and our uncertainty remained. Where were we really but with our uncertainty, waiting for nothing. There is that strange elongated feeling as you wait for the sun to rise, but in the embrace of the Earth and the breath of the sky the sun has already risen. There was nothing to wait for as we embraced our uncertainty and breathed in our waiting. A long day was passing with countless feet as someone appeared looking through our shirts, one, two shirts on their arm, a third, looking, deciding, a fourth and then a fifth, a smile and a thank you, along with our uncertainty.

CIRCLING IN

My mother was in the center bed of a shadowy, high-ceilinged, three-bed room at the care center. The blinds were closed to keep out the fierce heat on the west side of the building in the afternoon. The other beds were empty. On the chest of drawers across from the foot of her bed was her TV. This narrow slot of territory was now her world; she would be living in between the narrow territories of others in one room or another for the rest of her life. She had held out as long as she could, but Rob and I had been called down to Phoenix to move her from her apartment to the care center at her retirement community.

Behind the neurological mask that Parkinson's syndrome was slowly imposing on her face, she seemed bitter, bewildered, and betrayed, betrayed by her own body no longer willing to connect with her mind, betrayed by all the props she had clung to all her life, and betrayed by doctors whose medications she never trusted. The summer Olympics were on TV, and precisely at this moment, as I stood beside her bed, both of us feeling helpless about her situation in so many ways, Mohammed Ali heroically with faltering, courageous steps, carried the Olympic torch up a few almost insurmountable steps. My mother did not see.

Driving back from Phoenix, we were overwhelmed by the way our culture deals with old age and death. Rachel's cousins had talked about how we were all going to end up like Rachel's mom, as if they were taking comfort in believing that they would also end up in a care facility, debilitated and slowly losing their minds, all in an inevitable, secure hospital-like environment. We had made our lives so uncertain, stripped away all the supports of a normal life; it was almost too much to listen to her cousins' talk. It was difficult and even painful to embrace uncertainty. We were feeling the heaviness of our waiting, the weight of our path, the ache and the longing. We were looking for a different security, and in a different way.

By accident, we came across a copy of Suzi Gablik's new book, *Conversations Before the End of Time*. We were surprised to find our conversation of years past now part of a larger dialogue with other voices such as Leo Castelli and Hilton Kramer, James Hillman, Thomas Moore, and Theodore Rosak. It was truly strange after four years to hold a book that was engendered in some part by our actions and to touch on that time in our lives again. We still believed in what we said that night, but in a quieter way. We had changed, grown, and let go of so much, and our journey was far from over. We put the book aside and kept going.

A few weeks later, we heard from some friends who were opening a store in Durango, Colorado, and wanted to sell our shirts. When we delivered the shirts the area seemed vigorous and buoyant, revitalizing after our experiences in Phoenix. We wanted to spend time in retreat, so we looked for an inexpensive place there to rent for the winter, feeling that somewhere within the prayers of retreat we would receive a sign or a direction. We answered an ad about a trailer for lease in a small town north of Durango. The trailer was set apart from the owner's house, with open land, trees, and green pastures all around and the whole area was rimmed by tall mountains. It was quiet, simple, and cheap enough. When the owner said he only offered five-month leases, we knew that this was the right amount of time. We felt that this was a confirmation along the path, and we looked forward to a winter in the high country again, to the resourceful inwardness that cold temperatures and the purity of snow can bring.

As we settled into our retreat, we established a daily rhythm of meditating before and after breakfast, studying and reading after lunch, and meditating again in the evenings. The Durango library had a good collection of books on various spiritual paths, and there was a good bookstore in town. We read Rumi, Saint John of the Cross, *Mysticism* by Evelyn Underhill, Laurens Van der Post's *The Seed and the Sower*, and several books by Thich Nhat Hanh; as usual we were looking for clues. One of the most compelling clues we found was a portion of Chogyam Trungpa's commentary on the various visionary states in his introduction to *The Tibetan Book of the Dead*. Throughout our lives, these kinds of visionary experiences had arisen for us. We had found a few references to them in the lives of various saints, mystics, yogis, and shamans, and now, here was a doorway that resonated with our hearts; we recognized something familiar, the visions of the luminosity.

Rachel and I had gone to town on errands. At the Durango Library, I opened a book to a two-page photograph of a Tibetan Buddhist yogi meditating in a simple mud-walled cave. I knew this was an indication of our path, a spiritual practice in the wilderness, a memory revisited: the uncontrived simplicity of the earthen-walled shelter with a shelf carved into the clay wall for firewood, a small place to cook with some food stored nearby. The roof was a piece of corrugated steel, and the front wall was a tarp. I left this book along with a stack of others in the truck and went on an errand. While I was away, Rachel returned to the truck. She had finished her errands and sat in the truck looking through the books. She too landed on this photograph, and when I returned she excitedly showed me this picture saying, "Did you see this?!"

When we got home, we looked at the photograph again together, noticing the details, the yogi's simple tins of food, a few eggs, and a small sack of rice, the earthen walls, and the firewood. The earthen walls were clearly the most compelling part; we recognized something there. In the figure of the yogi sitting in his cave, we saw something else that went beyond the photograph, something we recognized deep in ourselves, a presence, an inward translucent focus, quiet, plain, like a stone that has been tossed and has found its place in a luminous depth, that has found the source of its rings. But we both knew as we looked at his shaven head that we did not want to cut off our hair.

The photo of the yogi was touching a memory within us: a way and a place where the wilderness and the luminosity could come together.

In late winter, a Tracker friend called us and asked if we would house-sit his place in Placerville, California, while it was for sale. He needed us to come at the beginning of March, which would be when our five-month lease would end. The timing was perfect, and we had a strong feeling that we were getting closer to something; the invitation to move back to California carried a sense of fulfillment and an opening.

Rob and I stood by the window in the dim light of the closed venetian blinds in the hospital room in Phoenix. The nurse standing nearby had just told us how much it helped patients to have family around, when behind us my mother let out a long deep wailing "Noooooo!" The three of us turned around to see her raised up partially in the bed. Her arms were stretched out straight in the air in front of her, and her hands were limp. It was as if an invisible energy was pulling her to sit up in the bed by her wrists. She wailed "Noooooo!" again. She had been hospitalized for a hairline pelvic fracture from a fall. She could barely move in bed without pain, and now the upper part of her body was raised up from the bed with no support and she was motionless, except for her cries.

I went to her and wrapped my arms around her shoulders. I could feel Rob holding me. My mother's arms were still outstretched and taunt, her hands limp. She was held in a dialogue with her memories. Another nurse came in; they called for the neurologist, for a stronger sedative. My mother did not know that any of us were there; she was in her own world, alone with her vivid images, and as I held her, I heard myself calling out "Mommy" in a voice that startled me.

The nurses arrived with the sedative. We watched my mother slowly relax, sinking deeper and deeper into a remote peace, growing softer and younger as the sedative took hold. Her mask and the familiar underlying thoughts and feelings drained from her face until she was resting on the shore of a deep dreamless sleep. Her face was suddenly very beautiful, her nose, her cheek, the curve of her lips, revealed a loveliness that had been hidden all these years inside the overlay of responses of who she thought she was.

That evening I called a friend in Santa Fe, and when I told her what we had experienced, especially in my mother's face, she suggested we read *The Tibetan Book of Living and Dying* by Sogyal Rinpoche. She said a friend of hers who was involved in hospice work back East found it very helpful.

The snowflakes of blessings fall in countless ways. They fall not only in moments of quiet wonderment and grace; they fall also in the midst of the heat of confusion and pain of our own and others' lives. Blessings connect with other blessings, forming endless links of intent in the way we accept what is offered, through the choices we make.

As we began to pack up once again to move to Placerville, we once again made offerings. All through our wandering and our waiting, we had given things away, and we had acquired new things and given many of them away too. Now we shipped batik banners and quilts we had made during our tee shirt career to an AIDS hospice in Santa Fe. Then we heard about a woman in Durango who was opening a thrift store to raise money for a no-kill animal shelter, and for Elliot we offered special treasures for the opening of the store, things we had held onto through the years, and other things that had come to us more recently, including some treasures from Rachel's mother to link her to the blessings of this giving too. By the time we left for Placerville, we were down to whatever essentials fit in the low camper shell on the back of our truck, and the no-kill shelter thrift store had opened with a reputation for good stuff.

There was an air of expectancy, of something positive arising as we tried to settle into another new place. The first week we were in Placerville, we went to a local bookstore and found a copy of the *Tibetan Book of Living and Dying* by Sogyal Rinpoche. We were both very touched by the quotes from mystics of many traditions and the chapters on the Innermost Essence and Intrinsic Radiance. We knew we had found what we had been looking for in his description of the path of Trekchö/Tögal. So many of our experiences were confirmed in his descriptions of the practice of the luminosity, the clear light, we were joyous.

We called the Rigpa center in San Francisco. Sogyal Rinpoche would be giving a weekend teaching on *The Way of the Bodhisattva* in the Bay Area in three weeks. We signed up for the class. He would also be speaking a week later at another center in northern California. We called them and signed up for this weekend too, and asked the woman on the phone if she could send us something about their group.

A few days later, we received a thick manila envelope from Rigdzin Ling filled with all kinds of newsletters, brochures, and pictures detailing the activities of their founder Chagdud Tulku Rinpoche, with a little post-it note saying, "I don't know why, but I'm sending you all of this." We went through everything in the packet carefully, and the image that really stood out for us was a very small photograph of a western lama sitting with a child. The man's face was hard to see in the small photograph, but we both said to each other, "If he teaches we could learn from him."

We took Sogyal Rinpoche's class in Berkeley. In our practice in the wilderness and in letting go of our land, we had felt a strong purpose outside of self, and so we felt a resonance with the way of the bodhisattva, but we knew that our connection lay with another teacher. A week later, we again received teachings from Sogyal Rinpoche, this time at the local school auditorium in a small historic gold mining town near the Gonpa, as Rigdzin Ling was called. We stayed at the center and drove into town for the teachings.

The woman we had spoken with over the phone had said that the Gonpa was still pretty raw, but they had a large Guru Rinpoche statue and a few stupas, and they were trying to settle in. There were photos of road graders and bulldozers in the newsletters, and we were expecting a stark construction site. We were surprised and charmed as we approached the office on a narrow woodland drive, catching sight of prayer flags high up in the trees, moss-covered shingled roofs, and the glowing pastels of rhododendron flowers in full bloom in the shadows of the tall trees. We checked in and received a small map of the grounds, and as we drove further up the narrow driveway on our way toward the camping area, the landscape suddenly opened out and we got our first look at "moonland."

The rest of the Gonpa was on the site of an old placer mine, in the huge hollow gaping space where the side of a thickly forested mountain had been carved away. The barren hill beside the campground and the much taller red cliffs behind the main building with its brightly colored Tibetan-style roof connected a curve of Earth no longer here. Only the sterile shattered and crushed gray cinder rock of the excavated mining floor remained. The people at the Gonpa were working hard to reclaim portions of this damaged land, but clearly it would take many more years of effort to knit the islands of green lawns and flower beds, the statue, the red-roofed buildings, the empty pond, and the long rows of prayer flags into a nurturing whole.

We pitched our tent and went back to the office to see if we could help out. The office was more crowded now. The resident staff and other people who had arrived early for the weekend teachings and were also helping out were friendly but very busy coordinating all the activities and logistics for a large event. As new people arrived, we were all folded into the general flow of tasks to be done, a pattern that seemed well established here, part family, part small town, part community college, part work camp. The level of commotion was intense, but there was another feeling, in the silent presence of the tall fir trees on the forested slopes of the wilderness that surrounded the Gonpa on all sides, that we were at last coming to something we had been slowly remembering our whole lives, in the opportunity to connect with the Dzogchen teachings again. The long trail we had been following was approaching home.

We walked over to the shrine room very early the next day before puja, the daily morning practice, was to begin. A thick fog enveloped the land. The dark green forest all around the edges of moonland had melted away. No one else was at the shrine room. We removed our shoes and went inside to sit for a while. The almost bewildering play of colors, decorative designs, and vigorous imagery was held suspended within the soft silence and the early light.

Someone came in and began to empty the water-offering bowls on the shrine as we sat. The rhythmic sound of the water being poured into a bucket from one bowl after another in the long line had a holiness of its own, another kind of prayer blending with the spacious stillness of the dawn.

A second person arrived, sat down at one of the big gong-like hanging drums and began a series of chants in a low rapid voice punctuated by a smaller hand drum.

The sky began to clear and the pace of the day sped up dramatically at breakfast time. The soft silence of the fog and the water's prayers in the early light receded into the background of a busy weekend. Even the shrine room would be crowded for pujas the next few days.

The teachings began in the evening. Sogyal Rinpoche's topic for this weekend was caring for the dying from the Dzogchen perspective, emphasizing the futility of grasping and the need for letting go to reach an open, sky-like mind. He ended the evening with a question to ask ourselves overnight, what are you here for? We found ourselves also asking our hearts whether we wanted to live here.

His teachings were confirmations of the resonance we had felt reading his book, but what drew our attention this time was his introduction of Lama Drimed, the western man in the small photograph.

That night we asked to speak with Lama Drimed, who, we had learned, was Chagdud Rinpoche's successor and head of Rigdzin Ling. We introduced ourselves, and he said that he had noticed us at the morning pujas and the teachings. He had a soft voice and a laid-back manner that was both friendly and reserved at the same time, but it was soon clear that as Lupon or head of the Gonpa he held a level of control over the lives of the residents there that was surprising. A young woman interrupted our interview to ask if she could go to return some of the equipment rented for the weekend. She said she wanted to spend the night and come back the next day. The lama asked her who she was going to go with. She gave a man's name and blushed. The lama paused for a long moment, and then said it was fine. She looked pleased and a bit flustered and left.

We told him of our experiences with the light, and how we were drawn to Trekchö/Tögal, the path of the luminosity. He said that our subtle bodies were very open and that we had already done a lot of work. We asked if we could live at the Gonpa, and he said yes. He said that the energy here might feel coarse to us, that Chagdud Rinpoche was coming soon to spend the summer and that while he was here it would be a busy, active place, but the winter would be much quieter. We told him that what we really wanted was to be in retreat. He said that people usually wait for a while before going into retreat, but he added, "I can tell you I have looked everywhere, and there is nothing else like the Dzogchen teachings."

The weekend we were at the Gonpa the real estate agents found a buyer for our friend's house. We had called friends in California when we arrived in Placerville, telling them we had returned from our wanderings and would be staying in touch. Now we were going away again, on another kind of journey.

A Circle Is Drawn

RETREAT

The Gonpa was in turmoil when we came back to stay. Rinpoche was in the midst of a medical crisis; he would not be coming up from Brazil this summer, and the lama was in retreat. Everyone was in a state of upheaval. There were extra practices for Rinpoche's health and elaborate preparations for the two drubchens, the ceremonial group practice events that were going to be held as planned even in Rinpoche's absence, on top of all the daily activities involved in running a busy dharma center. We worked in the kitchen and on the construction of the new stupas.

A little over a month had passed. On the morning of the summer solstice, five years to the day since a full-length article on our decision to give up everything to live life as a prayer appeared on the front page of the Santa Fe New Mexican, we asked the lama if we could speak with him. The three of us sat under the tall fir trees not far from the entrance to the shrine room; we told him we wanted to be in retreat. He said we were certainly ready but there were no cabins available. We told him that we knew how to build a simple underground shelter and that we had lived in one in the Pine Barrens. The lama was enthusiastic and said, "Yes, do it!" He suggested places for us to look for sites above the Gonpa. He also said we were ready to receive the Dzogchen teachings, although we would have to complete the preliminary practices first.

We were overjoyed to be going into retreat at last. During the coming weeks, we searched the mountain when we could get the time. The land was very steep, and it was hard to find a small knoll that shed water on all four sides. We finally found a site, a twenty-five-minute hike uphill from the Gonpa, on a small, nearly level terrace of mostly madrone and fir. Through the screen of trees growing on the steeper slope below and the tall trunks of trees closer around us, the gray and brown furrowed columns of Douglas fir and the curving red-barked muscular shapes of madrone, we could see small patches of brightness from the sky and the narrow river valley farther below. It was not exactly an overlook, but there was a gentler opening here, a place where we felt the elementals were inviting us to stay, and we prayed for this land and our retreat, feeling a sense of blessing, an auspicious warmth surrounding us. We explored further, and a quarter mile down an old deer trail we found a hidden area along a small creek that had escaped the damage of the mining and logging years, a healing fertile place with stands of horsetail, wild ginger, and other medicinal plants under grand old moss-covered maples and oaks where we could go for water each day.

We moved up the mountain in mid-August right after a week of empowerments and teachings for the preliminary practices, pitched a small backpacking tent, and started digging. We dug down two and half feet when we hit a hard layer of shale, so we modified our design and built a pit dwelling instead, half in and half out of the earth. The circular hole was fourteen feet across. In the center we set four posts, seven feet apart and seven feet high, joined with more beams, creating a square frame with a tapering chimney shape above. We laid long peeled poles against the frame in a circle, making a low teepee shape that extended three feet past the excavated area on all sides. Then we tacked peeled branches around the outside of the poles, making a kind of basket, leaving a smoke hole in the center. As in the Pine Barrens, there was no supply of appropriate bark here to use for the roof, so we added a layer of black plastic. We bermed the outside with all the earth we had dug out of the hole and heaped a thick layer of fallen leaves, twigs, and small branches over the earth. We had built a cave.

Inside the protective insulating layers of forest debris and earth there was always a soft light from the smoke hole during the day, and in the warm glow of candle light, the peeled poles were like golden rays pouring down from the center of the roof. Even the black plastic had a beauty then, like the night sky showing between the branches and the beams. The air moved through the space from two small, screened openings above the door up to the smoke hole and later a screened cupola. It was a tight fit but we had room for a shrine, a cot-like bed for each of us to sleep and practice on, an earthen shelf all around to store our belongings in plastic bins, and eventually a tiny woodstove in the center with just enough space on either side to do prostrations. It was comfortable enough, shed rain, and held the steady temperatures of the earth: cool in summer, warm in winter, never dropping below fifty-two degrees. In order to keep our animal and insect house guests to a minimum, we cooked under a tarp a good distance away. Beyond our future woodstove, the only modern convenience in the shelter was a four-foot-tall hinged door. The round domed shape with a low entryway to the east reminded us of the turtle in the Pine Barrens. We were home.

Soon after we moved into the shelter in late September, it began to rain, the beginning of a hundred-year El Niño winter of exceptionally heavy rainfall. On a drizzly foggy morning, we hiked down to the Gonpa to get supplies. As we crossed the open space near the stupas, we caught sight of the lama's truck rounding the curve. He stopped, and we chatted for a while about the rain. We asked him if it usually tapered off by April, but he said, "Well, then there's May." We let that sink in, then we told him about our experience with the turtle, and the reverent gesture of its breath, and afterward we all rested in a vast space listening to the soft sounds of the light rain. After a while he said, "I don't think I ever asked you if you have any money to live on." We told him we had sold our truck to buy food for the winter, and he said that he had a sponsor for us. It was all coming together, the blessings of a long road leading us into a life in deep retreat.

We knew that this retreat was our way to the Dzogchen teachings on luminous awareness and the visions of inner radiance. Here was our avenue to the sacred where we could open within the heart of the Earth. It was a place of return, a place to nourish ourselves, to delve within and allow ourselves to open to the heart essence.

We were grateful we had taken the time to learn traditional ways of living with the Earth, embracing the knowledge that we are one with the Earth and we could abide with her, letting go of the fear that holds contemporary man apart. We felt a freedom within our daily lives from knowing we were an aspect of this natural wholeness, something the yogis of old who practiced in the wilderness or charnel grounds would have been familiar with since childhood.

We were still confronted by the growing catastrophe of our modern world; the solitude and practice only made us more sensitive to it. It was close by, in the ongoing reverberation of trucks, cars, and motorcycles echoing along the highway on the other side of the river in this narrow valley, a constant reminder of the pounding suffering of our times.

The word "retreat" can be misleading. Withdrawal, defeat and avoidance of difficulty or danger are all listed first in the dictionary before the meanings of seclusion, reflection and prayer, and none of these definitions come close to evoking the dynamic, intense process that true retreat entails. The term "cloister" is perhaps a better choice: an enclosed sacred space as a destination and the suggestion of movement within that enclosure along a passageway, a commitment in time as well as place for a total spiritual transformation. But the aura of ordained monastic rule does not quite fit with the equally committed but outwardly different lives of yogi lay practitioners, so retreat was the word that had come most easily into use here, for the immense and sometimes difficult grace of this path.

It was understood that our boundaries for retreat were to stay "in" for as long as it took to reach the fruition of the path. We rarely left the Gonpa, except for a few teachings and for medical emergencies. There was a tangible support in the energetic bond with our place in this land, the knoll, the shelter, the creek, the trail we took to get water, and with our practice, a visceral elastic force, an intention to recognize. There was a support of another kind in the sameness and simplicity of the days, boundaries in time as well as space. We would get up very early before dawn for a full practice session before breakfast, have a second long session before lunch, do a few chores after lunch as needed, then another session in the late afternoon, followed by a light meal and a longer session into the night, finishing with special practices as you go to sleep. We would rise early and begin again, with no vacations, no holidays, no weekends, and no days off.

This was the basic schedule of our days, but there is a fine art to shaping your practice in retreat as there is in meditation itself. When you sit, you need to be both unmoving and relaxed. The tenseness of rigidity is a movement of its own, a constant holding to the inverse of movement. The way you shape your time is similar; extreme punctuality can be as much of a distraction as laziness. Just as in the studio when we were artists, we were here for a purpose deep in our hearts. That was the compass point, the guiding force. Everything else falls into place in relation to that overriding purpose, the burning need to recognize and return to the utter completeness of essence.

All the daily routines and practices can open into a spaciousness unseen before, but the process can also be hard, tedious work. Your habits and emotions are all there, along with ailments, illnesses, and upwellings of subtle energy. These and other difficult experiences can arise for you, not against you, to help you on the path. You can see firsthand how much it is the holding, grasping, and denial that imprison you, not the difficulties themselves, and you let go. This is the crucial shift, the gap that allows a spacious open heart to become more evident, sky-like, empty, yet filled with intrinsic grace.

We were both middle aged when we entered retreat, and we knew this was our last chance. Hauling water or supplies in the rain, even when we were sick or tired, we still had to go uphill yet again. We just kept going. The simplicity of our life, uncluttered and lean, was the ground, the basis on which we placed our practice, and the constant presence of the forest, the Earth, the rain, the simple tasks, became not only a strength encouraging us along the path, but a natural reflection of the practice itself.

We were choosing to do all this. This was the way the opportunity to immerse ourselves in the teachings had arisen for us, and our hearts were grateful beyond measure, even though our bodies at times found it hard to haul food buckets out to the kitchen tarp again, setting up for the third meal of the day in freezing pouring rain. You can experience the absence of familiar comfort in so many ways, and that discontinuity, held now within the structure of retreat, steadily transforms every moment, every aspect of your life, your relations with family, your memories, your pain and frustrations, everything. Our hardships did not have the exhilarating drama or beauty of being snowbound on a high mountain. We were faced instead with gray skies and rain, and the mildew, mold, and damp of a forest enclosure as a context for the final stage of our long process of letting go, along with aches and pains and changes of what we increasingly referred to as "middle age, sickness, and death." The hardest part was being cut off from the sky, but even that became at last saturated with true joy, a quiet wild delight rooted in the very essence of being, as we found the sky-like freedom we sought in our practice instead.

REFUGE

The rain that started in September our first year in retreat was relentless: it continued day after day. We were planning to heat our shelter with an open pit fire, but the rain was too heavy. We had to stretch a piece of plastic over the smoke hole and wait until the weather cleared enough to build a cupola and install a woodstove. We waited until June. In the meantime, we lit candles and wore a lot of clothes.

It was very early morning and still dark as we began our first practice session of the day. With the sound of a heavy downpour that had been going on all night, we felt under water. We began another round of prostrations, and then I noticed a rivulet of water under my cot. We stopped and quickly moved the cot and found water beginning to pour out of the earthen wall like water bursting through a breach in a dike. It was as if Rachel and I were back on the prairie trying to save our adobe during a thunderstorm, but there was no lightning or thunder, just the sound of the ocean coming in. Now instead of wearing away we were filling up. We sprang into action with old towels and rags, and mopped and bailed, throwing buckets of water out the door. We worked until dawn when the rain began to slack off.

The water was coming in at the only low spot around the shelter, and we were able to fix it easily, but it kept raining. The shelter without heat was wet; it was incredible, beyond incredible; you could call it the deep. Everything was wet, even when we were dry we were wet. Going out to our kitchen tarp was like river rafting; we had to put on rain gear and enter a waterfall just to heat water for a hot water bottle. Once I reached the tarp having brought a jug of water, water was everywhere! I stumbled around in the pitch black of the night and the blowing rain guided only by a small wobbly circle of reality from the flashlight held in my mouth. I finally succeed in firing up our camp stove, and boiling water! I'm sweating, drenched with rain blowing in all around me, salivating with the flashlight in my mouth. We were under water, too deep for snorkels. The water in the pot was hot enough. With wet soaking hands of rain and sweat, I returned with a hot water bottle to our very damp but absolute refuge.

There was no doubt that even in the most awful circumstances we always felt that this moment, this place of practice, was our refuge. It was refuge from a culture gone mad and in taking this refuge we were honoring all the yogis, all the mystics, all those who willingly walked into the charnel ground on the inner demand to seek a truth and allow the heart to blossom. To enter the charnel ground, the wilderness, is to be embraced and literally flooded with blessings.

During the most difficult times, we would suddenly start to laugh. We would laugh without words, laugh with this world, laugh with its joy and laugh with the dark, laugh with all the men and women who have found the heart essence alive within the charnel ground, alive with the rain, alive to the fluid, spontaneous arising in our own forms as we changed from young to old.

The staccato sounds of heavy rain on the plastic over the smoke hole were almost blurred by the muffled roar of the downpour on the forest floor and the debris of the roof. Inside our shelter, we were not dry, but we were wet in quieter ways, with sweat and tears, with practicing, with being bundled up in so many layers of clothes. The earth was damp, the air was damp, our rain gear never dried. All absorbent objects in the room were softening, accepting water, the preliminary to mold. Condensation had set in, appearing and reappearing endlessly, dripping on the beds, but inside these quiet or unquiet cycles of water surrounding us everywhere, we were held in a kindliness beyond comfort, within our practice, within the enduring accepting witness of the Earth. The small space of our damp shelter was actually peaceful, supportive, and secure. It was a sacred place, and we were making a life of all that was offered here, as a sacrament.

Rob and I had our prostration mats lined up together in the narrow area between the narrow beds. We were standing, kneeling, gliding forward, and raising ourselves again in unison, almost.

Then into the wholeness of the steady rhythms of our motions and the moisture and the reverent silence of the Earth, a rising edginess intervened. I began to rip my clothes off; I had only a few seconds left. I dove through the low doorway half-naked into the cold rain, heat rolling up my body, out from my face, massive waves of heat, blazing in the pouring rain. A few months into retreat, I hit menopause.

I was not a woman anymore. I was a volcano. I was molten Earth. I had major incandescent hot flashes every forty-five minutes day and night. Volcanoes do not get regular sleep. They are involved in vast insistent elemental cycles instead. I woke up again and again in the night with just thirty seconds to rip out of the covers before being enveloped in waves of heat and soaked with sweat. Volcanoes do not like zippers or turtlenecks. Volcanoes erupt. I broke every zipper on every piece of clothing that had one, getting out of my clothes so fast. I gave away all my shirts that had tight necks. Volcanoes are unsettled and unsettling. They surprise themselves. I would be sitting quietly practicing, and suddenly my mind would begin to shift, looking uneasily around inside itself to find a reason for the rising tide of adrenaline. There would be no threatening inner thought, no outer event, just adrenaline welling up on its own, running wild. You would think I would get used to it, but it remained perversely fresh and new, an ambush every time.

The lava flows were cooling down. I was not a volcano anymore. The explosive almost exuberant freedom of unlimited heat had given way to a different energy, a centripetal force, the colossal gravity of Earth, a unifying, gathering restraint. It felt terrible at first, and it was harder to understand. Volcanoes have an overt primal quality; they spew forth. Now I was another Earth, the gravel bed of a runaway truck ramp on a steep mountain road with a brakeless eighteen-wheeler grinding down into me. I was the truck too, caught in heaviness and momentum it could only escape by plunging headlong into an inertial grace placed along the way with the intent to save. I had never driven a big rig white-knuckled into a gravel bed, but I was certain I knew how it felt, from both sides. You were no longer road and rocks and wheels, no longer weight moving or in repose; you were forces, natural, direct. You were the moment they collide, not just intersect. You were a woman in menopause.

The whole of my life's energy for embodiment was coming to a halt, closing the door to the womb from the inside. Complex primordial cycles of birth and death, of creation and destruction of worlds, were playing out with oceanic magnitude. My cells were bigger than I was. There was a terrible earnestness as various parts of my biology struggled to jump-start the ovaries or to resist the call. There was a great sadness in the quiet voice of the remaining eggs relinquishing all hope. This was high drama. All the most effortful and holding aspects of your personality can be caught up in the play of all this molecular and elemental striving. There can be a temptation to take it as your own, or to run away. Or you can be a witness instead, like the Earth, you can accept, absorb, endure. Your emotions, your intuition, and your body no longer provide familiar support. Your inner truth sense can seem to disappear. This was sacred unknown territory. Wisdom blood was disengaging from material nurturing and attachment, pulling apart, ready to be stored inside, to nourish an inward life, to give birth to a livingness that transcends life. I craved silence; I craved a simple secluded life. I was already in retreat; I was greatly blessed.

Rachel and I had begun our retreat by selling our truck to buy food. So I began not driving. Through the trees, I could see pieces of a road and reflections and movement, cars moving, people driving. We sat, and every now and then, the glint of the sun off the cars in the distance came to rest on my eyes, but you could always hear people driving: a simple family car, a conservative engine with a conservative speed and a uniform sound, the logging trucks racing both ways, trucks moving goods west in the morning, and trucks moving east in the evening. In the summer, you could hear the far-off rumble, summer thunder of Harleys in a pack moving west, rumbling, gunning a roar that goes on for a long time. The sounds would go by as I continued to sit, jake breaking, drag racing, gunning engines passing RVs as large as middle class homes.

Not driving is not easily defined beyond the fact that I was not driving anymore. It would seem a simple passing memory in one's life, but since driving had been a daily experience, one that took Rachel and me to many different parts of the country; it held a pivotal place in my mind.

The meandering drive through beautiful country, cool and refreshing. The shock finding you have no brakes, a tire is flat, or the lights on the dashboard have all gone red. There was driving on gravel, worrying about a stone cracking your oil pan, and driving on sand, not too fast, not too deep. There seemed so many ways to drive, in so many different circumstances. There was the fast drive between two eighteen-wheelers, the proper noble drive through Beverly Hills, the driving over train tracks so fast they seemed smooth, the hot rolling drive in the hot dry wind with long distances between not much, the stopping and going in traffic for hours and hours, the hair-raising split-second decisions on turnpikes, parkways, and toll roads. The long narrow tunnels, the short tunnels in and out, in and out, and in and out. There was driving in the fifties, driving in the sixties, the seventies, the eighties, and the nineties, all memories of driving now, but the '00s, '01, '02, '03, '04, and '05 they grew and grew, becoming more and more not having driven.

Driving along route 66 the summer of '65. The slow descending drive into the depths. The straight, smooth interstates, to the rolling state highways, from the organic to the GMO turnpikes, and parkways. They all held memories, directions, and intent. And now I was not driving. Not driving, even though it is nothing whatsoever, still encompasses your whole being. You can experience not driving within every moment; you need only be aware of it. There is not driving while doing the dishes, not driving while sitting formally doing Trekchö, and there is not driving whenever you realize that you are no longer driving. Maybe it was the highway across the narrow valley from where we sat. Throughout the year the sounds of trucks, motorcycles, and cars along with the personalities of the drivers went by endlessly. There were lulls within this seemingly continuous flow, summer roadwork and the occasional winter snowstorm. In any case, as the days turned to another season and as my mind looked back at itself, I could only say with a slight assurance that I was not driving.

This morning it was the Pacific Coast Highway again, an endless gliding mellow forever sound. Yesterday was the engine room of the Titanic with the Volga boatmen full speed ahead. These were not the tape loop replays of memories of movie music, or inner echoes of the sound of the traffic on the road that comes more distantly to my ears than to Rob's, or the meditator's bane, the song whose lyrics will not go away that we sometimes sing aloud to each other to break the spell. This was actual sound arising in my ears that I actually heard. I heard it all the time except in sleep.

I tried at first to understand. Countless possible conditions presented themselves. I changed my diet repeatedly. I took hormones for a while. I kept practicing. I got acupuncture. I took Chinese herbs. I kept practicing. The various physical and energetic interventions sometimes modulated the sounds, but I returned always to the practice as my anchor, my support.

The weather would change, and before it did, before the high front or the low front showed itself, I would hear it in my ears. The sky had been blazingly clear for days; the forest was crisp and dry, and we were melting in the heat. Then the engine room and the boatmen would begin to fire up; the weather was going to change. I would wait until tomorrow to see the clouds I had been hearing for half a day or to see the patch of blue sky that would lift the rain; it went either way. I kept practicing.

I had heard the ringing call of Tibetan horns in the rushing mountain river at the picnic at the end of our first year Dzogchen retreat, and when we sat for a month of Trekchö afterwards, I began to hear much more. Gradually I realized I was hearing a tapestry of overlapping inward sound and subtle energy, my own and the world's. I heard heartbeats and tiny capillaries at the tips of fingers and toes. I heard weather, I heard whole careers, I heard whole lives. I heard banging, pounding, pumping, slamming, whooshing, splashing, zinging, whirring sounds all overlaid. I heard flute-like tones of exquisite purity beyond sound. I heard the heavy incessant cadence of the lowest notes on a piano hammered over and over. The only thing I rarely heard was the simple, perhaps even more oppressive high-pitched continuous sound known as ringing in the ears.

I struggled with this unexpected addition to my life. It was one of my teachers now. I used it to feel the changes in the weather, to listen to my body, to listen to my feelings. I used it for our practice. It was an actual opening in my heart, beyond visualization, a crack between the worlds. I was hearing landscapes of energies that engendered lives. I was hearing the rhythms of millions of beings trudging both ways across an endless dusty plain, carrying their last few belongings, clutching tightly, not wanting to let go, trudging hopelessly, going nowhere, already lost. I heard a sublime celestial ongoing sound as if curving arcs of light were moving across each other, the music of shimmering spheres. I heard the whole range in between. I heard the sounds of energies that drove people to do cruel things. I heard the energies that fall in love. I heard the fabric and the strands of the warp and weave of countless lives wanting to be free, not seeing how they were caught.

My life was woven of these same energies. I was not separate. The unseen sounds were always there reminding me of the cries of the world, a claustrophobic hollow space or a spacious parallel expanse. They were with me as I sat and as I ate. They fell away at the edge of sleep. They returned more slowly as I awoke and helped me identify more and more the bright transcendent shore that opens there. They were a tremendous support to practice. I was more aware of them then, an all-inclusive backdrop of energies beyond form, nothing not nothing, an expression of the ephemeral arising nature of all experience right there in my ears, continuously.

PATH OF JOY

Bubbles form all across the still pond in a light rain. They arise suddenly, and linger for a while. Some mass together while others drift away. Liquid rainbow colors swirl across curving surfaces becoming more and more delicate, becoming luminous nets growing thinner and thinner until they burst, temporary structures of time and space returning just as suddenly as they appeared— essence, sphere, essence.

The whole process of return is all around us, infinitely patiently teaching us to recognize. After following a path of letting go, learning the way of an open heart and an allowing mind and recognizing luminous awareness, you come to a beginning, a threshold. The seed in your heart initiates the final path. Through the practice of Tögal, it is as if you become a sphere riding upon the essence, becoming less and less held by time, space, shape, and distance, more and more a unity beyond separation, a unity of all experience, all phenomena, that resolves in an instant—essence, essence, essence.

The visions of Tögal have always been. They are primordial; they are the first and most radiant aspect of manifestation closest to the essence. They are not random. They arise in the same way and in the same progression for everyone. The complete path of return is organic and natural. The ancient ones followed the signs and cycles of Earth, water, and sky, moon and sun and seed. They found the luminous seed in their hearts through the vision that is this life and rays of the sun, through the water of their eyes and the light of their hearts. They watched, they waited, they allowed, they followed their hearts without hurrying—allowing the visions of inner radiance.

> —*To Return as a Circle Is Drawn,*
> *A Guidance Manual for the*
> *Preliminaries and Practice of Tögal,*
> by Robert and Rachel Olds

A few years into our retreat, deep in wintertime, we received the empowerments and teachings for Tögal. We felt so blessed. We had come at last to the Path of Joy. This was what we had so long awaited, and we had a deep knowing that this practice would guide us to fruition in this life. All the clues, the dreams, and our artwork had been leading us back to Tögal. We went outside in the cold winter rain and watched in wonder as the raindrops made concentric circles and bubbles on a small stream. We were seeing into the very fabric of the vision that is this life and the unity of this life and the visions of inner radiance, and we were just at the beginning.

The Dzogchen heart essence teachings on Tögal, the union of luminous awareness and the visions of inner radiance, are very simple. So are the pith instructions on recognition or pointing out, but to be fully open to this disarming simplicity, you need a lot of preparation, a lot of miles already covered in one way or another along the spiritual path. Our true preliminaries had been our whole lives, an ongoing motion of letting go, of remembering, and return. Our wandering years especially, with no respectable identity or formal spiritual path to provide a new security, had forced us to intensify our trust in the receptive, allowing openness that we had nurtured as artists, a natural preparation for the Dzogchen path.

The practice of Tögal is a dynamic and intense form of letting go, parallel to the process of death, the ultimate form of letting go. You are so open in this practice. There is a freedom similar to the experience after leaving the confines of the body at death that creates a fluid space where the luminous visions arise. If you are still holding and grasping to self and other, emotions and habits of mind, then all your stuff floods into that free space, arising vividly and compellingly, making it impossible for what is naturally abiding in your heart to come forth. This is why you must pare away all that is unnecessary, all that you hold onto in this life. You need to let go of everything, even yourself, to clean the slate of your very being. It is as if you were pivoting between this life and the moment after death over and over, steadying yourself to recognize the fluid wash of luminous organic being.

The practices of the heart essence arose out of direct experience in the wilderness long before they were known as Mahasandhi, Maha Ati, Dzogchen, or the Great Perfection. The complete path of the heart essence involves the union of luminous awareness and the visions of inner radiance. The practice of this union, Tögal, is not widely taught or experienced, and requires years in deep retreat and many more years of letting go before embracing this practice. Yet the same essence manifesting as the visions of inner radiance also manifests as the natural world, and if our hearts are open and our minds are allowing, we can begin to touch the qualities of inner radiance that are here all around us.

We are surrounded by teachings. The natural world arises from the same source as the Tögal visions, and for the same reason, to provide an avenue for return. This spiritual return is a natural movement, a path of return from the point of origin, and just as a circle is drawn with the energy of a line sweeping around and curving back to merge seamlessly with itself, the completion is inherent in the path from the beginning. Circles and cycles are the basis of all expressions of the intent of the essence, both the Tögal visions and this vision we call life. Circles and cycles from the point of origin are apparent everywhere: bubbles form on water in a light rain; rainbows bloom in a misty sky; seeds sprout, grow upward, mature and set seed again; waters flow in rivulets and mountain streams into larger rivers leading to the sea, then rise into sky and clouds, and fall as rain on mountaintops again.

In the practice of Tögal, the luminous seed in your heart initiates the cycle of the four visions, and the growth of the visions is very similar to the way a seed sprouts in nutrient-rich soil and rises up out of the ground. When one has come to genuine renunciation, and an open heart and an allowing mind, there is a potential developing within one's heart seed; the seed of light quickens with an energy delicate yet endowed with the strength to push upward toward the portal where the visions become evident. The seedling of light rises out of the soil of your heart, out of all your renunciation, love, and compassion, which then nourish its growth. Tögal is a living, evolving cycle that needs to be nurtured; you need to give everything to the practice to keep it going. Tögal requires being in long term retreat. If the visions begin to arise, they are a sacred demand. A very rare and precious gift is opening in your heart.

Tögal requires a deep faith in one's heart, a commitment to the practice, and the courage to keep going with a kindly diligence and perseverance that are nurturing and whole. Open, allowing, and fluid, you do not hold to anything, and the luminous rainbow color visions naturally pour from your heart and move you to fruition. It is the practice of inexplicable astounding joy, the joy of the fruition itself already present, interwoven seamlessly with each step along the way.

Tögal visions are not mind experiences or visualizations; they are direct perception of the true nature of phenomena outside of words. All words are symbolic markers that at best can only allude to experiences beyond themselves. The word Tögal has been translated in various ways: leaping over, surpassing the peak, surpassing the pinnacle, crossing over, direct crossing, and all-surpassing realization. These terms point to an experience that is outside the range of normal human perception. Returning to the luminous awareness of your heart takes you to the natural expansiveness within your familiar experience. Tögal shifts your experience entirely: slowly, gently, quietly, steadily, Tögal literally goes beyond all experience, taking as the path the manifesting energy of the essence itself.

We had just finished our early morning practice. A small stream of light from the rising sun illuminated the details of our shelter, and as we gathered the food buckets that we needed for making breakfast, we noticed an insect the size of a large cricket crawling near the entrance, a slow thick-bodied bug moving stiffly in the dust with an ancient heaviness. We brought the insect outside and watched the cicada slowly crawl onto the bark of a large fir tree, as if finding something long awaited. Then the cicada stopped and held onto the bark.

We came back after breakfast before hauling water. The cicada was still holding tight; it seemed like the light had gone out in the small form. Then we noticed a crack down the back, and as we stood there we could see the crack widening and the barest shimmer of birth appearing from inside. This moment, this little being, was a metamorphosis, a grace, and we were the witness. The crack widened more, beginning to reveal a luminous rainbow-tinged body. The upper part of the body emerged from the old shell. Pulling and straining to free the legs, stretching farther and farther, the cicada arched back into space in a gesture of rapture and total faith. Then with the legs free, holding onto the former self, the cicada pulled out the lower abdomen to fully reveal a translucent mother of pearl body with nascent iridescent wings, a dew drop breathing out into space, a fulfillment of being in light and form as the wings grew and refined to clear gossamer fans. The cicada had a pleasant broad little face and bright eyes that were filled with a purpose, climbing away from the shell and again clinging to the tree, the transformation almost complete, taking a moment to appreciate the radiance in what arises.

So many years below the surface, so many changes within the sacred Earth to ascend into the open air, searching for a safe place to completely open oneself, to reveal one's inner being so delicate and vulnerable. A moment so precious, so open it requires being set apart, removed, to allow the molten heart out.

We would find many other cicadas just out of the ground, held completely within the process of their transformation, needing to find a place that would allow what was already happening to come forth. There is a feeling deep within you, a knowing as sharp and demanding as being close to death. You must follow your heart, you must get within your cloister as your former being cracks open. This openness allows what is already in your heart to evolve and your mind to become the very fabric of being, a molten fluid oneness. Blessings and their intent are there, like the air we breathe, surrounding us, waiting only to be witnessed.

We had willingly left so much behind, following our inner call. Both Rob and I were already deep within our own process of metamorphosis before we entered retreat, and especially now as the Tögal visions were beginning to ripen, we had to be here; this was our time to do this. Our choices were clear to us. We knew why we were here, but it was hard for our families, especially our aging mothers, to understand: Why won't you come visit me? They were moving within the imperatives of their transformations too.

From the beginning of our retreat, my mother and I had written letters to each other, but as her Parkinson's progressed I had made arrangements to hike to a phone and call her instead. My mother's voice sounded more quavery and uncertain than usual when she answered the phone for our weekly call. She did not say that she felt troubled, but she hinted that she was aware of feeling things that did not quite relate to what was going on around her. I wanted to help her.

I was hundreds of miles away, and even if we were in the same room together, neither of us could hear very well. We heard each other's voices better amplified over the phone. The calls from retreat had become an unexpected vehicle for an intimacy and appreciation between us after all these years. Sometimes she asked the same questions, as if following a script. Sometimes she was hearing voices in the air-conditioning or was staying in imaginary hotels. The slow dementia that had accompanied her Parkinson's had not dimmed her mind, but she was less anchored, unmoored at times like her hands and feet and legs from her intent. She asked simpler questions now about our daily life. She no longer asked, as Rob's mother still did, what are you going to do with whatever it is that you are learning there? My mother's judgments no longer held well enough in her mind to give them weight. We rested instead in what we had both come to recognize as our love for each other, expressed in chitchat. Sometimes like today, there would be an opening, a gap, when her acknowledgment of her situation to herself allowed her to be more real for a while.

I said, "Sometimes feelings and memories come up from before. They don't quite match what is going on now, but they affect you anyway."

We both paused; I waited. Then she said, "How good of you to know that." There was another pause. Silence was also part of what we listened to in each other now.

Then she spoke, her frail voice more certain now, "Don't ever grow old." We were talking in code, shorthand, talking between and beyond the words. She meant, do not ever find yourself as I am now, overwhelmed by memories and feelings that you do not understand.

I said, "Mom, that's why we're in retreat, to look at those things before we get old, to look at them while we can." So that no one may ever have to feel that way again, I also meant, but did not say. I was keeping to one idea at a time so that she could follow.

The pause was huge now, filled with my mother's silence growing brighter. She had always preferred to live quietly, finding simple joys in a sheltered life. Now she was processing something, enveloped in the dawning of an idea she had not considered in this way before. I knew she understood and that this moment on the phone extended for her far outside time. She understood more than I said. She understood retreat.

Months later, I was sitting outside by myself, surrounded by brilliant sunlight and a profusion of bright-colored flowers for a tsok, a ceremonial offering practice. I was wearing a colorful sweater knitted in patches of yellow, red, purple, and pink. I smiled from inside all this multihued effusive display at the bright sunlit air in front of me and all around me. I was a portrait for my mother; I was sitting as her daughter with the flowers and the sunlight as a picture for her. I had just heard that she died, and I was sure that she was here with me.

She had gone into a coma the day before a ten-day Chetzun Nyingtik group sadhana practice began. She had been resting peacefully in hospice care surrounded by my cousins in Phoenix as we and the others gathered for the annual ritual that supported our heart practice. I could not imagine a better time for her to pass, enfolded also in the hearts and prayers of the blessings here. I was very joyful for her.

The insistent cadence of the small hand drums and the bells blended with the tsok verse and became a continuous sound. The shrine was heaped with offerings, and the tsok plates had almost all been filled. The rich, complex aromas of incense, pickle juice, cookies, roasted meats, perfume, flowers, ripe fruit, spiced crackers, and sweet liqueur enveloped the room. The big platter heaped with anise Springerles, the traditional Christmas cookies my mother's mother loved to make, had been divided up, a huge portion for the shrine and a cookie for every tsok plate. I had made a big batch of these cookies before the ten-day practice began. I knew my mother would be going then, and I had complete faith that she would come here to be with me. The cookies were an offering to connect her with our practice.

My mother sat in front of me, intangible in one way yet very present to my heart. She was glowing, looking at me with total love, a love she could not touch so openly in this life. I told her I made the cookies for her. She smiled and said I would have come to see you without the cookies. We love each other very much. I cried. No matter how our love had expressed itself through the years, I knew that we had always loved each other.

After the tsok Rob told me he saw her too; she looked younger, radiant, and although she was still very much focused on me, he said it was as if she had taken off her persona of this life like an old overcoat.

My mom had suffered greatly in her last few months. She no longer wanted to be who she was; she was ready to move on, which helped. So does prayer. True prayer is more than words, although they can be a support. True prayer is wordless, from your heart: It is luminous awareness coupled with your love.

Our path down to the creek was narrow, meandering at first through trees on the nearly level area around our shelter. As you pass the tarp and the old stump, the trail cuts between two large fir trees to a small opening, then curves to the right and descends to the creek. So many days and nights we have walked this trail with water jugs, backpacks, and a load of our minds. In all our wanderings we had given up so much not only of our possessions but also of our habits and desires. Things arose during our retreat, but they never remained on our trail, obstructing our way. We always kept going, never looking back. We had known for many years that all we wanted was retreat, keeping our path fairly clear.

In the summer of 1994, three years before we came to the Gonpa, we had reached an important crossroads in our lives. Rachel and I were talking in the underground shelter we had built in the Pine Barrens, protected from the heat and humidity and the biting flies hovering above the small entrance. We spoke of our intent to go as far as we could on the spiritual path: that was all we wanted in this life. We talked about living a celibate life. From early childhood and as a young man, I had considered a cloistered life, but I never felt comfortable with any organized order or rule. Ever since her visionary experiences in the winter in Vermont, Rachel's heart was calling her to an inner cloister but not as a monastic.

As we lay beside each other I still had sexual desire, but it was to the side of my path. There was a power in voicing this idea of staying together in a spiritual union of two solitudes, and in taking responsibility for our path and our lives as we saw them.

When we lived in the world, I was constantly confronted by a society obsessed with sexually indulgent behavior. I was not closing my eyes to the sensual but igniting my intent like a flare in the night; intent was a force demanding to be recognized.

Nothing on the path to liberation is easy or smooth. We did not feel we were restricting ourselves; rather a choice arose within our renunciation, cutting the ties, breaking the web of sexual delusion that is so omnipresent today. Our act of celibacy, like the cleaning of the hide, the burning of our art work, and the selling of our land, was a form of letting go, stepping out of the confines of ordinary perception and beliefs. Celibacy within a constructed order, no matter how exalted, was not the point for us: the impetus had to arise, as it did, naturally, organically; it was not a shield or a concept to promote spiritual power but a reordering, giving way to a free space, an open avenue.

Renunciation arose naturally out of our joy within this grand vision arising to fulfill its own reflection. This is fluidity, an

241

effulgent dance, finding our intent deep in our hearts and allowing renunciation to flow, to dissolve the grasping and clinging as we continued along our path.

Spring sometimes seems like it will never arrive, and when it does, it can resemble summer in every respect except the month. Life in retreat can be seasonal and wave up and down, and you never really know what season you will be in, but in general there are good days and bad days.

Good days can arise out of sudden perception of meditative experience that had been going on for a while; you just have to catch up to it. That's recognition. We were hauling water one morning, and the sun had just risen above the mountains. It was mid April, and it had been dry for about five days. As we walked down the path to the creek, the sun was coming through the trees in bright shafts, blurring the woods. Today there seemed something more, something we had not taken notice of before. It was in the air, a telling wave coming to us. We stopped and looked at the light pouring over the mountains, filling up the day; the light was revealing and illuminating a great moment in spring. Down toward the creek within the curtain of light there was a cloud, brilliant and shimmering, a mist of pinkish white blossoms, as if the heavy snowflakes of winter were held in just this one spot. You can breathe in this grace, and it lives with you for a time, a tall old cherry tree in full bloom, growing alone in the woods, a vision arising, abiding, lightening the load on our hearts. These are the good days remembered within the fibers of your existence, warming you long after the spectacle has faded. You can return to them in your mind to soften what inevitably comes and are known as the bad days.

The bad days can arrive after having touched the splendor of practice, the taste of one's mind changing and the heart opening to recognize, like those moments finding a flowering tree dazzling in the morning light. Now this blessing has faded, closed down, you're

242

caught in the claustrophobic, endless tape loop of stupidity, your stuff is in your face, you're miserable, it's continuous, yes there's permanence, there's no hope, endless infinite dread.

Early one fall Rachel and I had a new neighbor, a rock squirrel who took up lodging under a dead madrone tree close by. He was very comfortable with our coming and going; he just kept collecting dry leaves and generally outfitting his home for the winter. One day after dinner as I was walking down to our compost, I saw the movement of an animal nearby, so I stopped. Then the rock squirrel ran up toward me on the trail, but he too stopped and looked up at me, sitting back on his rear legs. His cheeks were puffed out like little balloons. He looked up at me as if trying to decide how to deal with an embarrassing social encounter. His little front paws were at his sides with his wrists propped up at his waist: Now what do you want? I was about to get out of his way when he took his left paw and placed it behind his left cheek and pushed forward, ejecting the contents of his pouch onto the trail between us. Yuk, I thought. He did this again with his right pouch and then placed his hands to his waist as if to say, so there, you can have your carrot peelings! And off he went. His gesture came to symbolize for us the bad days, the dreadful times that just seem to go on and on.

How was your day? One of us would ask silently with our eyes, and for reply, all we had to do was lift one hand behind the side of our face and push forward in a slow-motion version of the rock squirrel's gesture. It was enough to make us laugh, to keep going, to lift our hearts. There, you can have your carrots!

Our life in retreat was most exemplified by our choice to haul water. This decision certainly did not make things easier, but it put us in daily contact with a very fundamental gift of this life, the chance to make one's way to the elemental source of this sacred dream. The shelter was one way, with the Earth embracing us, not just the physical mass of the Earth but its absorbing depth. And for another essential aspect of our spiritual life to arise we felt we also needed to walk every morning to the source of our water. Every day, no matter what kind of weather we were having, we had to go for water. It became for us a sacrament reflecting the whole of the spiritual path, the whole of this amazing arising vision.

The morning was cold with a strong wind from the south as we gathered up our plastic water jugs. The rain had lessened, but there was a continuous chorus of rain hitting the debris on the forest floor. The madrones near our shelter shed the rain quickly, but the firs along the path to the creek would release a flood of raindrops with each breeze.

There was a spot along the creek where the earth dropped down a few feet, just enough for us to rest our jugs beneath the flow of water. There was a light green in the woods along the creek even during winter in northern California, the barest beginning of tiny seed leaves dotting the whole area, an enlivening presence spread upon the winter ground.

As we moved across this carpet of green beneath the bare dogwood branches, we came to the sound of water, a small and delicate offering. We reached our gift and offered thanks in return. As we come to water, we return to the source, we return again and again to the heart breath of a spacious mind, filling our jugs with an acceptance of this vision, opening up with a grateful hand at the source of such a simple gift as water flowing from the Earth.

The rain began to pour down. We were surrounded by the vibrancy of water, falling from the sky, pouring from the trees, running from the gravelly soil to enter our jugs. Then we slowly began our way back up the trail. Here along this trail, the small journey to the source is joy, the joy found within this sacred play unfolding, brilliant, vivid, and alive. It manifests and offers and blesses us when we are happy and positive about our practice and when we are down with our stuff in our face. We are given this great chance to live with and accept the joy.

In accepting these elemental wonders, they formed a place, a beginning, a staging point like water jugs along our trail filled with blessings. They helped us remember, helped us recognize the boundless openness arising in this experience. Within this play and joy there arises a luminous sky-like mind from the seed of inner radiance, like flowers in late spring. The mind blossoms forth spontaneously, open and vast; this is confidence born of the heart, like a flower opening to reveal a delicate scent, again and again blossoming, billowing, vast spacious radiance.

Another morning comes, in another season, to walk down to the source. So many, many times before, luminous awareness had blossomed and then closed like a flower at sunset, but now it remained, vibrant, aware sky-like mind, all that is, as it is.

You have crossed that earthen bridge along the trail to the source, returned to a knowing within the source, letting go into the current, flowing as the source, and through the brilliance becoming the illumined before the blue-black depth of all, the absolute source within you.

Going for water, part way down the trail, a phrase from a tantra, looks through my eyes, Whose eyes? Who looking? Me looking through the eyes of awareness? Luminous awareness looking through my eyes. Something deep inside comes to a stop, motionless on the trail, everything vividly present, grand and gentle, simply there. I walk a few steps and stop again, it takes a long time to get to water, inseparable from wonder. The derelict simplicity of the old water tank, the aliveness of flowing water and nothing needing to be done about any of it, it's all already there, now moving softly through whatever arises like a fading dream, awareness ongoing even in that. 9/30/02

I still had a hard time remembering who received which drinks, as my brother John and I served cocktails to the guests. Being only eight years old, I didn't understand the connection between a type of cocktail, how it was mixed, and the person who ordered it. My dad would tell me, vodka and soda is for Barbara; she's on the couch. Uncle Alden is having a dry vodka martini, and he's sitting next to Aunt Francis, who is having bourbon and water. They were the regulars, but although I had seen all of these people before at other parties, I was unsure about names and habits. I went back and forth with the drinks. Soon the hors d'oeuvres would be ready. I was more interested in eating some, but I knew I would have to wait until all the guests had been served. There were about twenty-five people here, talking, drinking, and smoking, and as if I were floating in a surreal world, as I handed each person their drink, they would age. I watched as their skin wrinkled and lost its color, their hair thinned and turned white, their skin became thin and sores appeared. Finally, their voices would change and quiver. They would look more feeble until they vanished. I went around my parents' living room, so elegant and refined, serving drinks to people, and witnessing anew all that I had experienced of them, all that my early memories could offer me. I looked back at everyone at those parties, and they had all passed away. The living room was empty and then the living room itself changed, the furniture dispersed, different people playing the piano. So many people, so many hopes and fears. These thoughts rushed through my mind as our friend went out to call the doctor. Rachel stayed with me; it was now 2:30 a.m. I felt I was dying, the weight of mountains pressing down on me. I asked Rachel if she would not mind staying home, doing our heart practice while I was taken to the hospital.

The day before, Rachel and I had spoken of the possibility that I had a fatal illness, and we had spoken of our love for each other, not only in this lifetime, but in the many in which we had been partners on the path. Our heart practice was in our blood, and I wanted Rachel to be immersed in it at the time I passed. I knew I would feel it. I had no regret having gone only halfway in the practice. The inner radiance was stable, and I was going to experience whatever came, witnessing the last marvels arising from grace in countless ways. Rachel and I held each other for what could be the last time, or was this a memory of past lives where we inevitably parted in manifest form knowing a oneness and union beyond parting?

It was still dark when I got to the hospital, and I could feel that whatever my condition, it was progressing rapidly. I was able to walk from the car into the emergency room and was greeted by a friendly attendant. He helped me into a gown and onto an examining table. I somehow felt good about the situation, but at the same time, I could feel my limbs were streams of water flowing to my center. I knew something would have to be done soon, or I would certainly die.

I was resting at home, having returned from the hospital that same morning, grateful they had saved my life. I was nodding off as Rachel held another series of Jin Shin Jyutsu points. I was still going over the events of the last two days, feeling them, knowing myself to be different, having experienced the edge of death with no regrets. We had taken a big step in the practice by saying goodbye, knowing the depth of union, but the intent to complete the path propelled me back to our practice together. The boy passing out the drinks seemed so far away now, yet so clear are my memories, like the clink of ice in a crystal glass.

Rob was sitting up in bed in the late evening, supported by a pile of pillows. It had been a long day since he left for the emergency room, and yet, enfolded in the practice while he was away, a tenderness beyond union and separation.

As if suspended in the moment between breathing out and breathing in again, we were resting in the aftermath, just quietly being here. I was holding Jin Shin points on his shoulder and his hand. His head fell back into the pillows; his long silvery hair floated gently beside his face, following the curve of the pillows, merging with his long grizzled beard. His eyes closed, and his jaw opened wide from within the flowing hair. I was very close to his mouth, looking straight inside a gaping hollow space, a cavern growing huge as a mountaintop, a black and glittering night, primordial and immense as all of space.

We were both at the threshold of sleep. The familiar anchoring forms of the bodies of the waking dream of this life were falling away. Within the vastness unfolding from his open mouth, Rob was dissolving, expanding into sleep, and I was going with him into the unknown reaches of that deepening space, a timeless night that was also mine, and for a moment I was seeing it with waking eyes.

Then suddenly he raised his head. His eyes opened, the mouth closed. He looked slowly around the room, then in the soft voice of someone who has returned from a far place, he asked, "Did I fall asleep?"

Days passed, the full moon rose through the trees. Seasons turned, the full moon rose again, over and over: summer moons low in the south, following the path of the winter sun; winter moons high overhead, traveling the arc of summer sun. Each time, the full moon rose pearlescent, luminous, and watery, like a reflection of itself floating in the clear night sky. As the moonlight spread softly through the forest air, sifting through the trees and gathering in small bright places on the forest floor like newly fallen snow, shadows and bright outlines of things partially revealed fused together in a single blessing inside this cool translucent light.

The essence is the compelling, limpid moon and its reflected light. The essence is the timeless blue-black darkness of the night and the shattering brilliance of the rainbow sun that endlessly illuminates the moon. The essence is the secret sun and moon in the sky of your heart. The essence is your heart, and the only reason that the outer guides in all their myriad forms appear in your life is to show you this, so that you return to the resplendent wisdom of the radiance and reflection that you already are.

ISLE OF GOLD

Nothing to understand or explain, today water bowls at Vima House, Rob and I pausing at the door before we leave, looking around the room, a feeling there, quiet, sweet, a little empty, looking at it like a child seeing a temple for the first time, or like a person who knows they will never see this place again, no longing, just a feeling quiet and sweet and a little empty like the room, then Rob says feels like we we'll never see this place again, I say yes, then we leave, Vimilamitra is everywhere. So much dropping away from the mind, resolving, exhausted, falling away in mid air, finished or unfinished, so very natural to turn to light again, a simple process, open and quiet, like the room. 8/6/04.

Sitting with Rachel before gazing, looking around the cabin like at Vima house yesterday. The early morning light coming from a crack in the curtains, everything falling away, just the light with a sphere of knowing, nothing else, seeing the mandalas is an embrace with the immaculate's own. 8/7/04

The autumn air was cool and still; a few whispers of fine white clouds were drifting across the surface of the clear blue sky, high and far away above the tops of the trees. The narrow draw along the creek was a blaze of yellow leaves. The glowing golds of oaks and big-leafed maples in the upper canopy, and the more delicate yellows of the alders and dogwoods in the thickets close around the stream, were ornamented here and there with the lingering green of wild syringa and the dark red heart-shaped leaves of wild grape. We walked the narrow trail through this corridor of living grace, surrounded by the gentle tides of clear saps, sweet liquid energies pulling inward, down, deep, towards hidden roots, revealing in the sudden glory of the gleaming golden and red leaves the lifelong secret practice of the plants and trees, their union with the light.

We were walking single file, walking briskly, our afternoon exercise. Rob was a few steps ahead. A robin-size bird, one of the towhees perhaps, who had been moving in a thicket of yellow leaves beside the trail, suddenly flew straight between us at chest level as if we were not there. I felt the wing beats curving through my heart like waves of sound moving through deep water. Quietly, steadily, day by day, we were dissolving away.

We had given our whole lives to the practice of Tögal, and as the visions matured, the veneer of solidity overlaid on the forms of our experience fell away, so smoothly and thoroughly, beyond concept or language, a oneness, a seamless molten space beyond fixed dimensions, yet not separate from the simplest, most intimate details of daily life. The yellow autumn leaves were no more or less amazing than the tall red cliffs of clayey earth suddenly bursting into translucent rainbow lights, or the countless universes suddenly unfolding from the vaporous shell of a collection of perceptions that a moment before had been an elbow or a hand.

If anything, this world of all-inclusive wholeness, fluid, subtle, permeable, neither holding to nor keeping separate any aspect of the enormous scope of possible experience, is far more tangible and real than ordinary waking life, bound as it is by illusions of separation, solidity, and duration. Generous, innocent, spontaneous, direct visceral experience, buddhafields, rainbow lights, deities, autumn leaves, the transparent, sparkling eyes of an ancient teacher, or the soft gray wings of a small bird in flight, we moved in worlds beyond words, immersed in a wholeness inconceivable, becoming the radiance.

The visions arise through day and night practice that extends over a period of years, and as the habits of mind, emotions, lives of weighted actions, and deep-seated concepts of time and space slowly dissolve away, you see directly how this world manifests out of essence, an experience of light, shape, and color that is all encompassing. Your physical form and the world around you are turning to light and yet you still go for water, cook food, and take care of your daily needs. As you walk down to the creek, the land

and the plants glow with light, it is naturally the way of all things, so simple, just as your hand is made of light as it lifts the jug of water.

The four visions of Tögal unfold in the same way as the growth cycle of a plant. The seedling of light that emerges from the luminous seed in your heart puts out seed leaves as the onset of the first vision. The seedling grows, puts out more leaves and the first buds of flowers as the second vision, and then matures and blossoms as the total effulgence of the third vision. The energy then turns inward, concentrating the dynamic force of the essence to set seed in the fourth vision, which brings you to the ultimate resolution of all phenomena as a seamless whole. There are specific landmarks along the path, but the four visions are not single events, they are whole arenas of experience, each with their own texture.

The experience of the fourth vision is very similar to the transformations of a plant going to seed. The plant no longer sets buds and the final delicate flower petals dry into furling shapes of darkening and opaque color. All the energy of the plant goes toward the seed. With the same inexorable power that drove their increase, slowly, unerringly, the visions recede from the limitless horizons of the full expanse of the third vision. There is a quietness, an inward turning, light returning to the point of origin. This is the most profound of all the visions. It is easy for the last vestiges of manifest identity to ride the visions outward, surrendering to the glory and the wonder of ever increasing experience, like a waxing moon reaching an effulgence without limit, the mountaintop beyond all mountaintops, the sky beyond all sky. Having embraced the full scope of all experience, as the visions turn that vastness inward, condensing it into the now awakened seed, the last bit of identity still residing as a body rides the vision inward and downward, in the last surrendering, surrendering even the expanse of the radiance.

All your experience is now seamless. Simple gestures of nature, the colors of autumn leaves, dewdrops on a blade of grass, an apple by candlelight, are just as wondrous as the visions or the bursts of light. There is a complete acceptance of all levels of experience as a unity forever beyond sundering, and with this unity come a softness and a depth like the endless bottom of the sea, a massive oceanic tenderness, relentless, fluid, and immense. The four great qualities that support the practice, openness, transcendence, oneness, and spontaneous presence are all one now; they are the same, no longer divisible into four, the perfection of the single sphere.

The vision is truly like waves subsiding on an ocean—the wave of vision can be incredible with color and forms, buddhafields etc then slowly they subside. There is a feeling of being drawn beyond form into light—a knowing within a single sphere. 9/25

Clear sense of the radiance turning inward, gently indrawn, still focused but in such a soft and quiet way, same quality as when the single sphere arises, beyond words, expansive but inward, a real oneness—seamless, no divisions, no big display, just indwelling potential, so kind, serene, and effortless. 10/02/04

During the last week I've been experiencing the inexpressible nature resolved to a single sphere—the mind is inwardly directed and lucid—an extremely subtle experience like a black light—an illuminated experience of essence. 10/03/04

Walking the trail, massive trunks of two big sugar pines at the curve up ahead seem to move past each other as we approach, illusion of 3D so convincing, so enticingly "real", space, the last great ignorance, in front, behind, near, far, all depend on point of view, in perspective drawing the point is at a distance, the vanishing point, in direct perception the vanishing point is you, the arising of the single sphere erasing all sense of in between. 10/10/04

From early on in our practice of Tögal, the potency and tremendous sense of presence within the shimmering visionary fields of this path were clear to us. One morning, late in summer, when Rob and I were still near the beginning of our innermost journey and the practice and the summer heat had melted all sense of time, I was suddenly enveloped from within by a soaring wave of gratitude, inseparable from the practice itself. An overwhelming thankfulness poured through me as I recognized the depth of the luminous tenderness within the visions, and where that tenderness was guiding us. My heart was filled to overflowing, grateful for everything that had led us to the practice of Tögal, grateful for the practice itself, and I was also gratefully aware of the overlapping waves of intention and prayer that had brought us here. Not only our own prayers, but a certainty in my heart that aging mothers or grown children in lives long ago had prayed strongly to bring us to this path. So many others, in the countless interactions through which we learn and grow along the path spanning the many lives in which we come and go, had also offered prayers: countless gestures, countless prayers, in the voices of the wind and waters, in the turn of a leaf, the curve of a flower petal, the touch of a hand.

Gratitude is an essential aspect of the path of Tögal. Tögal is profoundly a practice of the approach of grace, a relationship, an embrace. The energy of gratitude opens your heart to receive the blessings and is an expression of the natural openness that is your heart: grateful recognition, the surrender and release, the natural dissolving acceptance of a great goodness reflected in your heart and the fabric of all being. Moments of gratitude are crucial on the spiritual path. They are powerful expressions of the energy of the return, the intent of the essence calling from within your heart and the heart of the world. I cried within the glowing embrace of blessing, receptive, joyful tears, grateful water returning knowingly to light.

Early on in our lives, there were so many moments that were marked along a map already drawn out, an incredible map encompassing the infinite web of being. It is a map of return, a way, a suction pulling us, waving signs of myriad forms and sounds across this trail, letting us know we are going the right way. It is countless experience, countless lifetimes, involved with all beings in unbounded space.

We open to this simple, vast luminous being as a three-year-old boy in church, a four-year-old girl watching the sunrise, the light through a window, the reflections of Buddhas upon a wall, the glistening play of light on rippling water. The fabric of this whole experience we are in is sacred, is potent, is active arising intent to reflect itself, and we are this fabric of being too. It is found in the shock and horror, in the calm peaceful times; it is an abrupt, destructive, nurturing, explosive, loving, revolting beatitude of anything and everything, limitless possibility, universal oceanic depth found within your heart, an inner radiance, your inner guru.

It is a flare, brilliant and cutting in the night, and the warm assurance of knowing deep within you. The inner guru, your heart, is the essence; it is its own intent calling you to recognize, guiding you to and through experience. All you need to do is become aware of its call and have the courage to follow it. Its voice is within the wind, sounding from the stars, in your own heart.

You can search for immeasurable time and you will never find anything that is not this call to return. All arises for us to hear the call, always the call, never ending. You cannot run from it, it will run you down. It is absolute patience. A luminous tone of absolute space touching you like the early morning sun in spring or like death in a car crash, always the call. We heard this call so many times. We followed it in ways most people found hard to comprehend. We followed our hearts, our inner guru, all across the country with our money running out, our families increasingly concerned with our seemingly reckless behavior. We followed it to the south and up to the north, to the southwest, to the east, to the north, to the west, and we waited after waiting so long, and finally knew it was time, and the outer guru was there.

The inner guru never dissolves away; the outer guru, your guide, points out what you already have and lays out the instruction, the last steps on a long road, moments in a dance played out through offerings and acknowledgment, through gratitude to the essence that pulls us, calls to us and then teaches us, pointing, prodding, pushing us to recognize. The flowers, the offerings, the praise, all the carpets of gold fade to nothing compared to recognizing and following that simple act of pointing at the moon.

It had been in summer, and we were bathed in the practice of the heart essence, walking our last path, the most exalted trail, in the blazing heat and sun. It was after lunch or was it while hauling water or walking out to practice? Was it as we slept or when we saw the dawn? It had all come together like a blossom in the mind, the vast simple scent of being unfolded and remained, all that is, as it is, oceanic joy, knowing the call, listening as the call.

We found ourselves together on this luminous trail, in the current taken by the wave, our minds allowing within all that is allowed, in the sacred play unfolding, embracing the heart essence of Tögal as a circle is drawn, no brush, no ink, no beginning or end, fluid, molten, effulgent luminosity that just is, nothing more, reaching a moment outside of time, a space beyond, the ultimate return, the source, the essence, the call.

Beyond nothing needing to be done, abiding naturally, effortlessly, organically, nothing has changed yet in reference to past experience everything has changed. 12/5/04

A feeling of the body going away, a sensation, then, no body there, even the vision goes away, like no one watching or experiencing, nothing, then I'm back again. 12/7/04

Depth of oneness, for about a week or so I've been experiencing states while gazing, difficult to put into words, primordial, vast sense of oneness, this sense of oneness, pervades yet in a physical reaction, losing the body, dissolving all phenomena into the deep with no reference point, deep calm oceanic oneness. Rachel has also characterized this experience in a similar way. 12/23/04

Rob mentions he is feeling a shift too, a deepness like an ocean he says, and not dependant on what you see, much the same for me, the deep and soft and wide feeling, a quality very different now, walking, washing dishes, gazing, all within the same deep soft embrace, the deepness especially, so familiar, and so elusive to words. 12/25/04

R and R comparing notes, something physical and visceral, a shift, a speed bump, a black hole, and then what, beyond wordless, beyond any perception at all, a space, a fraction of an instant everything rolls up, collapses inward, all gone, then it all comes back, you and everything else, but so much softer, a gentle settling like a mist, R and R talking with each other, hard to verbalize, takes a while, moving our hands a lot searching in the air for words, both of us making the same gestures. 1/17/05

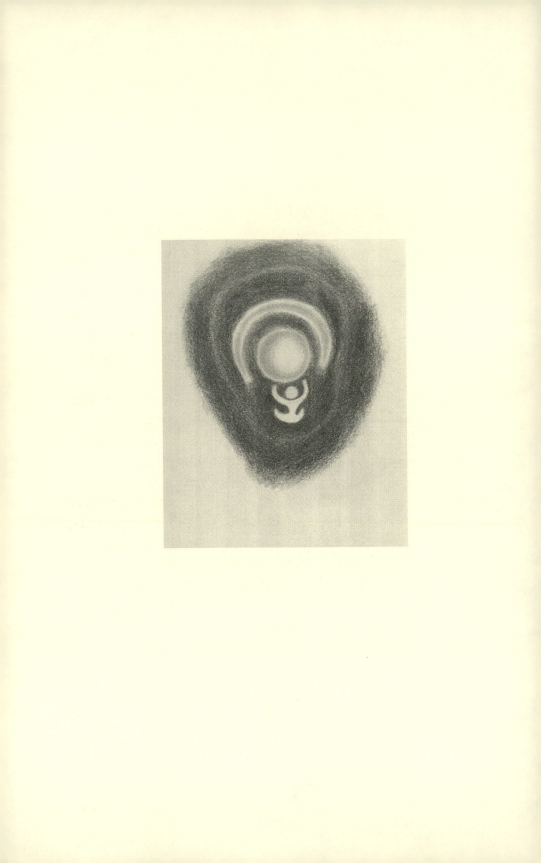

Outside of words, a depth beyond any kind of depth, no mind or body or world. Like a single low tone from a timpani drum. Time has dissolved, with space and words no more, beyond timelessness, nothing not nothing.

Then the return, as if one whole being, all of experience, begins to pulsate with blood again, suddenly, seamlessly, reappearing, remanifesting, nothing came back, and yet a memory held in every cell, a blue-black known with an intent both personal and outside of being, inexpressible yet its return is all appearances.

That morning we heard the final call and knew we were back until another death claims these forms. We walk outside in the bright spring air, talking quietly with each other. We talk as before of experience, though our eyes look now through this depth and see only its reflection. Everything is the vision, experience so deep and unassailable, so utterly beyond any function of mind, your bones know it, your eyes know it, your heart knows it, your hair, nothing that is not now suspended in a vast tenderness beyond all knowing. We are no more, yet we perceive and function as an essence embraced. All words, all thoughts are bright bubbles, bits of foam, floating on the surface of immeasurable radiant depths.

FULL CIRCLE

The early spring air was soft and bright. The shadows held the lingering cold of winter, but the mid morning sunlight laid a kindly warmth on our shoulders as we stood on the grassy bank of the old logging road cut into the side of the mountain. The huge old madrone rooted on the slope nearby was still laden with an overabundance of bright red berries, but its usually glossy green leaves were withering; the old sentinel was dying. We looked out over the steep narrow valley that had been our cloister for eight years. The flank of the mountain dropped off sharply below us, and through a gap between tall grey trunks of Douglas fir, we could see the river sparkling in the morning light and cars moving along the highway that followed the river's winding on the other shore. We heard the familiar rumble of heavy machinery from the rock quarry as a dump truck came into view far below; like a slow-bodied beetle or a toy truck it crawled across the uneven floor of the gravel pit. The rugged mountains that held this valley in a tight embrace were still covered with snow, but the willows along the river were beginning to quicken with a breath of green in their swelling buds.

The day before, we had completed the path of Tögal. After years of intense practice and many more years of letting go, we had reached the true return, the point of origin, the beginning and the end. Now we stood on the old logging road in the warm sun, in the earliest moments of spring enfolded in the earliest moments of our return. We were embraced within a great joy, a joy all encompassing, inseparable from all experience: the morning light, the river, the valley, the trees, the new stems of green grass and shoots of wild flowers pushing up through dried leaves of last year's growth, the sudden explosive sounds of the rock crusher in the quarry pit and the jake braking logging trucks on the highway below reverberating in the soft spring air so full of awakening life, all the hopes and anguish of this world all manifesting together as a seamless whole, the effulgent grace of the heart essence.

Each moment filled to the brim is also a message and a plea, a reflection of the essence manifesting as all life and its possible end. Immersed in the simple generous joy of being, we also feel the anguish and futility all around us of human insistence on separation from the Earth.

The Earth is the basic ground on which our lives and our spiritual practice evolve. It is the intent of the essence manifesting for all beings to seek and find the path of return. This expression of the essence is like a dream, although it appears as if solid and real. All experience, all phenomena, are as evanescent as a mist in the mid-day sun, but this does not in any way diminish the inherent holiness of this manifest vision we call life. The whole of this wondrous world arises for us to follow the signs guiding, opening, and gentling us, helping us to let go and surrender to the embrace of the essence.

Unfortunately, human ignorance is reaching dangerous proportions and is threatening the whole of this amazing offering. We have lived too long with the sense of separation and forget our kinship with all life. We have lived too long with the idea of unending expansion as a measure of progress; we forget our cyclical roots and the necessity and inevitability of decay and renewal. Now is the time to return to origin, to embrace the teachings that are all around us manifesting naturally as the vision that is this life, let go of separation, reconnect with the Earth and recognize our indwelling heart of light within the context of the natural world.

Just as the visions of inner radiance begin to turn inward to complete the cycle of return, just as a plant puts all its energy toward setting seed as it reaches climax and begins to wither and die, this is a time to recognize the source and the potential for transformation within you, this is a time for setting seed. This is a time to prepare the ground for the future seed to grow. This is a time to focus not on the fears and uncertainties associated with the declining and decaying structures of our times but on the openings for renewal and regeneration that moments like these naturally offer. This is the time to plant the seeds of oneness, simplicity of life, and compassionate acts that affirm our kinship with all life, the bright seeds that embody our deepest connection with manifest essence.

We feel strongly the importance of sharing this perspective now, to inspire recognition that this vision, this Earth, this life, is sacred and is not to be taken lightly, and to encourage the seeds of a more kindly, harmonious future, so that all beings may abide in the embrace of oneness.

A gesture, the heart opens.

11037356R0

Made in the USA
Lexington, KY
05 September 2011